THE WEALTHY WRITER

How to earn a six-figure income
as a freelance writer
(No Kidding!)

by Michael Meanwell

WRITER'S DIGEST BOOKS

Cincinnati, Ohio

www.writersdigest.com

Visit our Web site at www.writersdigest.com for information on more resources for writers.

To receive a free weekly e-mail newsletter delivering tips and updates about writing and about Writer's Digest products, register directly at our Web site at http://newsletters.fwpublications.com.

08   07   06   05   04   5   4   3   2   1

Library of Congress Cataloging-in-Publication Data

Meanwell, Michael
  [Enterprising writer]
  The wealthy writer : how to earn a six-figure income as a freelance writer (no kidding!) / by Michael Meanwell.
    p.   cm.
  Originally published: The enterprising writer. Melbourne : Hardie Grant Books, 2003. Includes bibliographical references and index.
  ISBN 1-58297-299-0 (alk. paper) -- ISBN 1-58297-311-3 (pbk. : alk. paper)
    1. Freelance journalism. 2. Authorship. 3. Authorship -- Marketing. I. Title.

  PN4784.F76M43   2004
  808'.02'023--dc22   2004045646
                                                            CIP

Edited by Michelle Ruberg
Designed by Terri Eubanks
Cover designed by Lisa Buchanan
Production coordinated by Robin Richie

Under the title *The Enterprising Writer:* Published as an e-book in 2001 by Meanwell, Melbourne. Published in Australia in 2003 by Hardie Grant Books, Melbourne.

Disclaimer
    This publication is a guide and is not to be relied on as financial or investment advice. The subject matter presented has been obtained from independent sources as well as the author's personal experiences and is designed to aid readers in formulating their own conclusions. In all instances where another product has been recommended, recommendations have been made based on the author's experience, not incentive.
    Every effort has been made to ensure that the information is accurate and authoritative, and the author and publisher assume no responsibility for errors, omissions, or contrary interpretation. While the author believes that the information contained herein is accurate at the time of publication, readers should obtain independent advice and assistance to suit their circumstances.

ABOUT THE AUTHOR

Michael Meanwell was born in Australia in 1963. He began publishing articles in newspapers and magazines when he was seventeen. The following year, he wrote his first novel.

Since then, his career has evolved from working as a journalist and freelance writer for Australian publications including the *Daily News, Herald Sun*, *New Idea, People*, and *Small Business Success* to serving as a public relations and marketing consultant for a variety of companies, including Ford Motor Company, Kodak, Simplot, and Royal Selangor as well as Cross Writing Instruments, VDO, Océ, Honda, and PACCAR Australia.

Michael has also produced and hosted a weekly radio show and written and presented a series of inspirational television programs.

He was born in Sydney, raised in Brisbane, and lives in Melbourne, Australia, with his wife, Yianna.

For Yianna,
My inspiration, my motivation,
my adoration

ACKNOWLEDGMENTS

This book is the result of twenty-plus years' experience as a professional writer. Along the way, I have known and worked with some extraordinary people, all of whom have played an indirect role in the shaping of this book.

But, in particular, I offer my heartfelt appreciation to my friends and colleagues Ken Silver, Csilla Coffey, and Chris Ryall and to my father, John Meanwell, for their tireless enthusiasm and advice. Also to Chris Wiles, legendary writer and loyal friend.

A special thanks to my friend and confidante on the other side of the Pacific, Barb Bressi-Donohue, for her encouragement. To Elaine Miller for her objective eye and invaluable comments. To Michelle Ruberg and the team at Writer's Digest Books for bringing this book to life. Also to my agent, Al Zuckerman, for making this possible.

Finally, to my wife and best friend, Yianna, for her undying support beyond the call of duty.

CONTENTS

What's in this Book

You cannot teach a man anything;
you can only help him to find it
within himself.

Galileo Galilei (1564-1642)

What's In This Book

This book is divided into several parts, each of which comprises a number of chapters.

For some, the "hardest" part of the book will be the first few chapters in the *Getting Started* section. They contain all of the tough, soul-searching issues such as:

- Your suitability as a full-time writer
- Your aptitude for running your own business
- Developing a business plan

The *Getting Organized* section gives you the tools you need to turbocharge your business by helping you develop a system for every aspect of your day-to-day operations. You get the hard stuff up front so you can enjoy the pleasures of the art of writing and being in business—the cream—later on.

In the next section, *Write What You Like*, we examine various hot markets for writers. Each of these specialized markets calls for a different approach to your craft. The proven tips and techniques provided allow you to adapt your style to succeed in these niche fields. In addition, I will show you the best places to look for work and how to create work that pays better than advertised jobs. For many, this section is a favorite, which is why it commands the largest part of the book. Being able to do the work is only part of the equation. You need to be able to attract clients and keep them, just as much as you need to earn and use money effectively. The next part of the book, *Getting Down to Business*, looks at methods of attracting new business, improving your work style, promoting your own business and handling bad debts. To make things even easier, I've included a series of templates that you can customize to automate various processes in your business.

The last section, *Working Smarter, Writing Faster*, shows you how to beat writer's block with a range of techniques that have worked well for me and other writers. We will also examine ways you can find the time to write and to improve your productivity. And, just as important, we explore how to look after the most vital resource you have in business—you.

In addition, you'll be invited into my writing world, where I have spent the past twenty-plus years. I'll share various things that have happened to me along the way as well as solutions to problems, which you can apply in your own business.

The essence of being an enterprising writer is knowing how to write profitably and earn what you are truly worth. If you work at it and apply the principles and techniques in this book, you can earn $100,000 a year or more, as I do. You can also generate extra revenue by subcontracting work you can't or don't want to handle (something I'll detail in a later chapter).

The best news is that you've already taken the first step, simply by choosing this book. Welcome aboard . . . I hope you enjoy the journey!

Introduction

Most people live and die with their music still
unplayed. They never dare to try.

Mary Kay Ash (1915–2001)

Getting into print—that was the big goal for all of us when we began writing. But, while it's still a thrill to get a byline, particularly in one of the more prestigious publications, it's no longer enough to enthuse our bank managers. We need to profit from our craft.

This book is designed to show you how to make a living from writing and still have a life worth living away from the keyboard. It's based on proven techniques I've learned from associates and mentors as well as my own experience writing professionally for more than two decades (almost half this time has been spent running my own business).

Whether you're new to the world of writing or ready to advance to a new level, this book will give you the motivation as well as the tools and techniques you need to make serious money from writing what you like, when you like.

Investing in Yourself

This book will also show you how to develop and manage your business. This is an important skill, and failing to master it is the main reason why many writers are not financially successful in their work. There's no magic wand for making money from words. Like any business, you need to invest in yourself by developing your skills, and then invest in your business by discovering new opportunities, determining markets, cultivating clients, and always delivering a quality product and service.

One secret is to diversify. This means broadening your skills to encompass a range of services—anything from journalism, scripts and books to Web content, marketing collateral and even lecturing on your craft. Marketing collateral, which is an industry term for marketing material, refers to any type of promotional device, from media releases, newsletters and brochures to general advertising, sales letters, and videos. The more tasks you are able and willing to take on, the more markets for your writing.

It's been said that the first five years in business are the hardest—that is, until you get through them. Then, the experts say, the next five are even more difficult. I can attest to both of these claims. The establishment of a business, a reputation and a quality methodology in the first five years was challenging. It's a real eye-opener to be completely responsible for your own income. But it's even more frightening to be responsible for other people's income. That's what happened over the next five years as I saw my business expand in clients and in staff.

Today, no business or individual can afford to rest on past achievements. There will always be someone offering a better mousetrap. My reality check is that I'm only as good as my last invoice. No matter what kind of relationship you've built with your clients, you'll need to continue to motivate them to do business with you in the future.

Riding the Roller Coaster

Being a freelance writer can be an extremely interesting, rewarding, and satisfying career. But, like any business, it can deliver as many famines as feasts. The trick is learning how to ride the roller coaster.

Feasts sound good, but there can sometimes be a downside to them. Clients usually want their projects completed "yesterday"—and there just aren't enough yesterdays in a week. That means you run the risk of disappointing some clients and losing future work, or losing a lot of sleep and possibly not completing the jobs professionally. Many other things can force you to rethink your plans. These may be events in your personal life or factors outside your control.

I started my writing business on my own and gained a partner who also happened to be my first wife. As we became more successful, we added more and more staff and built a lucrative business in the first five years, only to see it evaporate through divorce.

Believe it or not, it's possible to find opportunities even in such a devastating experience. It all depends on how you approach your business and your life in general. I've been on my own again since September 1996, and these years have been my most productive and profitable.

"Kiss" Your Business

Above all else, I have learned that it's best to follow the KISS principle— keep it simple, stupid. It's an oldie, but it still applies as much to the work we do as to the way we run our business.

In the beginning, as my business grew, I hired more staff. But when the market contracted, I was faced with the dilemma of letting go loyal people. Most employers say the hardest thing in business is letting go of good staff, and that was true for me, too. I would often put off the inevitable while madly searching for extra work to cover their wages. Since 1996, I have been on my own again and have found a much better alternative. Now I outsource work when it's there, just as my clients outsource work to me. It's so simple yet so empowering. It gives me the ability to work on my own and the flexibility to handle bigger projects or hand over others to professionals I know and trust.

Writing is my life. I've been doing it for over two decades, and I expect to do it for another two or more. But you don't need to have that kind of passion to benefit from this book. All you need are three things: drive, ability, and responsibility.

- You need the drive to get things done on time, to brief, and within budget; you need to run the extra mile when others can't or won't.
- You need to have the ability to handle a variety of projects and clients' demands so you can capitalize on any opportunity.
- You need to take responsibility not only for your business but also for your life by finding a balance between work and play and enjoying the fruits of your labor.

I've found that balance and I'd like to share it with you. Are you ready?

CHAPTER 1

Commercial Writing: A Freelancer's Dream

You are never given a wish without also being
given the power to make it true. You may
have to work for it, however.

Richard Bach (1936–)

There are more than twenty-four million writers in the U.S., and yet just 5 percent have been published.[1] Regrettably, a far smaller number actually make a comfortable living from their profession. Many freelancers spend an inordinate amount of time searching, querying, and writing for newspapers and magazines that often pay relatively little for the effort required—and usually without any promise of ongoing work. Worse still, every year, competition grows and markets shrink. But what if I could show you a viable alternative? One that is far more profitable, less competitive, and delivers ongoing work, usually after completing one or more successful assignments. Interested? Commercial writing—writing communications for businesses—can give you all of this and more. It can be as challenging and varied as you want to make it with as much work as you wish to handle, plus it offers assignments that you can do from home or abroad. It's literally up to you. But before we get ahead of ourselves, let's take a step back and consider what commercial writing offers compared with "traditional" freelance writing.

The major advantage of writing for businesses is the income. Whether large corporations or small firms, businesses generally pay more handsomely than freelancing for newspapers and magazines. Once you have established yourself with an organization, you may have the opportunity to write a wide variety of communications. This could include customer sales letters, speeches, and video scripts as well as internal and external newsletters, brochures, ads, and more. That's the potential with just one solid business client. So, you can see how lucrative this line of work can be with a handful of clients.

Now, using that same principle, if you have one magazine as your client, that publication will work with a string of writers, including staff and freelancers. Whether you write an occasional article or a series of articles, it's unlikely you will gain the volume of work and income from one magazine that you would from a healthy company.

I have handled one-off writing projects for organizations, but in most cases one job has led to a long-term relationship. With some clients, I manage several projects a year. With others, I work for them on a regular basis, and there's a few who I speak with virtually on a daily basis. That's one of the great things about being a commercial writer—the work is consistent, and it's also interesting because it's varied.

As you can see, writing for businesses versus writing for publications, can be a far more profitable and stable exercise. And, once you have a number of clients, the amount of effort required to gain new assignments is far less because existing clients will call you, rather than you calling them for work.

Another advantage to writing for businesses is the amount of time and energy required to produce your work. If you're writing for publications, generally it's up to you to identify stories and gather your own leads. When writing for businesses, often your client will have a ready supply of writing activities. The company, for example, may be releasing a new suite of products that require press releases, ads, direct mail letters, and brochures. Depending on how well you're briefed, your client will provide base information and contact names for you to gather more details. Essentially, much of the groundwork is already done for you.

The Benefits of Freelance Work

There will always be plenty of work for good writers. Communication is the oxygen of society. We cannot exist without it. And, as society continues to develop new and more cost-effective ways of communicating, the need for good communicators will also continue. We've witnessed this in our lifetime. Many people thought the demise of afternoon newspapers, in favor of packaged television news, would spell the beginning of the end for journalists. But as one market shrinks, another expands. Today, we are bombarded by information around the clock and from around the world. News and advertising messages are delivered to us via every conceivable medium, from billboards, cabs and trains to software, mobile phones and the Internet. This new attitude toward communication owes much of its success to the ubiquitous Internet. And this continues to be a goldmine for Web-savvy writers.

Your Next Assignment Is Just a Mouse Click Away

Today, there's an abundance of opportunities for online writers, from writing for e-zines to publishing e-books. For the first time, you have access to global markets and opportunities. For the first time, it doesn't matter what country or time zone you live in—your next job could materialize right in front of you, on your computer monitor.

There's also a virtually untapped niche market on the Internet: writing copy for Web sites. Next time you are surfing, take the time to read the text thoroughly. You'll find that even on some of the more professional Web sites, there's room for improvement, not just in correcting typos and grammatical errors, but also in creating compelling copy with a "call to action." And, with more than three billion sites online and increasing daily, there are plenty of opportunities for editing, rewriting, or drafting Web copy from scratch.

Opportunities in Every Medium

There is—and always will be—a wealth of work out there for good writers generated from the Internet and countless other sources. Think about it. Every time you turn on the television or radio, pick up a newspaper or magazine, or even buy your favorite box of cereal—there's a writer behind each message you're reading or hearing. I currently work with a number of large companies that choose to outsource specific tasks, such as technical writing, media releases, brochures, newsletters, and speechwriting. In addition, I occasionally write stories for various newspapers and magazines.

As you develop your skills and your services, you will find that the lines blur between advertising copywriter, direct marketer, PR consultant, journalist, and fiction writer. It's all a matter of adapting your skills to suit your clients' needs and the requirements of the target audience. The point is, that with more than six billion people on the planet and a plethora of interest, products and services available, there is and always will be a need for good communicators, educators, and marketers—roles you can comfortably fill as a freelance writer.

Company Advantages in Using a Freelancer

When pitching yourself to a company, remember to include the advantages that freelancers offer over internal staff:

- **Objectivity:** You are not part of the corporate culture, so you can provide a more objective and often more creative viewpoint.
- **Accountability:** You don't get paid until the job is done, so there's a vested interest in working fast, sticking to deadlines, and exceeding expectations.
- **Experience:** Writing is your specialty, so you can often complete projects more quickly and more professionally than internal staff who have other job commitments and less expertise.
- **Cost-effectiveness:** Because you're not on staff, you're not on the payroll, which offers certain advantages to companies in terms of annual leave and other benefits, tax, office space, and other considerations.
- **Relief/Assistance:** You can assist internal staff with projects when people are on leave or handling other tasks.

Personal Advantages in Being a Freelancer

Being a freelance writer also offers several advantages to you:

- **Flexibility:** If you become stalled or hit a block with a certain project, you can change gears by taking on a different project. Often that's enough to remove the block and reinvigorate you.
- **Working your own hours:** Because you work for yourself, you have the ability to work when it suits you. This gives you the option to enjoy time off while others are working or invest some time over the

weekend or at night, if required. Either way, your office is open when you need it, not when the boss demands it.

- **Being your own boss:** You have significant control over the projects that you take on and the way you want to handle them. You can pick and choose your projects and your clients. You don't have to work with someone if you don't like the conditions, the pay, or their approach. (This may appear arrogant, but I think you'll agree that when you work for yourself, it's vital that you enjoy your work. I see myself as in partnership with my clients, sharing expertise and responsibilities. If a company insists on treating its suppliers as slaves, or otherwise exploiting the business relationship, it's counterproductive for both parties.)
- **Doing what you love, loving what you do:** At the end of the day, you are writing and getting paid for it. If you're like all the writers I know, you won't be thinking of it as work, you'll be seeing it as your dream job.

GETTING STARTED

Now it's time to roll up your sleeves, answer some tough questions, and lay the foundation for your writing career. As with anything worth doing, the greater the investment you make now, the greater the rewards you can expect in the future.

CHAPTER 2

The Right Stuff
for Business

If writers were good businessmen, they'd
have too much sense to be writers.

Irvin S. Cobb (1876–1944)

Next to owning a house, running a business is one of the most sought-after goals. But before you leap into your own business, you need to think about your time, your financial position, and what running a business really involves. It's time to consider the good, the bad, and the risky.

Evaluate Your Capabilities and Skills

Start by asking yourself the following questions:

Can I work from my home?

Depending on where you live, you may need special permits or licenses to run your business from your home. Contact relevant state or local government authorities regarding regulations, or visit http://biz.findlaw .com to download legal forms relevant to your metropolitan area or county. Also, www.businesslaw.gov offers guides written in plain English on starting and running a small business as well as links to information, organizations, and services in each state.

Do I have enough time to commit to this business?

You don't just need time to write; you also need time to establish a presence and manage your enterprise. That means allowing time for developing new markets, prospecting for new clients, bookkeeping, and planning for future growth.

The bottom line is that when you run your own business, you will value your time differently. Maintaining your business also requires a lot more of your time than working for someone else ever did. In the beginning, you'll have to start work early, finish late, and often work on the weekends. You'll need to be able to strike a balance between your home business and your home life. Be realistic about the amount of time you can invest, especially if you have young children.

Do I have the skills to run a business?

It's not enough to be a good writer. You need to have skills in other areas to run a successful business. This includes expertise in sales, business management, and interpersonal relations. There are short courses you can take to bone up on the specifics. A good place to start online is http://dir.yahoo.com/business_and_economy. Click on the appropriate category or use the search engine to link to a range of providers and courses. You can also gain a wealth of general information at your local library.

It's also important to surround yourself with good advice. Even after more than a dozen years in business, I still have an accountant for financial planning and annual tax returns and a bookkeeper to handle my day-to-day business affairs. I have tried to have the best of both worlds by acquiring a working knowledge of business management and accounting as well as employing experts in these fields when I need them. I could invest considerable time in learning and understanding *all* the ins and outs of accounting, but that would eat into my earning time.

It's best to strike a balance between working *in* the business and working *on* the business. That's why I hire specialists when I haven't the time, inclination, or ability to handle their tasks. Tax rules and business regulations are forever changing, so it's wise to seek professional advice while still maintaining control of your business.

Do I have the money to begin?

You have two options—you can finance your business from savings or get a loan. Either way, you need to have enough funds not only to cover your salary, pension, and insurance but also to cover other ongoing costs in addition to setup expenses. These include telecommunications (phone, fax, and

Internet service), running costs for your car, stationery, postage, and so on.

It's best to be conservative when starting out. Allow for a slow start so you don't encounter cash flow problems from day one. Clear as much personal debt as possible, including credit card expenses and loans. When I started my business, I was fortunate in that my wife was drawing a regular salary and we were living with relatives. Savings from the sale of our house also helped to fund our growth in the early days and provided a safety net. Whether you have that advantage or not, I would recommend that you play it safe in the beginning. Try to fund your business from savings and control your credit cards. It's easy to rack up debt with the swipe of a card but not so easy to pay it back when business is slow.

As part of running lean, try to purchase items such as furniture and equipment second-hand. Many financial advisers would disagree with me, but I never lease anything. My reason, again, is cash flow. It's better to pay for something outright, if you can afford it now, than to pay it off every month. You never know when you're going to have a bad month, especially in the beginning.

My basic philosophy in business is to prepare for the best by planning for the worst. This way, there shouldn't be any surprises because you will have contingencies in place to handle rough financial times. Building up a little reserve in your personal bank account will assist with lean times when the business can't afford to pay its Managing Director on time.

It's always a good idea to start with a business plan (we'll discuss this in the next chapter). That plan needs to accommodate your current lifestyle— what sort of income is necessary to maintain it? You and your family have certain needs and should enjoy certain luxuries. You must be confident that your work will pay as much as you are currently earning, or you will need to make certain sacrifices to increase your income or reduce your needs through lifestyle changes.

Are You Ready for Business?

There are other aspects of your personal situation that you should consider to determine whether you are suited for business.

Are you willing to dedicate long hours for low wages?

I'm not trying to pour cold water on the idea of owning your own business. I've had the most fun working for myself, and I couldn't imagine ever working for anyone else. But I've also had to make sacrifices and tough decisions to ensure the future of my business. In the beginning, it's even tougher. Much like a plane taking off, a lot of energy is required in the launch phase. Once it's going well and navigation is confirmed, much less energy is required to maintain altitude. You will need to put in the hard yards in the beginning, but the going will get easier as time passes and your expertise and business presence increase.

Are you healthy?

Working hard requires plenty of energy and good health. Your body and mind are the engines driving your enterprise. If you're not in good shape, how can you expect your business to excel? It's important to eat right, exercise regularly, and enjoy a balanced life.

There will be times when you feel you haven't got the time to take care of yourself. Remember the consequences of pushing that envelope too hard or too often—your actions will one day catch up with you. So be sure to take time off when you can rather than be sidelined with illness when you really can't afford it.

Is your family supportive?

There's no point starting a new career if your family isn't 100 percent behind you. It's important to discuss all of the pros and cons of starting a business for you and all members of your family. You all need to share goals and reach agreement on all vital issues so you can work as a team.

Have you ever been self-employed?

This is not a prerequisite, but it does help to know what to expect. If you haven't, ask family and friends who are self-employed about the pros and cons. Running a home office with a staff of one can be a lonely affair. In our profession, many hours are spent working in silence without conversation or collaboration. For some, this kind of work style can be soul destroying. For others, it can be invigorating.

Have you worked as a full-time writer before?

Again, this is not a prerequisite, but if you have done this type of work before, whether freelance or as a member of an in-house staff for a company or publication, you're more likely to know if you have the stamina and the interest to be a professional wordsmith. It's easier to be a success if you honestly enjoy your job.

Are you disciplined with money?

If you find it hard to make ends meet, if you find it hard to pay bills on time, if you find your paycheck is virtually gone the moment you get it, it may be wise to reconsider working for yourself. There are many different ways of running a business, but most successful people would say that the key word is "discipline." Many a successful enterprise has been destroyed through a lack of financial management.

Are you disciplined with time?

Remember Benjamin Franklin's advice to a young tradesman, "Time is money"? Time is your most important resource. You need to be a good manager of time, and you also have to be time conscious in meeting your customers' expectations. Every working journalist knows all too well the value of meeting deadlines. When you are totally responsible for meeting customers' needs and your company's revenue, deadlines take on even more critical importance.

A good way to stay on track is to plan each day in advance. "Plan your work, then work your plan," as the adage goes. "If you fail to plan, then you plan to fail," says business consultant Jim Rohn. Both are true.

Even when I am not officially working, I still plan my day. There are always chores to do in and around the house. By writing them down in a separate list, you give them a separate slot in your day. If those tasks are accomplished during "downtime," there's no excuse to be doing them when you should be in your office. Likewise, when you are in your office, ensure that every hour is effective by prioritizing every task that has to be done. If a task isn't completed today, it goes on tomorrow's list.

Are you self-motivated?

Being your own boss means ensuring you're getting maximum benefit from time and effort. You have to be able to set goals and plan how to achieve them, because if you're the boss, there's no one else to provide either the incentives or the means of achieving them! The best entrepreneurs are self-starters who are customer focused and goal oriented. They know what they want, and they know that to get it they must exceed their customers' demands.

Are you good with people?

You may be good with words, but you also need to be good with people, whether you intend to make a living as a journalist, PR person, or any other type of scribe. Communicating with and relating to people is a necessity in all commercial life, and *effective* communication is one of the cornerstones of success.

Are you a good leader?

Just because you're working for yourself doesn't mean you don't need leadership skills. You may have a staff of one, but there will be times when you'll need the services of others. Even though I no longer employ staff, I still hire freelance writers, artists, photographers, and other professionals for various client projects—sometimes a whole team.

Even if your enterprise never gets to this stage, there will be many occasions when good leadership skills will give you a decided advantage. Discover them, develop them, and exercise them so they become a natural part of your working life.

Are you responsible?

Taking responsibility for everything that crosses your desk is vital for your success. The buck must stop with you.

Whenever I'm involved in a project, I take full responsibility for every aspect. You cannot always be involved in every aspect, such as printing a brochure or shooting the photos for a catalog, but you can certainly manage the process to ensure a successful outcome. Hire good people with proven track records. Determine and discuss objectives up front with both your suppliers and your clients, and keep all parties continually updated.

It's a good idea to develop a "work in progress" schedule, listing each of the tasks required, attributing responsibility, and attaching a deadline for its completion. That way, everyone stays informed about who's doing what and by which date. It also allows you to stay on top of the project and take action the day a task falls behind schedule.

Are you a good decision-maker?

Procrastination not only wastes time, it can sometimes cost you everything. So ask all the right questions and gather all of the facts. If you'd like more information but are unlikely to get it, you may have to rely on your instincts and base your decision on the information you have.

Building a Business Begins With Solid Foundations

If you answered "yes" to most of these questions, you probably have the skills to be a commercial success. Where you have answered "no," you now have an insight into areas that require some training.

Okay, you've done some soul-searching and answered some questions you probably had never thought to ask. Resolve any potential roadblocks and get ready to dig a little deeper. It's now time to lay the foundation for your new business—something that should last a lifetime if you plan with foresight and build correctly.

CHAPTER 3

A Business Plan for Success

Don't be too busy earning a
living to make any money.

Joe Karbo (1925–1980)

When you're finally ready to start something new, the last thing you want to do is develop a plan—you just want to leap right in and get going, right? Well, if you want your business to continue beyond the first big splash, you'll need some solid planning before the big day and continued planning for the rest of your business life.

If you've read this far, you've decided you're right for business. So let's begin planning how you will make waves around the world.

Questions to Ask to Make Your Business Seaworthy

To start off, research and answer the following basic questions. There are many books you can consult for ideas and information.

What field will you service?

Consider the fields in which you'll be involved. Will you focus on one field, such as public relations, or will you diversify and cover a range of areas, such as freelance journalism, ad copywriting, and e-publishing? If you intend to focus on more than one field, you will need to assess each individually, as each has a unique set of issues. When assessing a field, you also need to decide whether you will be targeting it as a whole or specializing in certain segments. For example, if you plan to service the PR field, will you focus on developing communications for the information technology sector or the transport or medical sector? If it's freelance journalism, are you going to focus on being a travel writer, an entertainment reporter, or a feature writer? As you're writing your business plan, it's important to decide so both you and your energies remain focused.

Who is your competition?

An important part of assessing the field is also assessing your competition. What do your competitors offer clients? How can your business provide improvements on their services? Are there specific niches that are not being fulfilled that you can fulfill easily, cost-effectively, or at some greater benefit to your potential clients?

There is a range of information available online, as well as various publications, associations, and market research that will give you greater insight into specific industries and the opportunities that exist. A good place to start is your local library or newsstand where you can pick up a few copies of magazines, such as *Advertising Age, Adweek*, and *Mediaweek*, which are the leading industry publications for advertising and marketing in the U.S. In addition to keeping professionals informed about changing accounts, new campaigns, and personnel appointments, they offer a rich source of information for enterprising writers. You can learn firsthand about the latest trends, issues, and attitudes and how specific businesses are marketing themselves. Not only will you gain a greater understanding of the inner workings of the industry, you'll be brimming with ideas and opportunities to exploit.

Professional associations, such as the American Advertising Federation, the Direct Marketing Association, and the International Association of Business Communicators, offer a range of courses, books, and events where you can network with like-minded people. In addition, the National Writers Union (www.nwu.org) is the only labor union in the U.S. that represents all freelance writers. It offers wordsmiths of all genres and media a range of useful services, including contract advice, writer alerts (regarding unscrupulous employers and media outlets), an employment hotline, and health and professional liability insurance.

For those who prefer to let their fingers do the work, there are a growing number of Web sites offering news and information about various industries. You can find them by typing simple keyword phrases into a search engine, such as "PR industry" or "market research," or narrow your focus by searching specific business categories of YellowPages.com. The keywords "market research" will identify an array of market research companies. Then simply use the business name as a keyword in your search engine to locate the most appropriate site. You'll find that many company Web sites, such as ACNielsen.com, provide market intelligence in the form of industry analysis and reports on trends and surveys, as well as a comprehensive news archive for a longer-term perspective.

What advantages do you have over the competition?

Once you know the industry and your competition, you will know which category you fit as an industry supplier. There will, of course, be large firms providing a wider range of services at a higher rate. There will be smaller firms specializing in one or more distinct areas, and there will be sole operators, some of whom are writing as a hobby and others who are serious and have the credentials and the client list to prove it. Whatever the competition, it's important to understand which niche you can fill. This will assist you in distinguishing yourself from the others in the eyes of prospective clients.

When formulating your business plan and putting together sales letters, it's best to see things through the eyes of others:

- Why should a company hire you?
- What do you offer that others do not?
- What's the benefit in using your services?
- Are you cheaper?
- Are you quicker?
- Do you guarantee a better quality product, service, or some other advantage?

You should consider each of these questions both now and throughout your commercial life. Just because you have clients doesn't mean you'll keep them. You'll only keep them if you continue to satisfy them. Having a business plan and continually reviewing and improving on it will help keep you on course and keep clients on your books.

Can you deliver a better product, service, or solution?

I think this is worthy of further thought. What I am asking you to do is develop what marketers call a "USP"—a unique selling proposition. I am asking you to differentiate yourself from others in the market. What makes you special? Or, more importantly, how you can offer a greater benefit to your clients compared with the competition?

Let's face it, there are a lot of people who want to write and a lot who already write well. You have plenty of competition, but you also have plenty of opportunities to make a good living. The key is not only finding out what you enjoy doing and are good at but convincing others they need your unique service.

When you discover this, you should have enough information to write your mission statement, a single sentence or paragraph that will capture the essence of your business, your philosophy, and your promise to clients. This mission statement can help you in many ways. You can use it to develop a slogan, and you can use it as a running theme in sales letters, pitches, brochures, newsletters, or any other marketing collateral you eventually create to promote yourself. When my partner left the business some years ago, I took the opportunity to change the name to reflect the new direction I was taking. I decided in late 1996 to focus on developing business-to-business marketing communications for the corporate market. I changed the name to Marketzing. And my mission statement? *To put more zing in your marketing.*

What are your skills and experience, and how can they benefit the business?

Since you are starting out alone, the job of fulfilling the goals of your business falls on your shoulders. You are its greatest asset, so it's important to objectively evaluate your background, skills, experience, and expertise and determine how they can best be used to meet client needs. If you haven't already done it, now is a good time to do a SWOT (strengths, weaknesses, opportunities, and threats) analysis on you and your firm. Then you can promote the positives and work on the negatives.

What is the best legal structure for the business?

There are essentially four different legal structures you can adopt when establishing your business: a sole proprietorship, partnership, corporation, or limited liability company (LLC). Sole proprietorships and partnerships (for more than one owner) are the least expensive and easiest structures to register in the U.S. You should, however, discuss this matter with your accountant or financial adviser. Consider all of the options—the cheapest is not always the best.

How should you keep your business records?

Again, you can seek advice on this. My personal preference is to use a computer accounting system (I have used MYOB for years and have never had a problem). When I first set up my company, I used a paper-based, manual system. Then, as the business grew, it was easier and more cost-effective to automate the process.

Today, I enter the data for my invoices, print them out, and pay the bills, but I leave all the other tasks—entering the accounts receivable, bank reconciliations, and so on—to my bookkeeper. To keep me on track, she communicates regularly with the accountant who handles my taxes, and the three of us get together each quarter to complete various reports and the annual tax return. This approach suits me because I am far from being a financial whiz. In fact, I really hate anything to do with figures, but I'm living proof that you can still make money and keep it, even if you hate counting it. If you gain some perverse enjoyment from reconciling accounts, more power to you. If not, hire a competent professional you can trust. You'll sleep better at night and have more time to make money, rather than accounting for it.

What insurance do you need?

Again, this is something you should discuss with an adviser who understands your needs. My advice is that you will need to insure all of your business equipment. It would also be wise to have income protection insurance that protects you against long-term illness or disability.

Some people in our business have professional indemnity or liability insurance, which protects them against any legal claim resulting from substandard or negligent service. I considered getting this when I first started but chose not to for a couple of reasons: The insurance is generally very expensive and I was fairly certain I wouldn't need it. Although my main work came from PR and corporate communications—potentially the most litigious literary areas—I chose not to get professional insurance because I did not intend to make the type of mistakes that would expose me to a civil action.

That may sound foolish or arrogant, but my reasoning was that I had been conducting PR for some years for a previous employer, as well as having several years' experience in journalism. In that time, I'd learned how to report accurately and how to protect myself by obtaining signed approval of copy before releasing it to the media. I've never had one case—or even one bit of trouble—over what I've written on behalf of a client or third party. Having said that, whether you get this kind of insurance will depend on many things: the industries you service, your clients, and the way you conduct business. Being careful is part of the solution. Being formal and getting everything in writing is the other part.

How will you attract business?

Whether you have decided to focus on PR and marketing communications or some other writing markets, you have an advantage over other people starting businesses, because a large part of prospecting involves the written word. Growing a business can take various forms, ranging from developing a referral system and publishing a regular newsletter to promoting yourself as an expert by writing for specialist publications or hitting the lecture circuit. Alternatively, you can issue direct mailers or "cold call" editors and companies promoting your services. You can also advertise in marketing publications, establish strategic alliances with like-minded businesses, build a Web site, or network at various functions.

There are many ways to get your name out there and attract favorable attention. The secret to all good marketing is "test marketing." Try a few approaches, review the results, tweak the system, and then test it again. If it works, stick with it. If it doesn't, try another strategy.

I've tried all of the above prospecting tools, but the most effective over the years has been getting referrals from satisfied clients. Let's face it—clients are walking, talking advertisements for you, and those advertisements get results because people trust people. Word-of-mouth advertising cuts through other forms of promotion because it's credible. You heard about XYZ Company when a friend recommended them to you—there was no gimmick, no sales pitch, and no hidden agenda, just one friend helping out another. So what does that tell you? It's yet another good reason to offer your clients the best service and value for money. Not only will they keep coming back to you, they'll also tell others. But word of mouth is a double-edged sword. If you do a poor job, not only will you ultimately lose the client, you will lose other opportunities. A customer will tell five colleagues about exceptionally good service but will tell ten people about exceptionally bad service. Many marketing experts[2] have made this point over the years, and most of us can confirm it from our own experiences. Keep in mind, however, that it's not enough to expect or wait for your satisfied clients to tell others. You need to encourage them by developing a referral system (see chapter fifteen).

How will you operate?

You need to consider work practices, policies, and procedures for conducting business:

- How will you work on a day-to-day basis?
- Will you start each day with a preconceived plan of action?
- Will you evaluate each project before, during, and after?
- How will you learn from mistakes?
- How can you save time?
- How can you ensure that you will keep the client after the first job or the last job?
- How will you appease disgruntled clients?
- How will you handle queries regarding your services, abilities, and background?
- How will you manage people who don't pay on time or at all?

These are interesting questions to consider. I find the best way to answer them is to work it out on paper. This can begin in your business plan and end in an operations manual, if you really wish to formalize the strategy. An operations manual contains all of the systems in your armory. Having procedures to follow allows you to ensure that your daily operations are carried out correctly, efficiently, and professionally. It may seem a little premature for an enterprise that's just starting, but if you ever expand, it could be vital to your survival.

When my firm grew to half a dozen people, the operations manual became our bible. Today, my operations manual has evolved to suit my new circumstances, but it's still something I refer to when needed. It covers every aspect of my daily operations as well as procedures for prospecting, servicing new clients, preparing proposals, gaining referrals, and so on.

It's wise to begin answering the above questions and consulting with others at the very beginning of your enterprise. I will share more on this in chapter four.

Do you need a financial strategy?

Absolutely! Every business needs both a marketing strategy and a financial one, and they should complement each other. You need to calculate how many billable hours (if this is appropriate) or how many projects you can produce each day, week, month, and year. You need to calculate how much money you require to maintain your lifestyle, how much money you need to maintain the business, and what rate to charge your clients.

These are all personal questions. How do you set a rate as a consultant, freelance journalist, or any other type of professional writer? Should you lead the industry with the highest rate? Should you be the cheapest and undercut the competition? Or should you follow the norm?

Before you answer these questions, you need to know what the competition charge and what companies may be willing to pay for literary services. Consult industry organizations to get a general understanding of what you can charge. You can also check trade publications such as *Writer's Market* (accessible online at www.writersmarket.com), which provides guidelines on a wide range of marketing, editorial, and freelance jobs, both on a project and hourly basis. Also, see chapter six for a cost breakdown on specific writing projects I handle.

I think it's best to begin as a "price follower," offering the standard rate for your services. Once you become better known or decide to specialize, you can begin to educate the market about paying you a higher fee for a greater benefit, such as faster turnaround, improved quality, or better service, which equates to better value for money. Whatever rate you decide on, you first must know your break-even costs. And to know that, you need to determine your start-up costs and estimate your operating costs. Then, you need to develop a monthly operating plan for the first year. This will give you the information you need to ensure that the writing rates you set are acceptable, not just to your clients but also to you. There's no point in offering cheap rates if you don't make any money. Another important part of your financial strategy is setting terms and conditions. As you know, cash flow is the key to sound financial management, so you need to ensure that your clients pay you on time.

What is the industry standard for payment? It may be seven, fourteen, or thirty days from the date of invoice. Again, you can choose to follow the market or you can offer clients an incentive for paying early, if maintaining cash flow is of paramount importance. An incentive may be a 5 percent discount or some other enticement.

You also need to consider how and when you'll pay yourself and other creditors. I prefer to pay myself once a month, to assist with the business' cash flow. That can be hard to live with if you've been used to getting paid weekly or every two weeks, but it just gets down to discipline. You may also choose to use your credit card, rather than checks, for paying regular expenses. This gives you the flexibility of paying when cash flow permits and taking advantage of extra free credit, which some institutions offer. Use separate credit cards for business and personal expenses—it will make it easier when you are paying off your cards and reconciling your accounts.

What equipment will you need?

These days, it's virtually impossible to get by without a computer connected to the Internet. Add to that a fax machine for transferring manual documents and a mobile phone and answering machine so you're contactable anywhere at any time. Remember, you're in a service business, so you need to be accessible to your clients when it suits them, not you. Other items, such as a scanner or photocopier, may not be as essential to your business. If not, use them when you need them through the services of local businesses, such as a quick print shop.

What will you name your business?

This is another personal question. Should you go with something uninspiring like "John Smith & Associates?" That may sound okay for a law or accounting firm, but you're in a creative business, so reflect it in your business name. Unless you have a memorable name or you are a personality in your own right, I would steer clear of using your own name. Try for something that's memorable because it's short, sharp, and creative.

My company was initially called "The Write Advice." That was back in

1991, when "write" wasn't as overused as it is today. It was a catchy phrase for a PR and marketing communications company and had strong retention value years later. In 1996, I changed the name to "Market*zing*" to reflect the change in ownership and my new direction. I have a second business, simply called "Meanwell," specializing in assisting people to develop their latent talents. Meanwell is my surname (yes, it's a real name, and yes, I've got the birth certificate to prove it). In addition to being memorable, it also reflects the work I do in that business: helping people empower their lives through self-development programs, tapes, and literature.

When considering an appropriate name for your business, think about the work you do, personal traits you have, and how you would like to be remembered by clients. Remember, first impressions count, so make it a good one.

What space do you need to run a business?

You will spend most of your time in your workplace, so make sure that it's spacious, comfortable, quiet, and professional. This is business central for you. Dedicate a bedroom or other area as your new office—you'll need more than the kitchen table. Believe me, after one week, you will be sick of clearing your work each day to make room for dinner plates each night. If you haven't got the room, make the room. You can't skimp on your workspace.

Your Roadmap to Sustained Success

Should you set goals? Yes, but what goals you set are up to you. You certainly should set some financial goals for each week or each month so you meet your financial commitments. Beyond this, setting goals in other areas of your life will assist in defining what you desire, and in reminding you of what you're working toward in your commercial life. Where do you want to be—personally and professionally—in one, two, and three years' time? Don't just think about it; write about it. Flesh out your dreams into goals that can be broken down into a number of steps, each with a deadline for completion.

Reviewing your business plan

Some people go to all the trouble of developing a business plan only to shelve it a month later. This should be a living document, one that evolves as you and your business evolve. None of the information in your

---

business plan should be carved in stone. This is a plan based on your current knowledge and circumstances—and, as we both know, these are forever changing. Review and update your plan accordingly. This will keep you focused on the goals you've set, the objectives you have for your business, and the course you have fixed. If you decide to change direction—and you will, believe me—you can always make adjustments to the plan to meet your current situation.

What You Must Know Before You Plan

It may take you weeks or even months to research all of the parameters and consider all of the options before you complete your business plan. Just remember, whatever time you invest now will be worth it in the long run. Along the way, you will have plenty of time to consider the risk you are taking in starting your own operation. You will also have plenty of time to minimize the risk through thoughtful planning—formulating contingencies, and developing alliances with like-minded businesses—as well as doing your homework on the marketplace and the competition, your strengths, and any areas in need of improvement.

At the end of it all, you will know how much revenue you need to run the business and live comfortably. You will know how to measure your progress. You will know what you need to do to stay on target, and you will also know how to do it. Keep in mind, it's important to undertake this even if you are already in business.

I have produced a number of business plans since I went solo. I won't say I've written or updated the plan every year—that was the plan, but business got in the way. I have, however, read and reflected on the most recent business plan throughout each year.

When you've written a few, it's interesting to read over them and see how you, the captain of your destiny, have developed over the years. I've seen some dramatic shifts in both my attitudes and the course I've charted since that first fateful plan written back in April 1991, eight months before I set sail. Since then I've weathered countless storms and hazards that have thrown me off course, often into uncharted waters. But by having that trusty old business plan at hand, I've had the means to return to the original course or head out in a new direction.

GETTING ORGANIZED

Quality practitioners get it right the first time, every time. The secret of their success relates to systems: a set of procedures developed to ensure that every aspect of their business is coordinated professionally and efficiently.

You can use this approach in your business, not just to impress your clients but also to save you valuable time and money, and maybe win you some unexpected opportunities.

CHAPTER 4

Supercharge Your Business With Systems and Procedures

If one wants to write, one simply has to
organize one's life in a mass of little habits.

Graham Greene (1904–1991)

You've done all of the necessary planning—now you're ready to roll up your sleeves and begin organizing yourself so your business runs smoothly and efficiently from day one. As mentioned in chapter three, it's wise to develop systems, policies, and procedures that cover every facet of your business. This constitutes your operations manual. Here are some areas you can look at to improve your output.

Automating information

Develop a series of form letters that cover various aspects of your enterprise, including letters for prospecting, a basic script or bullet points for cold calling, and follow-up direct mail letters. In addition, develop systems that automate as much activity as possible.

Let's assume your system for attracting new clients is to mail a letter and brochure. Before you do this, create a system like the following so that each procedure is undertaken on time, every time.

1. Identify prospects from referrals, newspapers, and other sources.
2. Undertake basic research on a prospect's needs. (Visit the company's Web site to get an understanding of its products and services and what marketing communications are most appropriate.)

3. Issue a personal letter to the relevant decision-maker (e.g., General Editor or Marketing Manager).
4. Follow up the letter with a phone call (three days after receipt).
5. Arrange a meeting and present your portfolio.
6. Follow up the meeting with a proposal, letter, or phone call to close the deal (within a week).

Depending on your workload, these steps could be undertaken weekly or every two weeks. The point is that by developing systems like this, you can save time, keep the wheels in motion, and ensure that all necessary components of your system are carried out in a quality manner. You could develop similar procedures for maintaining contact with clients, referrals, debt collection—virtually any area of your business. By documenting every procedure, there's no need to rely on your memory to know what to do and when to do it.

Coding files for easy recall

One of the first things you discover in business is the amount of paper-work you have to deal with each day. That's not just correspondence you receive and periodicals you collect, but also the work you generate. I've found that the best way to maintain some order on the computer is to develop a three or four-letter code for each type of data file. For example:

PER   Personal Files pertain to your personal life
HSE   House Files pertain to your business, not clients
TWA   A three-letter acronym representing each client

This system, like all others, is designed to bring discipline to your office. But that discipline must begin and end with you. In the future, every time you create a file, save it beginning with the relevant three-letter acronym. It's also a good idea to add a date (month and year) to the end of the file name so you know when it was created, for example:

HSE   Mike's Tax 8-04

This is a good habit to get into. You'll thank yourself, especially the day you cannot find a specific file. Even if you don't know the name, you will now be able to find it by searching via your new code system. This system also makes it easy when it's time to file work.

Managing information on your desk and computer

Every time I start a new project—whether it's an article for a magazine or a newsletter for a company—I always start with a new manila folder (in fact, to make things even easier, I use different colored folders for different aspects of my business). By keeping all information in the file, I never lose anything; keeping just one file on my desk at a time, keeps my mind on the task at hand. I also avoid any confusion or duplication by maintaining the same files and folders on my computer.

Both Windows and Mac operating systems allow for the creation of files that can be stored in any number of folders organized in any of a number of ways. My personal preference is first to create two main folders. One contains all the Current Work—active files and work in progress. The other folder, Archives, contains all of the completed work. You can further categorize by clients within your Current Work folder and have a series of folders, each of which contains data relevant to your business, within each Client Folder, such as:

- Correspondence
- Background information
- Brochures
- Databases
- Media releases
- Newsletters
- Quotations
- Purchase orders
- Speeches

It won't be long before you have a large number of files within various folders. That's why it's important to clean out your Current Work file regularly, trashing some files and archiving others. Your Archives folder should reflect your Current Work folder so you can easily retrieve client files in years to come, if needed.

Like all systems, there's a fair bit of work involved in setting it up, but it's worth it in the long run. You'll always know where to find a specific file, based on its code and its folder. Here's how it works: When I'm not working on a specific job and it's still in progress, it goes back into the Current Work filing cabinet at my desk. When that job is done, I file relevant information, such as the final draft, the signed approval form, and any background information, in my Archives filing cabinet—whose contents, of course, have been categorized by client and by activity. One weekend a year is spent going through the Archives cabinet, sorting through material that I need to keep. This material finds its way into my garage and into another filing system for posterity.

It may sound like a lot of work, but it's not. Once you get into the habit, you'll be amazed at the difference it makes in your productivity. How many times have you blown an afternoon looking for an elusive file or tax receipt?

Dealing with snail mail and e-mail

Both kinds of mail should be sorted every day so there's no backlog to wade through at the end of each week. Postal mail can be sorted into piles, depending on its relevance and importance. Magazines can be placed into a pile for reading when you have time; correspondence that requires attention can be placed in an inbox. You should decide on the importance of the other mail you receive. Junk mail should be trashed immediately.

With e-mail, you can receive information any time of day rather than in one hit as with conventional mail. So it's even more important to stay on top of this through the use of discipline and systems. Delete junk mail, respond to important messages and file them in folders you've set up, based on client and activity. You should get into the habit of filing e-mail at the end of each day.

Backing up data

Backing up your computer data is one of the most important tasks you can undertake. For many, including me, the business would grind to a halt if the computer data were lost or corrupted. It is even more imperative to back up given the number of computer viruses that are unleashed around the world. But it's not enough to just back up your work on separate disks. What happens if your home is burglarized or, heaven forbid, destroyed?

That's why I maintain two sets of backup disks for all of my data. One set remains in the home office and the other in a secure location off-site. Each day, I back up the set of disks at home and then swap them with the other set. That way, there's no chance my business will go down even if the office does. I recommend you maintain two sets of backup disks and rotate them daily or weekly at the very least. One set can be kept at home and the other can be kept in an off-site location, such as a friend's home or a post office box, if you have one.

Handling office supplies and repairs

What happens if the fax machine breaks down or you run out of toner for your printer? Do you have the suppliers' details at your fingertips? You do if you maintain a file with contact details of all equipment suppliers, as well as the model and serial numbers of your equipment. This is also a good place to keep equipment manuals, warranties, and any technical information you may require. You can't control the amount of information that flows through your business, but you can manage it better by organizing yourself with systems.

Six Easy Habits for Improving Efficiency

1. **Keep it clean.** If your office or desk is a mess, you're probably a mess, too. Get into the habit of clearing and cleaning your desktop at the end of each day and your office at the end of each week. By keeping your workplace free of clutter, you'll start the day and any new tasks quicker and fresher.

2. **Plan each task and each day.** Often projects can appear insurmountable until you break them down into individual tasks and prioritize them. The same applies to your day. There's always so much to do, but what do you do first?

   Start each day with a "to do" list. Prioritize the most important tasks for the day and, if they are not completed, transfer them to the next day's list with an appropriate priority rating. In addition to a daily plan, keep weekly and monthly plans for longer-term or larger projects. Each week, review the list and transfer tasks to your daily lists, as required.

3. **Keep a shopping list.** When you're running low on supplies, add them to your shopping list to ensure that you have them when you need them.

4. **Get into a routine.** Discover when you work at peak efficiency—is it first thing in the morning or later in the afternoon? Allocate your most intensive tasks for these peak periods and choose to do other tasks, such as filing, research, and administration, at other times.

5. **Do tasks in batches.** Variety may be the spice of life, but you can often improve productivity by doing a number of the same tasks in batches, such as responding to correspondence, e-mail, and phone messages.

6. **When you're hot, don't stop.** When you're hitting those keys at a blistering pace, the last thing you want to do is stop, so avoid the temptation by turning the answering machine on so you can keep up the pace. Make sure, however, that you return all calls before the end of that day.

CHAPTER 5

Getting the Most Out of Working From Home

The writer is one who writes . . . He withdraws to
some quiet corner, a bedroom perhaps, or any
cubicle with a chair and a table, and applies himself
to his blank paper. Two hours a day are needed;
three hours are better; four are heroic.

Gerald Warner Brace (1901–1978)

There are both advantages and disadvantages to working from home. The good news is that you can save time in travelling costs, you can save money in terms of rent and operational expenses, and you can minimize your taxes. The bad news is that you miss out on the synergy that a good office offers. Even if you're working alone and sharing an office with other entrepreneurs, just having other people around you can be a good motivator. It does help, however, to be sharing space with the right people. I've been in situations where I've shared space with people whose presence was more disruptive than stimulating.

Turning a Spare Room Into a Productive Office

If you've decided to work from home, it's important to make your workplace as pleasant, professional, and conducive to working as possible. Here are some commonsense points you can apply.

1. **Make your workplace sacred.** Whatever area you deem to be your office—a bedroom, a spare room, or even the corner of a room—it should be sacred and off limits to "unauthorized personnel." This is your workplace, so other members of the family need to respect it.

2. **Stay flexible.** Whatever amount of space you have available, chances are you'll need more as your business grows. Invest in a larger desk than you currently need and install extra bookshelves. Keep less critical items, such as extra filing cabinets, supplies, and archived records, in a closet or garage.

3. **Get wired for work.** No doubt your office will contain a plethora of technological devices that require electrical outlets and/or phone jacks. Make sure you have enough of both for your needs now and in the future and that they are located close to your equipment.

4. **Light up your life.** Your office will need to be well lit. It's best for your eyesight (and usually your sanity) to have your desk face a window. When positioning your desk, make sure it takes full advantage of natural light without any glare on your computer screen. You can supplement natural light with a desk lamp and suitable ceiling lighting.

5. **Protect yourself.** Your office is now your livelihood, so safeguard it against "acts of God." Install surge protection equipment to protect your equipment from lightning strikes and power surges, which can fry electronic components. The equipment you now have in your home is among the most sought-after by burglars, so be sure to install a good alarm system.

6. **Think ergonomically.** Your workplace has to be safe, not only for your equipment but also for your body. If you expect to spend four or more hours a day at your desk, you need a workstation that promotes good posture. Start by investing in a good ergonomic chair that includes an adjustable back support and seat height to suit your body. Ideally, the chair should swivel and have castors for ease of use. Your computer screen should be placed directly in front of you at eye level and arm's reach. If needed, raise the height by placing the screen on a stand or even some stacked phonebooks.

7. **Make your office your haven.** The advantage of working from home is that you can put as much personality into your home office as you like. I spend a lot of time in my bedroom-turned-office, so I've made it into a haven—a home for my thoughts as much as my work. Serene pictures decorate the walls, soft instrumental music plays in the background, and often essences waft throughout the house all day long. It makes the office more tranquil and work more pleasant.

8. **Make sure the door works.** At the end of the business day, close the door to your office. This is also your home, so respect the personal needs of all who live there. Remember, you're working to live, not living to work.

How to Keep Your Mind on the Job

One of the things you'll find when working from home is that others may not consider that you're working at all. Often, because you're home, the perception is that you must be taking time off, that you're in between real jobs or just writing as a hobby. If you're not careful, you'll find friends and family dropping in for coffee or calling for a long chat on the phone during work hours. You need to educate them that this is work time. Make a point of seeing or speaking to them after hours, as you would if you were still working for an employer. Office hours are the time you should be working in the office or out seeing clients. You know this, but sometimes others need to be reminded of it.

That's not to say that your new home life is all work and no play. It's a matter of striking a balance. Because you're now working from home, you have the option of setting your own hours, to some degree. You can elect to start your day earlier to allow you time later in the day to go shopping or enjoy a long lunch with a friend while others are at work. In fact, it's good to give yourself a treat every now and then. There will be plenty of times when you're burning the midnight oil trying to finish a project on time.

Initially, I fell into the trap of letting my nine-to-five work spill over into nights and weekends. Before long, I was working every day and most nights. Apart from the fact that I didn't have much of a life, I was finding that it took me longer to complete tasks because I was not fresh at the start of each day.

We all need time to recharge the batteries, and we need to remind ourselves why we started our own business—for quality of life. So, while it's important to stay focused while you're working, you need to consider the big picture to ensure that neither you nor your family is missing out. You can do this by setting specific hours for business and allowing yourself time each day for a proper lunch break. You may wish to keep an answering machine on during these times so you can enjoy your break without interruptions. It's also important to get out of the house when you can. Even during a busy day, a quick walk around the block will not be time wasted. Your body and mind will thank you for it.

Dress for success

To maintain a professional image, dress for success. Yes, you could hang out in your bathrobe all day, and maybe no one would know except you. That's enough reason not to make a habit of it.

When I first began working from home, I would dress each day for work in a shirt and tie, like I did when working in a normal office. It made me feel like I really was at work. Now it's been several years, so I don't need external motivation to know I'm at work. Consequently, I dress a little more casually, unless I have a client meeting, and then it's back into the corporate attire.

Find the balance

Working from home can be a blessing or a curse. Like most things in life, it's really up to you. Your work and home environments can coexist, as long as you find a balance between work and play and respect the boundaries of each.

CHAPTER 6

The Cost of Doing Business

Writing is the only profession where
no one considers you ridiculous if you
earn no money.

Jules Renard (1864–1910)

How much you charge your clients depends on a great many variables, ranging from your overheads and experience to the complexity of the individual tasks and a client's ability to afford your services.

Tell Them What You're Worth

Whatever rates you set, you should promote them in introductory literature and any communication with prospective clients. This is a good way to qualify inquiries—it gives serious people an idea of the budget required, and it minimizes contact with "tire-kickers" and others who cannot afford you. In many instances, you will need to provide a quote on a job rather than give a standard fee. But often a client will want a ballpark figure. Wherever possible, provide a range of fees covering various jobs of interest. As I've said earlier, you need to know your financial position before you set your fees.

Consulting Fees: A Guideline

Factors to consider

Your commercial fees will depend on many factors, including:

- The caliber of your clients (you can earn more working with a large organization than a small business, as well as a company operating on the either coast or a major metropolitan area compared with the Midwest or a country town)

- The nature of the work (some areas, such as advertising and technical writing, pay better than other areas, such as PR and corporate communications)
- The complexity of the assignments (you can charge more for specialist tasks or jobs requiring technical knowledge)
- The duration of the projects (generally, you can charge more per hour for smaller, one-off jobs compared to longer-term projects. When quoting on assignments that will take several weeks or more, discount your daily or weekly rate by 10 to 20 percent—and make sure your client knows.)

Keep in mind that you can earn considerably more by working directly with organizations rather than through an agency. An advertising or PR agency will, of course, place a premium on your services before passing on the fee to the client. This can be anywhere from 30 to 100 percent. So, you can see, it pays to work directly for a company and cut out the middleman. However, freelancing for an agency can also pay, especially when you're starting out, in that you can generally be assured of a more consistent working relationship. In the long run, you will find that while it's safer to subcontract to an agency, it's smarter and more profitable to work directly with businesses. This way you are operating on a level playing field with agencies, which means you can not only charge more attractive fees, but you also have the opportunity to develop client relationships in terms of the services you offer and the work you handle.

At the end of the day, you are not offering a product or a conventional service that comes at a standard rate. You are selling *yourself*. And that's what you need to do—*sell* yourself and the benefits of working with you. What you are capable of earning will depend as much on the quality of your work, your experience in an industry (and your interaction with individual clients), and the way in which you conduct yourself.

As I said, there are many parameters to consider when determining consulting fees, including the individual writer's attitude and aptitude. To start you thinking, most commercial writing falls into a broad earning capability of $50 to $125 per hour (although some specialists operate in the rarefied stratosphere of up to $250 an hour). I personally calculate projects based on $100 to $125 per hour. This may sound like I am working at the top end, but I find that I generally can complete tasks faster than my competitors and, in some cases, offer the client specialist skills in niche markets. So, often my clients get a faster turnaround at a cheaper overall cost compared with competitors. Again, what you charge will depend on what you deliver, which is why I rarely reveal my hourly rate to clients when discussing the cost of a project. Hourly rates are "rubbery figures"— they're flexible, depending on the professional. What a client pays depends on the skills and speed of the writer. A slow writer may have a low hourly rate, which would appeal to a client until they get the bill. A faster writer may operate at a premium rate but complete the task in half the time, making him or her cheaper and quicker, which is why you need to talk in terms of the bottom line—the overall cost of the project and the overall benefits to the client.

You should also understand that you cannot charge clients for every hour you work. Generally speaking, I find that I bill around half of my working week. You need to take time out to organize your day, pay bills, write invoices, quote on jobs and handle any of a number of other administrative tasks. That's part of the cost of running a business—and that's why it's important to set reasonable fees, so you can afford the "downtime."

Typical fees

Here's a short list of fees for typical copywriting projects. This is merely a guideline to give you an understanding of what you can earn as an enterprising writer—ultimately, it's up to you:

Advertisements

Full printed page	$1,000–$2,000
Partial	$400–$1,000
Radio commercial	$500–$750

Public Relations

Media releases (1-2 typewritten pages)	$675–$800
Features (3 or more typewritten pages)	$900–$1,500

Corporate Communications

Product and service brochures	$500–$1,000 per printed page

Corporate profiles	$750–$1,000 per printed page
Newsletters	$500–$1,000 per printed page
Speeches and scripts	$100–$150 per speech minute

Direct Mail

| Sales letters (1-2 typewritten pages) | $500–$1,000 |

Web

| E-mail (1 typewritten page) | $500–$1,000 |
| Web site content | $500–$750 per Web page |

General Consulting

| Ad-hoc consulting | $100–$125 per hour |

For a more detailed list of commercial writing fees, consult *Writer's Market* (www.writersmarket.com).

In addition to consulting fees, you can elect to handle other tasks or manage an entire project, such as a publication. This would involve coordinating photography, graphic design, printing, distribution, and possibly other third-party services such as media relations and database management. As a general rule, I add an extra 10 to 30 percent to the cost of third-party services, which I on-sell to the client. My reasoning is that this profit margin allows for the extra time required for coordinating other contractors and project management. Adding a margin is standard operating procedure; however, the percentage varies. Some agencies charge upwards of 100 percent, depending on the services and the client involved.

Working with other contractors and even outsourcing writing tasks is a smart way to expand your services and improve your profitability (we'll discuss this more in chapter nineteen). But, if you decide to hire other contractors—be they other freelancers, designers, or photographers—you must accept responsibility for their actions and the quality of their work. If something goes wrong, your client will expect you to resolve it.

Fishing for Clients:
Know Which to Keep and Which to Throw Back

One last thing to consider when setting your rates is the kind of clients you intend to work with. My first boss in PR was fond of saying that "little fish are sweet," meaning that it's wise to have a handful of small regular clients rather than a few large clients. His reasoning was that it's easier to replace one or two smaller clients than one or two larger ones. I think everyone would agree with that, but I've never agreed with the philosophy of servicing just small clients. I saw in his consultancy how they took the major portion of the agency's time.

Often, you can invest as much time in a small project as a large one. Also, when dealing with smaller clients, it can sometimes be hard to educate them regarding the true cost of working with you, and you can wind up working at a lower rate and usually just as hard as you would for a larger business. In the beginning, you may not have a choice. The only clients you can attract may be small businesses, which is fine. Work with them while you develop your skills and reputation, but always keep an eye out for the big fish. You may have to change your tackle and bait to snare them, but you'll find in the long run that it's worth hooking a marlin rather than a mackerel.

How to Make Your Finances Work for You

No matter how successful you are in business, the trick to having money is not how much you make but how much you keep. That's right—saving—the ugly word most of us try to avoid our whole lives. Here are some relatively painless ways of putting the dollars back into *your* life.

I'm not going to spout wisdom about any wealth-creating strategies you can employ, and I'm not going to recommend a get-rich-quick scheme or even some swampland I've been meaning to offload. This section is about good old-fashioned financial planning and management techniques you can and *should* employ in your business *and* your life.

You know as well as I do that being in business is precarious enough without having to worry about a cloud of debt hanging over you. So allow for the flat times that come in every business. Allow for the big, unexpected bills that arrive when you can least afford them. Plan now by saving now or you'll pay for it later. And I'm not just talking about money.

Three Simple Tips to Keep You in the Black

Okay, I'm off the soapbox for now. Here are some commonsense tips that aren't so common in many people's lives. Why not make them part of yours?

Start budgeting

Whether you've been in business five minutes or five years, you will have some understanding of regular bills that are due next week, next month, or later in the year. Right? If not, now's the time to take note. In fact, you have all the information about your bills already at your fingertips. Whether you run a manual or computerized accounting system, you have a log of every bill that is paid by your business. In there will be a record of all your regular bills—things like car servicing and gasoline, communication costs and utilities, office equipment, maintenance, and consumables, computer software, hardware, repairs, and technical support. Categorize these any way you like, taking note of the cost and the times these bills arrived. Now take account of all the irregular or unexpected bills that your business has paid throughout the year. Categorize and note the times you paid these as well. Now you know the average cost of running your business for a year as well as on a monthly basis. You also know the peak months for bills.

You now know that you either need to make a certain amount in a certain month, or have that money in reserve if business is flat. Experience tells me it's good to allow for both. Allow for a certain level of "fat" in your business bank account, just in case you haven't got the earnings to cover your bills. For some, that means taking an initial pay cut; for others, it just means being more disciplined in spending. Whatever the case, this is a good business habit to get into.

There have been several times when I've worked hard and had a bumper business period. Then, for some unforeseen reason, business levels out or drops off. That used to be a great concern for me, but it isn't so much today. I cannot control market forces. I cannot control client strategies. But I can and *do* control my company's financial fitness by managing funds and allowing for rainy days, weeks or even months.

Stay debt-free

The first rule of budgeting is, of course, to spend less than you earn. If you want to stay in the black, you cannot afford to spend in the red. But you can use credit to your advantage, *if you are disciplined.*

I'm like everyone else. If I see something I like, I want it now. I don't always wait until I can afford it. My compromise is that I use credit cards wisely. I have two credit cards, one for personal use and one for business.

Most of my consumer items and domestic bills are paid by credit card, and the total amount is paid off at the end of the month. The same applies to my business credit card. I use it like an electronic checkbook, and why not? It gives me a certain number of credit-free days, it's accepted more widely than checks, and I get incentive points for using it. But, as I've said, the key to using it wisely is paying it off regularly.

Tithe 10 percent

Tithing is the old Christian practice of donating 10 percent of one's income to the church. A similar good practice is to invest 10 percent of your income (regularly—say, on a monthly basis) in a separate, interest-bearing account. Before long, the money will be worth something—maybe an annual vacation or, if you continue to save and add to it over the years, a sizeable retirement package. To me, it's the easiest and safest way to prepare financially for the future.

Money means different things to different people, but all freelancers would agree it offers them a safety net. Having money in the bank, in shares, or some other investment means you can ride out rough months. It means you can afford to take a break when others can't or shouldn't. It means you can slow down when you need to or want to. Having money affords you the luxury of time to reassess where you're going and to change course when it suits you. That is, after all, one of the great benefits of being a freelance writer—having the freedom to work your own hours, at your own pace, and on your own projects. Never forget that money makes it all happen, but only if you make money work for you.

WRITE WHAT YOU LIKE

Let's face it—you're a writer by choice. You chose this profession because you like the art of communication, so why not choose the areas of writing that you understand, are good at, and enjoy?

As discussed, there's a range of areas from which to choose. Other writers have dedicated volumes to addressing just one discipline. Over the following chapters, we'll examine some of the more profitable areas of writing you can choose to maximize your success.

CHAPTER 7

Get Technical and Tap
a Growing Market

If you're creating and selling information,
you'll never go out of business.

Michael LeBoeuf (1942–)

W hen was the last time you picked up an instruction booklet or technical manual and wondered what the author was trying to communicate? We've all had experiences where we've struggled to understand how to set a video recorder, figure out a computer program, or just assemble a child's toy. Some people choose to go it alone and only seek help from the instructions when they have to. Others try to work through the instructions and often become more confused. Either way you look at it, technical writing is a valuable skill. Some writers will see it as the most boring form of writing possible, but once they've handled a few technical assignments, most will agree it's one of the most financially rewarding.

It can take considerable skill to translate technical details into readable information for nontechnical people. And since technology is continually changing, there will always be a strong demand for good technical writers. Badly written technical communications will ultimately cost an organization money and maybe even market share. If customers cannot understand a manual, they will call the company's technical support staff, and extra support resources cost money. Alternatively, they will return the item for a refund or never buy from that company again. The repercussions for the company that does not invest in professional communications are quite significant.

Discover a Wealth of Opportunities

Technical writing takes in a broad variety of areas, from a cookbook, reference manual, or instruction book to an online help system, environmental impact report, or business prospectus. The purpose of any form of technical writing is to assist the reader in making decisions, fixing problems, or taking action. In fact, this very book you're reading is essentially a technical manual because we are discussing various processes and procedures for maximizing your potential in the writing business.

A lot has happened in this field in just twenty years. In the "old days," technical material was written for the technically minded and therefore was not very user-friendly. Today, more lay people are taking up the role of technician and, thankfully, the vast majority of technical communication is being written for this broader audience. You just have to look at today's computer manuals to see the evolution. These days, most are written in plain English instead of technospeak, and when you still can't understand the lingo, there's an abundance of third-party how-to manuals to help you, such as the *For Dummies* series.

This new form of technical communication has made the art more interesting for writers and, to some degree, a little harder. The easier it is to read, the more skill is required by the technical writer to translate gobbledygook into sensible prose. Another interesting trend that's occurred in the past few years has been the shift from using in-house technical writers to employing freelancers, as more organizations have downsized and are focusing on core activities.

Crack the Market and Make Real Money

As Peter Kent, author of *Making Money in Technical Writing*,[3] explains, there are three avenues for making money as a technical writer.

First, you can sell your services via an agency, which makes a handsome commission on each hour you work.

Second, you can beat the agency by going directly to the company in need. In both cases, you would work from their office and get paid as a salaried employee (but on a higher, casual rate).

The third and most profitable method is to approach companies as a freelancer and work from your own home office. While some larger companies may balk at hiring freelancers directly, most small- to medium-sized companies will not—and that's where the real wealth is. By cutting out the middleman, you'll be able to charge some, if not all, of the amount of their commission on top of your standard rate. To make the pot even sweeter, instead of quoting an hourly rate, you should carefully estimate the size of the project and quote on a total cost.

This requires a little experience, so it's best to begin with an hourly rate until you get a feel for the size and complexity of future jobs. Once you do, you can increase your rate without having to explain it to your client. This also suits the client, as most companies prefer to have an upfront understanding of the cost of a job before it is undertaken. I've always quoted a total fee for completing technical projects. Depending on how much time is required, you can invoice the client at various stages of its development or upon completion.

Which Technical Job Is Right for You?

Not only is there a great need for technical writing, there is also an enormous variety of areas from which to choose. Once you've decided you want to try your hand at technical communications, decide on the type you wish to target: writing software manuals, for example, which happens to be one of today's fastest growing areas.

You don't need to be an expert in a particular field to write a technical manual. If you have experience, it will help you get more work. But if you haven't, you'll still be able to write effectively because you are more likely to explain things other writers may take for granted. It's important to understand up front that technical writing requires a special breed of communicator: one who can write under pressure, write quickly, and above all else, understand technical data and know how to translate it into readable information for the nontechnically minded.

Before you say "yes, that's me," you'll need to consider a few factors that will be relevant to your success as a technical writer.

Identifying your interests

It's easier to break in and to write with passion if you have a natural interest or understanding of a particular area.

List your hobbies and areas of interest. These can be interests you have today, such as investing, past pursuits when you were growing up, such as surfing, and even things you'd like to do or learn when you have time, such as horticulture. Then think about technical, specialist, or general areas of knowledge, such as electrical engineering. Like all good brainstorming, think, don't judge—just jot down whatever springs to mind (there's an excellent brainstorming principle, called the Mind Map, which is covered in chapters eleven and twenty-one). Within a short time, you should have a dozen or more specialties or interests. That is, a dozen or more target areas for technical writing.

In fact, you can apply this principle to any and every area of commercial writing you offer to clients. Literally every industry, endeavor, and area of interest requires marketing services. That's the beauty of what we do. As writers, we are doing what we love, so it hardly feels like work. And when you write in an area that naturally interests you, well, it's hard to take your clients' money. I said hard, not impossible!

Approaching prospects

Once you've identified specific areas, you can target organizations working within those areas. These could be manufacturers developing products, industry bodies overseeing activities or corporations offering either business-to-business (B2B) or business-to-consumer (B2C) marketing solutions. When approaching these potential clients, highlight your skills and experience as a writer as well as your interest in and knowledge of their industry. If you have written articles or marketing material for their industry, this will improve your prospects.

Keep in mind that many organizations overlook the need to hire professional writers for manuals and other technical communications. Highlight the fact that quality communications can improve their corporate image and increase sales. Your skill at this may also help you get the job.

As mentioned earlier, don't be put off if you are not technically minded. This can work in your favor, in that you will be approaching the communication as a novice—much like your eventual reader. As such, you're more likely to explain processes carefully, simply, and correctly.

Honing these skills

Technical writing requires the skills of a journalist to identify and decipher information. You will need:

- **Interview skills** to be able to extract information from a variety of people, including management and technical staff. This can be somewhat challenging when dealing with technicians who have little idea of how to tell you what you need to know.
- **Organizational skills** to be able to prioritize tasks so the project stays on course and on deadline.
- **Knowledge**, even if you do not have specific knowledge of a particular product, it helps if you are familiar with the industry.

And, before you get the job, you will need to demonstrate that you are capable of handling it. That's where a portfolio documenting your past achievements and demonstrating your abilities is vital for success.

If you have never undertaken a technical communication before or have not produced work in a specific industry, you can gain experience and samples by creating a manual or other communication for a friend in the industry or for a nonprofit organization. In addition, you can accelerate training through numerous short courses available (see chapter two).

Eight Steps to Technical Writing Riches

If you think you're up to the task, let's examine what's required to ensure your technical communications stay focused and meet your clients' needs.

1. Establish ground rules. The first thing you need to do is to establish ground rules with your clients. Start by meeting the developers of the product or service, as well as management, to establish internal objectives and deadlines. Determine the size and style of the document, the audience, and the list of people who will be involved with the project.

2. Understand your objective. Before you type a word, you must understand the aim or purpose of the communication. What are you trying to communicate? Has your client launched a new product or upgrade, introduced a new service, or had a change in company policy? While your objective focuses on the subject matter you will be writing about, it should also cover what you expect to achieve for the reader. This could mean a clear understanding of the operating instructions for the new product, an improvement in employee safety or productivity, or a lift in the customers' perception of a company.

3. Know and understand your reader. Another rule of marketing is to know your target audience. When you know specifically who they are, you can better understand their needs and can tailor the communication to match their working knowledge, education, prejudices, preferences, and any other relevant criteria. This is one of the most important principles for writing any successful communication—perhaps *the* most important. How can you expect to communicate effectively with your readers when you have no idea of their needs and expectations? But ironically, it's the least utilized by technical writers and most other professional scribes today. The main reason technical writers do not know their audience is because the process involved in gaining that information appears daunting. In cases where your client does not provide adequate detail, you can develop a profile of your audience by gathering information from various sources, including surveys, questionnaires, focus groups, and existing customers. Once you have gathered this intelligence, determine your readers' level of technical know-how, education, and information needs, and weigh this against your client's objective with the communication.

4. Lay the foundation. Once you know your audience and your objective, you can begin gathering, structuring, and drafting the information so it can be presented in a logical, easy-to-understand manner. Where possible, include illustrations to support the documentation. Remember, we are visual creatures—it's easier to understand something if we can picture it. Your client may wish to provide photos or illustrations or may ask you to commission them. Always be clear about your responsibilities when negotiating the contract with the client.

5. Know what makes effective technical writing. Here are my three golden rules for solid gold technical writing:

- **Write to impress.** Just because you're writing about a technical subject doesn't mean you should always write like a technician. Present information in an interesting, clear, and warm manner. Use some discretion in your delivery: Employ a more conversational style when writing a software manual for the consumer market, as opposed to a specifications sheet on an air conditioning system for engineers.
- **Write for clarity.** Modify the KISS axiom to "keep it succinct and simple." That means using active language rather than passive, sub-

stituting everyday words for jargon and eliminating verbose phrases.

- **Be specific.** Whether you are writing for management, an industry specialist, or the general public, technical writing requires technical information, such as facts, figures, and recommendations. Wherever possible, be specific and support your claims with hard data.

6. Test it. You've finished the first draft. It looks good, but does it actually do the job? If you've written an instruction booklet on how to operate a piece of machinery, it's now time to put it to the test. Select someone who fits your audience profile and have them follow your instructions to determine the clarity and usefulness of the communication. This procedure will help you hone your communication and pinpoint any problems.

7. Get a technical review. Once you've incorporated the necessary revisions into the second draft, your manual is now ready to be validated by a company technician and any other relevant personnel to ensure that it covers all aspects of the subject being explained.

8. Confirm by testing the final draft. Following the third draft incorporating any technical, legal or corporate changes, the final phase is to test the document to ensure that it continues to meet the readers' requirements. This can be done through focus groups, surveys, and questionnaires.

Your technical communication has now gone full circle and is ready to go out into the real world.

Plenty of Opportunities for Good Communicators

Technical writing has received a bad reputation over the years. That's probably because in the early days, technicians and engineers drafted technical communications. Fortunately, more organizations are recognizing the need for clear, concise communications that not only help customers but also help the companies they represent.

That's good news. Even with healthy competition, technical communication continues to command one of the highest pay rates for writers. Every year there are new products on the market and new opportunities for writers to explain how they work. And remember, that's only one area of technical writing—there are plenty more where that came from.

As we've learned, technical communications can serve more than one purpose. In addition to explaining a process or providing instructions, they can also assist in breaking into new markets or enhancing a profile with existing customers.

One example of this is an instructional booklet, *How To Produce Your Own Newsletter*, which I created for Australia Post, the country's major postal service, as seen in image at right. Its corporate customers comprise a broad cross section of business, from small firms to large corporations. My task was to develop a value-added communication that achieved three objectives: To highlight the benefits of direct mail as an efficient communications and customer service tool; to provide simple, step-by-step instructions for developing an inexpensive, in-house newsletter; and to emphasize the benefits of Australia Post as a "marketing partner," providing a range of low-cost direct mail solutions for small businesses.

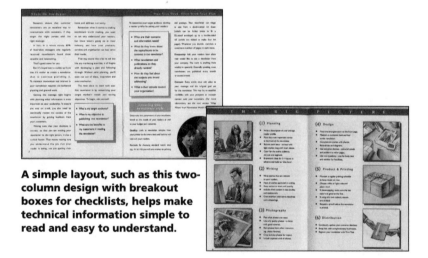

A simple layout, such as this two-column design with breakout boxes for checklists, helps make technical information simple to read and easy to understand.

The free, sixteen-page publication, which came with a recommended retail price of $7.95 (a simple method to obtain a perceived value), was a standard A5 booklet size (5⅞ inches by 8¼ inches). It featured a clean, two-column layout with a few breakout boxes for tips and checklists. It also included stock photos and line drawings to illustrate the major processes of newsletter production. The client preferred to use line drawings instead of conventional photography for two reasons: First, it was cheaper and quicker to produce several drawings than set up several location shots, and second, the client believed the drawings made the document more reader friendly.

A mix of stock photos and line drawings help ensure that this document is interesting to read and inexpensive to produce.

As stated in the introduction of *How To Produce Your Own Newsletter*, the booklet was not meant as the final word on newsletter publishing, but a starting point. It showed small businesses how to plan a newsletter, write and edit stories, and work with photographs. It also covered the basics of layout, design, and printing. And, finally (and most importantly from the client's viewpoint), it showed customers how they could save postage by using Australia Post's services.

The booklet achieved its objectives and became much sought-after by the customer base. It was direct mailed to several thousand active customers. A large number of leads were also generated by promoting the free booklet on Australia Post's Web site and in its customer newsletter.

The booklet also illustrates the point I have been making in this chapter: Always think outside the box when writing a technical document. Don't just settle for writing a how-to instruction, when you can develop a value-added communication. Consider the end user—the readers. What challenges do they face, what needs do they have? Include solutions—helpful product tips and techniques that improve productivity or client services which can save time and money. Thinking outside the box and beyond the brief is a win-win situation for all concerned. It will make a technical document more useful to read, more interesting to write, and a more valuable marketing tool for the client.

CHAPTER 8

Welcome to a New World: Writing for the Web

Make it simple. Make it memorable. Make it
inviting to look at. Make it fun to read.

Leo Burnett (1891–1971)

The World Wide Web, while still a relatively new communications medium, has undergone three significant stages of evolution.

Life online began with the word. Individuals initially used the Internet to share information. Then organizations large and small discovered the potential for global business. This second phase saw the Web's look transform from a bland, gray background filled with text to one with animated graphics, flashing banners, and online audio and video. During these "gold rush" days of the mid to late 1990s, all kinds of businesses scrambled to hang their shingles online. The problem was that the content of their Web sites was poor and, consequently, the majority has failed to capitalize on their investment.

Today, the Web is undergoing another evolution as a growing number of businesses reevaluate their content and develop more sophisticated ways of connecting with visitors.

What Is Content?

From a Web entrepreneur's viewpoint, content is literally everything you see and experience online—from information, audio/video streams, and links to the site's graphics, layout, and even its choice of colors. From a writer's viewpoint, content is literally every word that appears on a Web site—from news, reviews, and FAQs to e-zines, prescriptive information, and user forums.

One of the key "discoveries" by smart Web entrepreneurs is that content is king. Unfortunately, few realize that the written word remains the king of content. In fact, surveys have shown that the most effective Web sites in terms of hits or sales are those that focus less on design and more on content, particularly the clear presentation of information.[4]

Breaking Into the Industry

Today, the Internet appears to be at a crossroads with Web copy. Brick-and-mortar organizations tend to recycle marketing collateral for the Internet, while many dot-com enterprises are happy to leave content in the hands of advertising copywriters, marketers—or worse, Web developers. It's no wonder that the vast majority of Web sites don't achieve their potential, simply because they are not fit for their purpose. Given this, there exists an enormous opportunity for Web-savvy writers to enhance existing sites and play an integral role in the development of new sites.

The road to riches online is still a rocky one. You face an enormous challenge if you want to convince businesses of the need to invest in professional writers for the Web. But once you break through (we'll discuss strategies for doing this soon), you'll have an enormous choice of online writing markets, ranging from Web sites that feature news, information services, and consumer advice to e-zines on virtually any and every conceivable topic. And, once you've mastered them, new markets and opportunities await cyber scribes.

Discover Online Wealth in Eight Hot Markets

There are a number of lucrative online markets for writers, ranging from corporate communications to general interest articles and self-publishing. When working on the Web, you do not need to limit yourself to one market or, in fact, one skill set—you can be writer, editor, and publisher, one or all at the same time. The major markets include:

1. Web content providers. As we've discussed, a growing number of professional organizations are hiring writers to develop or edit content for their Web sites. Freelance opportunities exist with independent Web developers; there is also work available through agencies. Alternatively, you may wish to deal directly with clients. In addition to laying the foundation, you can also enjoy ongoing work as more smart organizations realize the need to update their content regularly.

Companies need writers who are well-versed in specific industries and who are also Web savvy. Ideally, it helps if you have some experience in HTML or XML Web programming languages, but this is generally not a prerequisite. In many cases, you will be required to work with a graphic designer or Web designer who would be responsible for site development. Copy can be e-mailed as standard text files and should include preferred headlines, subheads, and other editorial considerations. If you are responsible for photos, they should be sent either as JPEG or GIF files (check with the developer for the preferred format) with captions included.

2. E-zine producers. In just a few short years the e-zine market has exploded, with countless electronic publications produced on a wide range of topics. It seems that almost every professional Web site sports an e-zine, and the most successful are usually written by professionals. One simple way to gauge this market is to subscribe to e-zines on a particular interest or industry. You'll get an instant understanding of the scope and quality of the writing as well as acceptable styles. You'll also know which e-publications would benefit from your contributions—as we've discussed, the best way to attract business is to demonstrate your abilities.

An effective way to stimulate interest in your online writing services is to create your own e-zine that espouses the marketing advantages that an e-zine can offer—namely, raising awareness and building loyalty—and the role these play in improving the company's bottom line. This not only gives interested parties an information service that will be regarded as valuable and credible, it also establishes you as an expert. Who do you think they'll contact when they need help?

In addition to making a strong case for the value of using a professional e-zine writer, you can include beneficial hints and tips on how organizations can enhance their communication. This information can also form the basis of a query e-mail sent to prospects that have e-zines (or could have by using your services). The copy can also complement e-mail responses to Web visitors requesting more information or a quote on your services. Remember, with self-promotions such as this, you need to think about the old WIIFM adage—"What's in it for me?"—and make sure that what you're offering is of interest to your reader.

3. E-zine writers. Opportunities exist for writing news bites, opinion columns, and other articles, which can be placed with one or more e-zines directly or through online syndicates. Getting your name in cyber print also gives you valuable exposure, which will build your online profile and your portfolio and may also attract inquiries from potential customers.

4. Direct e-mail writers. There is also a growing market for writing online sales letters, auto-response e-mail copy, and other corporate communications as more organizations and their customers commit to e-commerce. A good place to begin is with your traditional clients, offering to add value to their marketing communications with direct e-mail to prospects, customers, shareholders, and the media. This has been a particularly lucrative area for me, as I've been maintaining contact with the media for my PR clients for several years. A natural extension of this has been to develop and deliver electronic communications to other target audiences.

5. Online writers. There are a number of literary as well as general Web sites that pay writers for original content. Also, a growing number of news services require freelancers to develop new material for their online outlets.

6. Electronic publishers. Print magazines and newsletters now have a viable cousin in the PDF publication. These can be read online or printed from any computer, they can be e-mailed quickly and simply downloaded from the Internet. In addition to promotional newsletters and magazines, freelancers can also create reports (known in business as "white papers"), specification sheets, and technical manuals using this universal format.

7. E-book authors. More writers are realizing the benefits of e-publishing. E-books can be marketed through sites such as Amazon.com, or authors can develop their own Web sites and reap all of the rewards. The most marketable e-books are technical or instructional manuals and workbooks, which can be priced up to ten times higher than fiction titles.

8. Online educational course providers. E-learning is one of the current trends online, and consequently the market for course developers is expanding rapidly. Online education sites need writers to transform dry material into palatable interactive tutorials and training packages.

Information and Opportunities Are Everywhere

Before you can capitalize on this virtual goldmine, you need to understand the difference between writing for traditional outlets and writing for online entities. Let's examine what works in the cyber world.

People visit Web sites for many reasons, ranging from technical support, product information, and general research to specialist advice, employment opportunities, and sales leads. They also go online to get the latest information on everything from news, weather, and industry gossip to sports scores, movie times, and stock quotes. Regardless of the type of information they're seeking, the number-one goal of Web users is to locate it as easily and quickly as possible. Consequently, Web sites live or die by the quality of the content they present.

Many studies indicate that users are less likely to read Web copy than to scan sentences and key words for information of interest to them. Content that is written concisely and objectively is generally considered more credible than, and is better remembered than, promotional hype, which makes up the majority of content on Web sites. Producing fresh content that stands out is not only the most effective way to attract traffic and establish user credibility but also to generate business leads, increase sales, and maintain loyalty.

Six Musts to Satisfy Web Users

Follow these key points for writing Web content that clicks.

1. Write clear and simple copy. Adopt an inviting, informal writing style. Even though people go online to gather information, many also want to be entertained, and everyone wants to feel welcome and not intimidated. Make sure your writing style engenders confidence, friendliness, and trust.

2. Keep it short. People don't like reading long, scrolling text on screen.[5] Write tight, concise, clear copy. Get your point across fast, keeping pages to two screen lengths or less. While this may mean more pages (you can provide hypertext links to related topics or more pages in an article), it will reduce the need to scroll.

3. Add a touch of humor. Humor can be an effective tool for maintaining a reader's interest, but it should be used sparingly and appropriately. Your brand of wit will not amuse every reader. Remember, Web visitors are an unknown quantity. Your site may attract people from all over the world, from different cultural and educational backgrounds as well as different age groups. When in doubt, play it straight.

4. Present information that's readable and scannable. Speed is the name of the game online. People want information fast, otherwise they'll click somewhere else. Employ elements to enhance your content's usability, such as headings, pullout quotes, bullet points, and highlighted text (bold or a different color). Use elements sparingly for effect.

5. Use a "newsy" style. The "inverted pyramid" style of writing, adopted by journalists, also suits the Web. If you place the major facts or conclusion first (appropriately known as "the lead") and the details and background later, readers will be able to gather information faster. Web users want to know up front whether the material is relevant to what they're looking for, especially if they're pressed for time. Write as if you only have a few minutes to make a point (with some visitors, that is all you'll get). Then, once you have your reader's attention, you can flesh out the piece with more details and background.

6. Create links to more info. One advantage of the Web is that you can insert links from one article or Web site to another, giving readers the choice of reading one article or several, simply by clicking on a hypertext link. This is also beneficial for the business behind the Web site. Links give the organization the ability to guide visitors easily to additional product information or sales.

What Makes a Good Content Provider?

If you wish to become a full-time content provider, or even if you just write for the Web occasionally, you should embrace the following attributes.

Integrity

Whether you're writing online reviews or sales content for an entire site, you should believe in what you're doing and write accordingly. Credibility is the most sought-after quality in Web communications.

Having integrity also means taking a stand with the work you undertake and the work you reject. As with offline writing, occasionally clients will want to "enhance" your work. There's nothing wrong with constructive criticism or legitimate rewriting, but if you firmly believe the editing devalues your work, you should say so. After all, you are being paid to be a communications consultant, so you have every right to express your views and make recommendations.

Confidence

Sadly, scribes have traditionally been low on the food chain. Whether as staff writers or freelancers, we have had to fight for reasonable pay rates and even the right to be treated as professionals. While many Web providers may be happy to continue this tradition, clearly times are changing. Content rules online. Writers who can produce fresh, exciting copy for the Net are much sought after in this increasingly competitive environment.

Aspiring content writers have to value themselves before they can expect respect from others. You must have faith in your abilities and the strength to walk away from a project if it appears to be illegal. Remember, there are plenty of dot-cons out there.

Organizational skills

Generally speaking, content budgets are fairly slim, so don't expect a lot of resources or support for your project. You need to be self-sufficient, disciplined, organized, and goal-oriented. You, or your client, will set deadlines for the completion of tasks. It's important to develop a schedule and ensure that you, your client, and any third parties stick to agreed deadlines. The responsibility for making this happen will probably end up on your shoulders, so you must be doubly proficient in managing your time and that of others.

Self-editing ability

Web sites usually cannot afford the luxury of an editor. When reviewing your own work, try to read it while wearing two different hats:

- **Management**, to be sure that it meets their objectives
- **Readers**, to ensure that the message will be understood, accepted and acted upon

Efficiency

The Web is all about speed. Content often needs to be written quickly and updated regularly. Turnaround times can sometimes be a matter of hours, so you need to be able to stay focused to meet tight deadlines.

Flexibility

It's been said that one year in the Internet world represents seven years in the offline business world. The Web is forever changing. Companies and their products can become overnight successes or failures, simply through online word of mouth. Conversely, new trends can become outmoded in a matter of weeks or months. To survive in this environment, it pays to be flexible. Keep your mind open to new ideas, methods, and attitudes.

Staying open, however, doesn't mean being gullible. When you come across new opportunities, it's important to validate them by researching the provider's financial status, history, and other relevant characteristics. Check online forums to see what experiences others may have had.

Interact With Your Visitors

The goal of all content is "usability"—how easy, enjoyable, and beneficial the Web site experience is for the user. And the key to usability is interactivity. People don't just soak up information like sponges; they need to be actively involved with it. Rather than simply presenting the Web visitor with a seemingly endless stream of text, it's important to develop an interactive Web site that encourages the user to participate in discussion forums, click on links, download materials, and respond to surveys and other devices.

Building an interactive site may be beyond your client's idea of what their Web site should be, but it's useful to "think interactive" and build this feature into your online communications wherever possible. The more interactive the site, the more meaningful and memorable it is for your visitors.

Establishing Context With Your Readers

If you pick up a textbook, brochure, or media release, you instantly know its purpose, its intended audience and, more than likely, the type of information it contains and its credibility. The physical, three-dimensional form and appearance of the document tells readers what they can expect to read.

While the Web provides the reader with a myriad of information at their fingertips, it's harder to discern context because there is nothing to distinguish one type of site from another, going by onscreen appearance alone. This is especially so when you consider that a visitor can arrive at any Web page from any point online. The visitor may have no idea whether their next click is going to take her to a corporate site, a personal home page, or a nonprofit association. Consequently, when writing for the Web, you need to supply more contextual information than is required for printed materials. Web content needs to convey to the reader the identity of the Web site, the type of information being presented, and for whom it is intended.

Online content expert Amy Gahran says that before you begin writing, you should examine the Web site where your work will appear to determine how much basic context it provides to readers.[6] The less content the site provides, the more you will need to include in your material. In addition, it's wise to review pages in the site that carry similar types of information to what you are writing. If you're writing a technical background paper on the inner workings of a product for a corporate site, check other technical pieces on the site to ensure that your writing is consistent and complementary.

Gahran says there are three simple but effective techniques you can employ to establish context:

1. **Mention your target audience in the headline or opening paragraph.** For example: "An increasing number of freelance writers are discovering the wide range of opportunities for working online."
2. **Link to the site's home page.** If the Web site has poor navigation characteristics, your readers will quickly become disoriented. So, to assist them with putting the site and your work in context, provide a link to the home page as part of your copy. For example: "Enterpris ingWriter.com offers a wealth of information to assist you in your writing business."
3. **Specifically mention the type of material being presented.** For example: "This book is designed to assist both beginning and experienced writers in becoming more productive, professional, and profitable."

Twenty Tactics for Successful Web Pages

Writing for the Web is a double-edged sword. On one side, your words have the potential to influence literally tens of millions of people online who are searching for information, ideas, and solutions. On the other side, your words ultimately compete with several billion Web pages throughout the world.

To be successful, your Web pages need to attract readers' fickle attention and maintain interest despite their short attention spans. It's good to remember that everyone's Web page is just a click away from success or failure. Here are the best ways I've found to ensure your cyber success.

1. Think of your reader as you write. Your job is first to communicate with and second to educate your reader. Before you can do either, you must know your readers' general needs, interests, and education level. Once you do, you can employ a context and terminology that are familiar to your audience, giving your message greater meaning and impact.

2. Write for speed. According to studies by usability expert Jacob Nielsen,[7] people read 25 percent slower from computer screens than from paper. In addition, the average time spent on a Web page is below one minute.[8]

To improve your chances of being read, as a general rule, write less than 50 percent of the copy you would ordinarily use for a printed piece. If you need to include more information, consider hypertext links to other pages.

3. Grab your reader's attention. As you know, cyber readers scan headlines, subheads, highlighted text, and bullet points, so use these to capture and motivate your reader. If you don't write these elements yourself or if you leave them for a Webmaster or designer, you run the risk of losing your readers early on. Aid readers who skim text by including short, highlighted subheads every few paragraphs. These can feature key words or brief quotes from the text that follows.

Research shows that eight out of ten readers scan pages,[9] so it pays to invest time in writing good headlines to stimulate interest. Make sure at least one headline is featured on each screen page. Also make headlines specific by including key words found in the text. With bullet points, keep the list between three and five items for improved scanning. If your list is too long, divide points into different categories that are segmented by text or combine several bullet points into one entry.

4. Use explanatory headings and page titles. You're not writing for an advertising agency, so smart, ironic, and teaser headlines are out. Write plain language attention-grabbers that complement the copy and meet the audience's expectations. Remember, the first thing a Web user sees is the page title and/or the headline, so invest more time in getting them right.

5. Give summaries to aid scanning. If you're checking for specific information in a large printed document, you can fan through the pages pretty quickly. If you want to do the same with a large online document, there's a better way than scrolling down each page, scanning the headlines, subheads, and bold text. If a one-paragraph summary is provided at the top of each page, your readers will know what to expect and whether it's of interest to them.

6. Use pullout quotes to improve scanability. Pullout quotes are picked up by the scanning eye, along with headlines and other elements. Keep highlighted quotes brief and relevant so they tell the reader something interesting about the content. Choose the quote that best captures the reader's attention. If it's too long, consider editing it to a dozen words or less.

7. Write like a journalist. As discussed earlier, the "inverted pyramid" style of journalism best suits Web writing. Readers want to gather information quickly, rather than wading through background material until they get to the meat at the end. The principles of a well-written lead can be adapted to the Web. The lead can kick off the story or be presented as a sidebar or an extended subhead positioned below the main headline. The lead could also be presented as a brief explanatory sentence accompanying a hyperlink on the links page. Or it could be a combination of these.

8. Use active language. Simple, concise, direct writing is far more effective onscreen than flamboyant marketing hyperbole. Straight, affirmative writing improves credibility, aids scanning, and conveys information more effectively.

9. Present one thought per paragraph. Again, think news when you're writing for the Web and write in headlines, as Ernest Hemingway once said. Use only one point or idea in each paragraph, and keep paragraphs to three or fewer sentences. Remember, short paragraphs mean white space, and that means visual breaks for the reader—a plus when you're looking at a screen for more than a few minutes.

10. Write as if you're having a conversation. The two extremes of writing—bureaucratic and market-ese—don't work online. If you write with an officious tone, your words will soon be ignored; if you write with too much of a promotional flair, you will suffer a similar fate.

Take an objective view of your writing and eliminate jargon, hyperbole, and the passive voice. Write with heart and use the second person ("you"). Make your words more personal and conversational, as if you are writing to a friend.

11. Use lists. Lists have become a popular element in newspapers and magazines because they provide a useful way of organizing information and attracting readers. In fact, even throughout this book, there are many examples of lists (including this one).

Web lists, like bullet points, work best when the lines are short for easy scanning. They have a variety of uses. You can have a list of links to other Web pages or sites. You can also list the contents of a large information piece (with links to specific topics or sections).

12. Use but don't abuse elements. Elements such as bullet points, lists, and pullout quotes are good in moderation, but don't overuse them or they will lose their effect. This is especially true when using bold to high-light key words and concepts. If overused, it makes reading harder and scanning virtually impossible.

13. For more information, link. That's the advantage of the Web. If you need more room to make a point or wish to include other references, you can link your Web page to others. Hypertext allows readers the choice of continuing to read your piece or clicking on to other information that expands upon a point.

The most effective ways of presenting links are either to embed them in the text of a document or to make a list of links at the end of the piece. The best way to embed links is to include the link in the natural course of the sentence (e.g., "For more information on the author, you can visit MichaelMeanwell.com"). This way, the sentence reads smoothly, whether the reader clicks on the link or continues to read the document.

The alternative is to present a number of links as a list. This allows readers to finish the document and then click on any links they choose.

If you decide to create a list of links, however, it's important to include a sentence describing what the reader can expect to find. And don't include too many links—you may run the risk of confusing the reader or diluting the message.

14. Allow for nonsequential content. There's no guarantee that your well-conceived document will be read sequentially, since Web visitors can arrive at virtually any page from any point on the Net. It's important to structure each of the Web pages that make up your document, like a cross-indexed reference book. Each document should be segmented into self-contained subjects so they can be read independently or as part of the whole. That means repeating contextual information on each Web page and including links to relevant information.

15. Write for different audiences. One of the main advantages online documents have over print documents is that you can write for different audiences and readers with different levels of understanding (i.e., beginner and expert). This is simply achieved through hypertext links. Your initial document can be written for both novices and professionals, with links to further information that can be tailored to suit the needs and levels of different audiences.

16. Don't capitalize all of your copy. Capitals SHOUT at the online reader. They also turn readers off and slow down their speed. However, you can use capitals sparingly, for example, if you are giving away a FREE item. JUST DON'T OVERDO IT!

17. Don't forget to edit. The same rules apply online as offline: Check for spelling, grammatical, and punctuation errors as well as for consistency of capitalization. Make sure all information is accurate and also test all hyperlinks (because the Web is a dynamic organism, links that worked yesterday may be obsolete today). Just when you think you're finished, check the final version on paper. It may seem ironic, but you'll find that if you print out your online writing you'll do a better job of picking up typos, poor structure, flow, meaning, and other communication errors. Better still, print it and then read it out loud. Web copy is supposed to be conversational, so it's best heard.

18. Take care with punctuation. Words appear on screen at a lower resolution than the printed word, and depending on the Web browser and computer monitor used, many punctuation marks can be misread or misunderstood online. Here are three general rules to follow:

- Replace colons and semicolons with dashes.
- Rework sentences where possible to avoid the use of apostrophes.
- Limit the use of hyphenated words.

19. Think local, write global. Your Web pages can be accessed from literally anywhere in the world. Even though English has become the new Esperanto language online, it's important to remove colloquialisms (e.g., Americanisms like "on the ball"; Briticisms like "on your jack"; or Australianisms like "offsider"). These local phrases may confuse readers from different countries and cultures, not to mention those readers whose first language is not English.

20. Keep your content fresh. View a Web site as an online magazine. You don't produce just one edition but a series of issues on a regular basis. Why? Not only to attract new readers but also to maintain the interest of existing readers.

New and updated information isn't just the domain of news sites; it should be the responsibility of every content provider. On a commercial site, new product information should be updated regularly, but it's also important to make new and interesting offers to customers and prospects in order to give them a reason to continue visiting the site. Current, quality content can transform the site itself into a valuable resource. Look at some of the large commercial sites, such as Apple.com, Microsoft.com, or Kodak.com. You'll find that their content is forever changing to maintain reader interest and motivate return visits. While your own Web site, or those of the companies you are working with, may not have the same resources as these multinationals, you can improve traffic to your site by modifying the appearance and by regularly adding new information and special features.

The Winning Formula for Online Reporting

When news services initially came online, the option was simply to "repurpose" news stories for the Web—in other words, copy and paste stories online. This is still the case for many smaller organizations, but a growing number of professional news services are presenting news stories and features that have been written specifically for the Web.

While the basic rules of writing print news also apply to Web news—chief among them the importance of the "inverted pyramid" style—Web stories generally should be half the length and pack just as much punch (if not more). The attention span of the average Web reader is far shorter than that of the average newspaper reader or television viewer. In many cases, you will either win or lose your visitor with your lead paragraph.

As we've discussed earlier, Web visitors read more slowly, remember less and don't enjoy digesting large slabs of text on screen. So, as a general rule, limit Web stories to half a dozen paragraphs or fewer. You can economize by using bullet points, which also make scanning easier. In addition, you can link to other stories, references, or further information on other Web pages or other sites.

If you are freelancing for an offline publication that also has a Web presence, you will need to draft two versions of the story for the two media. It's best to begin with the traditional piece first, as this will contain more information. Once you've completed the print version, you can rework it to suit the Web, refining the style and reducing the words. In a sense, it's like reworking a rough draft, editing it down to around half the size. This approach has worked best for me, but some writers prefer the reverse approach and write the Web version first, which serves as an outline for fleshing out the larger, print version. Try both approaches to see which best suits you.

As with other Web communications, you will need to take over some editorial responsibilities, such as including headlines and subheads in your copy as well as captions for photos, if appropriate.

The Future of Direct Response Is Already Here

Direct mail has been a successful tool for personalized communications with prospects and customers. The main problem, however, has been keeping costs down as mailing lists increase. That's where e-mail has a distinct advantage.

E-mail promises the same benefits for the entrepreneur as direct mail, but the difference is that costs do not rise in line with mailing list numbers. In addition to cost savings, e-mail offers timesaving benefits. You can set up auto-response functions, either through the e-mail application on your computer or through a Web-based service (many of which are free). This enables you to respond immediately to inquiries—even when you're not available. Apart from keeping in contact with your target audience anytime and anywhere, you can include links to more information on products and services as well as promote special offers on your own and other Web sites.

E-mail does, however, have some disadvantages compared with the humble direct mailer. Unless you're using HTML-enhanced e-mail, there are no eye-catching graphics or tangible involvement devices to attract the reader. And even then, your words have to work harder to sell your company and concepts. And because e-mail is so easy to send and perceived by many as a transitory form of communication, there's the temptation to write something on the fly without giving it proper thought. How often have you received e-mail messages filled with typos, missing words, and ungrammatical sentences? If you don't want your communications to join the junk e-mail pile, craft them with the same care you would give a query, sales letter, or anything else worth writing.

Ten Steps to Empower Your E-Mail

1. Write with care. Give your e-mail copy the same consideration you would give any other writing task. Make a list of important points you wish to address and ensure that you open the communication with the most important point.

2. Grab attention with your subject line. This one line can act as a strong motivator to either open or trash your e-mail. Your subject line should be compelling but should also honestly indicate the contents of your message. Most business people receive dozens of e-mails every day, so time has become more precious and competition more fierce. Your subject line has to cut through the clutter by signaling relevance and urgency to the recipient.

3. Be conversational. E-mail communications are not only personal; they're informal by nature. So, in your direct marketing communications, adopt a light, conversational style, making reference to the recipient personally throughout the message.

4. Be clear. Like Web readers, e-mail readers have limited time, short attention spans, and fickle natures. Get to the point immediately. Don't beat around the bush with a long, meandering introduction. Tell the reader what you want at the start, support it with facts or brief details, and finish with a compelling reason for the reader to take immediate action.

5. Call readers to action. Like any direct marketing communication, your e-mail should include a strong "call to action," prompting the reader to respond, buy or click on a link for more urgent information.

6. Present one message. Your e-mail message should address one issue, not several, so you don't confuse the reader or lose his or her interest. If you are selling an assortment of products, promote them individually in subsequent e-mails or consider developing a regular opt-in e-zine. This device affords you more space to discuss a range of issues as well as links to various Web pages for further information or sales.

7. Remember that presentation counts. Just as with other online communications, you only have a small amount of time and space to get your message across. Keep your sentences and paragraphs short (even shorter than Web pages, since the columns are much thinner) and include plenty of white space. Likewise, keep bullet points short in length and size.

8. Spell out the benefits. Your readers are investing valuable time to read your e-mail, so you had better make it worth their while. Your message should contain relevant, useful information or a special offer. In addition, ensure that your words spell out the benefits of working with your organization and what the reader stands to gain by responding to your offer.

9. Allow your reader to opt out. The most effective way of building an e-mail list is either through direct contact (such as via phone, coupons, or surveys) or through an opt-in facility on your Web site (where, for example, people can respond to an offer of more information, a free product, or an e-zine). Even though they have "opted in," most people still want the option of being removed from your list.

Complete your first, welcoming e-mail with a final paragraph offering the reader the opportunity to unsubscribe from the list. This message should be included in all bulk e-mails sent as well as e-zines, otherwise you run the risk of being labeled a "spammer" and may even attract "flaming" e-mails from unhappy readers. Recent Federal legislation now makes it illegal to send unsolicited e-mail. So make sure you include an opt-out notification at the end of your message.

10. Don't forget to proofread. When you've finished the piece, trim the fat, check for typos and spelling errors, and manually check any links you have to Web sites and any attachments you're sending with the e-mail.

Things to Know Before Working in Cyberspace
Quality counts

You can apply your usual writing principles to your new markets, but be doubly careful when it comes to editing and checking facts and accuracy. Because of the speed and nature of online publishing, there's less time and effort invested in editing submitted copy, so you should assume responsibility to protect your reputation and to ensure continued good favor with your clients.

How to win work

As in the offline world, you can apply for advertised positions (there are a number of literary and employment sites on the Net) or check the needs of conventional news services. Unlike the offline world, the query-to-publication time can be short—sometimes only a few hours or days rather than the traditional weeks or months. You can take a more proactive approach by targeting Web sites of interest and querying them with story ideas and content proposals. Keep in mind that the bulk of Web sites that require help with content often neither realize it nor value it, so you may need to educate them as to the value of employing a professional wordsmith. Needless to say, one query letter isn't going to achieve that for you. Developing new markets may require producing a proposal that not only contains the benefits of fresh, original content but also explains how you will research, produce, and implement it on their Web site—and, of course, tells the organization what it will save in resources and expenses.

As you can see, this approach requires a substantial investment from you up front. But keep in mind that we are talking about approaching companies that wouldn't ordinarily use a freelance content provider. Once you gain their attention, it's unlikely that you'll have competitors to deal with. Also, when you have completed the site, there's the opportunity of obtaining more work from the company in terms of ongoing writing to keep the site up-to-date, as well as referral business.

Skills for every season

Because of the diverse nature of Net writing, it pays to develop writing, editing, and Web-development skills. Editing is a particularly important skill to hone, given the need for speed in online work. The writing skills required can vary, depending on the company and its Web site or other needs. Again, diversity is the name of the game. Some companies may require industry-specific knowledge or a technical writing background, while others will be looking for a generalist or a writer with a marketing background.

If you plan to write general content for Web sites but have yet to get off the ground, demonstrate your abilities based on your experience in other writing fields. If you have already established yourself as a successful writer of marketing communications, such as direct mail, brochures, newsletters, or ad copy, this should differentiate you from many others. In addition, your experience offers the potential to convert your traditional clients into new online clients as they establish a Web presence.

Another advantage of writing for the Web is that it favors teleworking. You don't need to visit your client's office every day or even once—in fact, in some cases, you don't even need to be in the same city or country. Such is the beauty of working online. You and your client are just a mouse click away from each other.

How to be professional

As you can see, the World Wide Web offers a wealth of opportunities for savvy writers. It is attractive to writers because of its speed and universal reach. But it's important to exercise some caution with Web clients, particularly companies that are just starting out.

Before commencing work, check the company's history with Government authorities or the Better Business Bureau. The BBB (you can visit the bureau online at www.bbb.org) can keep you abreast of scams and also advise you about disreputable firms or individuals to avoid. As with other writing jobs, it's also wise to make sure a contract has been signed or that the client's purchase order or your quotation has been formally approved. Dot-com companies come and go pretty quickly, as we've seen in recent times. So make sure you have a chair if the music stops playing.

CASE STUDIES:
Web Communications That Click

The key element to the success of any Web communication is the writing, which generally requires a different approach than offline copywriting. That is, unless your communication has to pull double-duty as both a cyber and paper document.

Come2gether brochure on target—online and offline

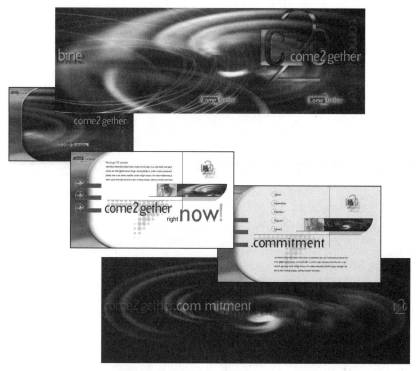

It's rare that brochure design dictates content, but Come2gether.com's Web site and brochure is one example.

A new Web design company, Come2gether.com, thought that the best way to promote itself was to demonstrate what it could produce for clients. The result is a paper and cyber brochure that is eye-catching, to say the least.

Generally speaking, copy comes first and design second. But when a client has already decided on a certain look, words are dictated by design. That was the case with the Come2gether.com brochure. The client already had the concept in mind. All that was needed were the right words to complement it. Admittedly, I am used to writing longer company profiles, but given the space restrictions and the fact that this brochure was meant as a "quick read" whether online or offline, I think the copy says it all. See what you think:

COME2GETHER.COM: "Bringing Together Business and Customers With Creative Multimedia Solutions"

You've got 30 seconds.

That's all it takes to win a sale or lose a potential customer on the Internet. Now, more than ever, you need clear, concise marketing communications that lift your profile, increase business, and encourage customer loyalty.

That's why smart companies work with Come2gether.com. A full-service Web development and marketing company that brings together talented communications specialists who know traditional and online media, and know how to make them work for *your* business.

Come2gether.com can design, build, and manage a range of multimedia solutions to suit any market or industry as well as any business need or budget.

With clients in retail, tourism, and other industries, Come2gether.com is well versed in all areas of business. We can deliver interactive Web sites featuring electronic catalogs, multimedia applications, and secure, easy-to-use e-commerce facilities. We can also handle all of your print requirements, from corporate identity and logo design to copywriting, illustration, and production of brochures, newsletters, and advertising.

Come2gether.com has the skills, capabilities, and resources to meet your requirements on time, to brief, and within budget.

Talent—Our business is based on in-depth experience across a broad range of disciplines, including advertising and PR; illustration and graphic design; photography, multimedia production, and artwork reproduction. We are also proficient in Internet strategy, support, and customer relationship programs. *Our team is at your service.*

Innovation—Whether you need to launch a new product, tap new markets, or improve corporate awareness, we can develop a dynamic Web site that's founded on leading-edge technology and sound business management principles. *Your Web site will be fit for e-business.*

Functionality—Our multimedia solutions are not only easy to understand, they're also practical for today's business. Whether it's a Web presence with secure, electronic shopping facilities, online chat and forums, or a four-color magazine, brochure, or eye-catching point of sale. *Whatever your needs, our approach will stimulate and maintain customer interest.*

Support—Business requirements and customer demands are forever growing and evolving. We are here—with you—every step of the way. We offer ongoing marketing and business consulting to ensure you re-

---

main responsive to your market and ahead of your competition. *You can be assured your promotions will continue to meet your goals and customers' demands.*

Synergy—At the end of the day, whatever you publish on paper or online is far more than a collection of marketing collateral. It makes a statement about you and your business. That's why we invest considerable time, so that we understand your business needs, goals, and direction. *By working as a partnership, we ensure your continued success.*

Come2gether.com means business. And so should you.

Call us today to find out how we can help you attract new business *and* keep it.

BureauScan company profile heads for cyberspace

Film and printing house BureauScan had operated a successful business for many years, primarily on word of mouth. But when it decided to establish a strategic alliance with several specialist firms to provide a complete marketing service, it was time to show customers exactly what it could do for their businesses.

The resulting four-color, corporate profile (seen above) was produced entirely in-house by the company and its strategic "partners"—and I was one of them. It became the company's premier sales tool, direct mailed to customers and presented to prospects. It also served as BureauScan's foray into cyberspace.

Here is the copy that appears online and offline:

BureauScan

Making first impressions lasting impressions.

Business: We Know What's on Your Mind

Undoubtedly the most important asset in business today is timely information.

BureauScan understands your needs and meets them with a total solution—a complete service for all your marketing communications today *and* tomorrow.

Established in 1990 as a specialist-scanning provider for the graphic arts and advertising industries, BureauScan has continued to expand its services to meet the changing needs of customers.

But, unlike your usual suppliers, we offer more than imaging, proofing, film, and printing. We provide a complete communications package—from concept, copywriting, and design right through to final print and beyond.

We have assembled a team of specialists in each critical phase, so that we can offer you the best advice, the most professional service, and outstanding results at an affordable cost. And we do this by pooling resources and expertise with a select number of expert suppliers.

We're an extension of your business, providing an efficient and cost-effective total communications solution.

Creative: We Understand Your Needs

Beyond the usual consideration of target audience and marketing strategies, you need to complement words with images and design to produce a coherent vehicle that gets your message across simply and effectively.

That's where BureauScan can help.

Rather than employing a number of suppliers to undertake various tasks, we assemble a team specific for your task, so you benefit from a coordinated approach from the beginning.

Copywriters who are experienced journalists work hand-in-hand with our commercial and industrial photographers to capture the essence of a new product range or complement the image you wish to portray.

Our designers can fuse text and photos into a graphic package that showcases your company's features and benefits to prospects and existing customers.

Whether you need a fresh corporate identity, display advertising, or a customer publication, BureauScan can handle the entire task or a portion of it, from idea to execution.

Production: Professionalism You Can Trust

Being satisfied with your corporate message on paper is only half the job. You need to ensure that it is conveyed accurately in the finished product.

Our business was built on specialist scanning and today we are still a premier provider of full service flatbed, drum and slide scanning, not to mention quality film and accurate proofs. That's because we only use state-of-the-art technology like Linotype-Hell imagesetting equipment and the fully integrated Heidelberg Delta Tower "in-RIP" trapping system.

And we back this technology with industry experience and technical expertise—and a considerable amount of resources in the early stages of production to guarantee that your job will be processed right the first time.

From the moment your electronic art is received by our Production Department, it undergoes a "preflight" analysis to check files for missing fonts, images for correct colors, and any other anomalies.

We have the capacity to convert almost any kind of file from both IBM and Macintosh platforms. Also for your convenience, you can download data via e-mail or our dedicated ISDN line for large files or interstate clients.

Choose from our full-service or ad-hoc services—we deliver efficiently and effectively.

Printing: We'll Make You Look Good on Paper

Whether you have a one-page, single-color brochure or a multi-page, four-color publication, BureauScan treats your job the same way—with care, attention to detail and a quality result.

Our high-capacity digital photocopiers and printers ensure faster and more effective turnaround of jobs.

State-of-the-art digital technology enables images to be scanned or transmitted electronically into memory where they can be stored for future use. Data need only be input once, reducing much of the setup time involved in traditional printing and copying methods. And less setup time means lower costs for you.

When it comes to finishing the task, BureauScan offers a range of options, from stapling, folding, or scoring to saddle stitching, perfect binding, or coil binding and laminating.

And, when you wish to publish on the Internet, BureauScan can help you get online with a minimum of fuss. We can develop simple, information-rich home pages or graphics-intensive Web sites that interact with your online audience.

Whichever option you choose, we'll make a good impression the first time, every time.

The Bottom Line: Our Business is Taking Care of Your Business

So what is BureauScan?

We are a full-service marketing communications center. So when you deal with us, you deal with only one Account Manager, give only one brief, and get only one invoice—and that means real savings in time and money.

Even better, your first impression on prospects will be a lasting impression.

And we can do this for you—just as well as we do it for our wide range of existing clients—by meeting your needs and exceeding your expectations.

On Time, on Brief, and on Budget

Call us anytime and find out how we can help you improve your bottom line today and tomorrow.

CHAPTER 9

The Anatomy of an E-Author

The self-publisher really has control
of his or her destiny to a much larger degree
than does a writer merely submitting a
manuscript [to a publisher].

Dan Poynter

There's more than one way to get published. If you're like me, you haven't got just one book inside of you, you've got a dozen screaming for attention. However, with just one in one thousand unsolicited manuscripts ever seeing the light of day (the figure is closer to one in ten thousand with the large New York publishers), it seems the easy part is to write the book—the hard part is to get it published. That's why a growing number of writers are turning to self-publishing.

Some people may see this as a poor alternative to traditional publishing, but it's important to remember that a string of best-sellers started life as self-published tomes. Well-known titles like *The Celestine Prophecy, What Color Is Your Parachute?*, and *The One Minute Manager* were all initially self-published. Once they became successful, traditional publishers picked them up and the rest is history.

This book was originally self-published in January 2001 and distributed on the Internet. Since then, my humble e-book has sold consistently around the world, primarily throughout the United States, United Kingdom, Australia, and New Zealand. It has also gained readers in unlikely locations, including Japan, Denmark, Georgia (formerly the Georgian Soviet Socialist Republic), and the Pacific island of Vanuatu. In addition, the e-book attracted widespread praise from critics, the media, and some best-selling authors. All this has led to publishing contacts in the U.S. and Australia, along with growing interest in my other work.

Who knows—the same fate may befall your opus. It's certainly easier, thanks to the Internet and Stephen King. King, as many will recall, produced the publisher's worst nightmare a few years ago when he posted his e-novella, *Riding the Bullet*, on the Internet and sold five hundred thousand copies in the first 48 hours. This not only sent

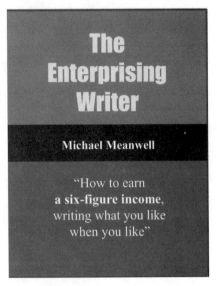

The original e-book cover for *The Enterprising Writer*.

shockwaves through traditional publishers, it also paved the way for published authors and newcomers. Almost immediately, submissions to e-publishers like DiskUs Publishing quadrupled, and e-book sales tripled. Now, I'm not suggesting you can replicate that effort, but it does open the door to a new market for mid-list and would-be authors eager to get a break.

E-publishing on the Internet has distinct advantages over traditional vanity publishing. For one, beyond your time, there's virtually no cost involved in producing a book. And you will have greater control over the marketing (if you wish) and a greater slice of the profits. Also, e-books sell better than almost any other commodity online. One of the reasons is that customers can purchase them and gain instant gratification by downloading and reading them immediately. With other products, they may have to wait days, weeks, or even months to receive them. Amazon.com started and built its multimillion-dollar enterprise by selling books. Today, many small-time authors are experiencing big success online.

Two Ways to Publish Online

There are many advantages to publishing, marketing, and selling your own e-books.

- There's no need to invest hundreds or thousands of dollars in printing. If you publish on the Web, your customer downloads a copy of the file, which can then be read on screen or printed.
- There's no need to lose a significant percentage of each sale in distribution fees or commission to wholesalers and retailers. Your e-book will have access to a global market via the Web, and it can be distributed with the click of a mouse button.
- You also retain the maximum profits from sales. By setting up your own Web site with a secure credit card payment facility, you can make sales around the world and around the clock—automatically.

There are two ways to sell your books online. You can sell them directly on your Web site, or you can sell them via one of the many Web sites dedicated to e-publishing. If you choose the latter approach, I recommend you visit www.booklocker.com, one of the most reputable e-publishers, which also offers some of the highest royalties in the industry.

When I decided to e-publish, I took both approaches. I developed my own e-bookstore, simply called Meanwellstore.com. And, within a few months of launching the site, I also offered my e-book to Booklocker.com. This way, I got the best of both worlds—the highest royalties from my own site and 70 percent through a third party, which offered wider exposure and potentially more sales.

Let's examine both approaches.

Becoming Your Own E-Publisher

There are a couple of reasons why you should establish your own Web site.

First, you retain the maximum percentage of profits. Once you've set up your site, you will only need to pay for your ongoing Web hosting and domain fees as well as charges for accepting payments via credit cards. Depending on which providers you select, these costs may represent 5 to 10 percent of the cost of each sale.

Second, by establishing your own site, you have the opportunity to not only promote and sell your books but also showcase your other literary works and skills, and attract more business.

While the rewards can be high, you will need to make a serious investment in understanding how Web marketing works and how to attract and convert visitors to customers—all before you see a serious financial return. If you decide to build your own site, there are many online tools that can help you as well as some good, low-cost, easy-to-use Web development packages.

As stated earlier, the key to Web site success, particularly in our profession, is to keep it simple. The added advantage in doing this is that you do not need to buy expensive Web development programs or hire a Web designer. Your priority should be to design simple Web pages, build credibility with quality products, stimulate interest with convincing copy, and have the ability to safely accept credit card payments and allow e-book downloads from your site. There's a significant investment to be made before you have a successful e-publishing venture, but I assure you that the long-term rewards far outweigh the initial investment.

If you're serious about the Web, I suggest you invest in three e-books. These are best-sellers on the Internet for good reason—they will give you all the information and expertise you need to develop information products, build a solid Web site, and kick-start your online business.

Read *Ebook Secrets* by Ken Silver. It was the first e-book I downloaded, and it's still among the most valuable in my growing e-library. Ken is a veteran journalist and newspaper publisher who offers a wealth of information and experience in his best-selling e-book. This is an ideal reference book for anyone considering publishing and selling their own information books. It includes practical information and loads of online links, not just on developing e-books but all you need to know to sell them online, including Web copy and design as well as online strategies and free tools for automating business processes.

I also recommend that you read *Make Your Site SELL!* by Dr. Ken Evoy, as well as *Make Your Words Sell!* by Dr. Ken Evoy and Joe Robson. Joe is a well-known and experienced copywriter and marketer. Ken is a general practitioner who struck gold online with his first Web how-to e-book, which is considered by many as the bible for Web site success. These two e-books cover similar territory to Ken Silver's, but they also include more detailed information on attracting, cultivating, and convincing people to buy from your site.

All three books are written in a friendly, easy-to-understand manner and will give you a well-rounded understanding of how to make the Net work for you.

Finding the Right E-Publisher

If it all sounds too technical, the simple alternative is to have your work available on one of the many Web sites dedicated to e-publishing. This will, of course, cost a slice of each book sale. How large the slice depends on how well you shop around.

If you choose to go with a co-op publisher, make sure you read their contract's fine print. Some e-publishers are nothing more than printers, offering little editorial guidance, marketing assistance and, often, achieve few sales for their e-authors. Be careful. Read anything contractual cautiously. There are many horror stories of writers who signed up with an e-publisher only to find that they had not received any sales and couldn't sell their book elsewhere because they couldn't buy back the rights.

Choosing the Best E-Book Format

Whichever road you take, you will still be responsible for the initial look and feel of your e-book, so begin by choosing the right e-book publishing program for your needs.

There are many packages on the market that enable you to present books in PDF, HTML, or plain text files. For my money, Adobe Acrobat's PDF is the most versatile and is the format I use for my e-books. Acrobat has quickly become the industry defacto standard because of its ease of use, flexibility (you can add images and live links to Web sites), and universality (files are readable on both PCs and Macs), and Adobe Reader is free.

You can publish PDF-based books several ways. The most straightforward approach is to draft the copy with your word processor and then save as a PDF file (Microsoft Word and other programs offer this facility). If you wish to produce a more sophisticated product, with pictures and graphics, you may need more sophisticated software. When I published *The Enterprising Writer* as an e-book, I drafted it in Microsoft Word, compiled the pictures and graphics in Adobe PageMaker, and then converted it to PDF. The whole process was made immensely easier with the help of *The 5-Minute PDF Creator*. Author Scot Dantzer has put together a no-

nonsense manual that covers all of the PDF basics as well as how to add bells and whistles, such as multimedia capabilities and security features. If you're serious about e-books, this e-book is a must-have.

Once you've produced your own e-book, you not only can distribute it via the Web, you can also e-mail it or save on CD or DVD for mail order. To improve download speeds, you should compress your PDF documents. Once they have been saved onto the customer's hard drive, they can be decompressed using one of two programs—WinZip for PC users or Aladdin's Stuffit for Mac users.

Pricing for Success

What value should you place on your e-book? That's a good question. In just a few years, e-books have exploded onto the market. Many are freely available for promotional purposes, while the majority range in price from $10 to $100. The price you place on your product will ultimately determine your success. Too high a price will drive potential customers away; too low a price may devalue it and create the same effect.

The most common approaches to pricing are:

- **Following the market**—offering a slightly lower price than competitive e-books. This sounds good in principle, but customers don't just buy on price; they are also motivated by their perception of the author, the quality of the product, and other factors.
- **Testing the market**—generally starting at a high price and gradually reducing it to determine the most popular price for sales. This "trial and error" approach also looks good on paper, but when your customers see the product for which they paid a premium is now available at a discount, they won't be happy and they'll let you know about it. Remember what complaining customers can do to sales.

These "safe" strategies are not always the most effective in determining the true value of your e-book or meeting the objective of your business. The following two strategies represent the current pricing models that work best online.

If you want to "own" the market, price your book to sell in volume. Offer your books at a lower price but still with a healthy margin so you will attract customers. By increasing the number of books sold, your profits will increase as well as your profile in the marketplace. And, since around 80 percent of buyers from successful sites become repeat customers, you will have a ready market for future e-books. This is the best approach to take if you wish to gain a large number of customers and secure a long-term future. The trade-off is a lower short-term profit, since you will need to offer your products at a lower cost than usual.

If your e-book is unique, you can name your price. This strategy is essentially the reverse of the first. By applying a premium price, you will naturally gain higher profits from sales but generally at the expense of the number of customers you attract. To succeed in the rarefied territory of $50, $80, or $100 plus per e-book, you need to not only have a unique product but also one that addresses a topic that is much in demand. You will also need more than a quality product; you'll need a quality sales approach to convince prospects to part with that amount of money.

But nothing lasts forever, especially online. You may have the e-book of the moment, but that moment will pass soon enough. You need to be aware of this and adjust your price accordingly. Needless to say, if it's too high for too long, you will lose sales and most probably lose out to a newcomer with a similar mousetrap at a more attractive price.

Eight Sure-Fire Ways to Produce a Best-Seller

Here are some final points to consider before sending your book out to the world:

1. Know your market. The larger your potential market, the more chance you have of ongoing sales. When determining your market, consider also who your potential customers are and their financial status. This may also determine your long-term success. If, for example, your e-book will appeal to high-income earners, you will have a greater chance of sustained growth. Also consider your competition in this market analysis. If you have a lot of competition, you will need to work harder at differentiating your e-book in the marketplace.

2. Quality counts. If you are looking for long-term success online, you need to produce quality work. This may seem obvious, but the vast majority of e-books available are not quality products. Despite this, e-books are increasing in popularity and credibility. But, until Web visitors have purchased, you and your e-books are an unknown quantity. Once they have handed over their credit card details, well they can sing your praises or spell your doom just as easily via countless online forums. Forums can create a buzz or destroy a reputation in a matter of hours. So, if you're going to live by the cyber sword, work hard to ensure that your e-book is the very best product you can deliver. Make sure that it meets the needs and exceeds the expectations of your customers by adding to their knowledge, solving a problem, or addressing a subject in a unique fashion.

3. Write what people want to read. To paraphrase Charles Dickens, write what you know or have an interest in. With more than six billion people on the planet, there's a viable market for literally anything you know or like. There is a wealth of e-books just waiting to be written in areas as diverse as:

- Health
- Hobbies
- Lifestyles
- Philosophy
- Business
- Wealth
- Success

I've found that some of the best material I've written has been that which has interested me, despite having no previous experience or knowledge. The fun part is researching a topic; the rewarding part is writing about it. I've gained the greatest education by sharing information with others. It's almost a sin to charge people to read it (well, almost).

Keep in mind that fiction does not sell as well as nonfiction, nor does it sell for the same price. The best-selling and highest-paying e-books are prescriptive "how-to" books that account for around 85 percent of the market.

4. Make your e-book live and breathe. Your e-book is very much a product of you, so it should contain elements of you in terms of personal experiences and opinions. As you know, throughout this book, I've added my own views and techniques, and I've relayed various personal experiences that are relevant to the subject matter. By giving you insight into my actions and my success, it will give you a greater understanding of your abilities and potential for success. It also makes reading easier, because we are naturally drawn to other people's personality and experiences.

5. When pricing, choose your numbers carefully. There's little monetary difference between $20 and $19.99, but there's a wealth of difference in perceived value to your customer. The prices with the most emotional appeal end in five, seven, eight, or nine. I'm fond of ninety-seven cents because it's essentially the same value as ninety-nine and ninety-five cents but not as over-used.

6. Make your e-book a credible package so your customer enjoys a bargain. We are all immediately attracted to words like FREE and BONUS. You can afford to raise the price of your e-book if you can raise its perceived value. One method is to include a bonus book at no additional price but with a perceived value of $20, for example. That way, your customers feel they are getting a real bargain with a $20 product for FREE.

If you have a number of titles, you can package like-minded volumes together and improve profits. For instance, you can offer a "starter pack" containing two e-books and a "professional pack" containing four volumes. If the two volumes each sell for $19.99, you could offer the package for $29.97, giving the customer a perceived saving of more than $10 and you an extra $10 you probably wouldn't have received otherwise. Similarly, with the "professional pack," you could elect to give away the fourth volume, giving the customer an extra $20 in value.

Your customers can—and will—judge an e-book by its cover. One of the advantages that printed books have is a colorful billboard. When you pick up a book, the cover instantly tells you what to expect inside (or it should). You can apply the same principle when you're ready to put your e-book on your Web page.

Studies have shown that e-books sales have increased simply by adding a cover graphic to a Web site. You can design a simple, colorful cover in a design program, like Adobe PhotoShop, and convert it to a GIF or JPEG file (the same as a photo file). You can also link the graphic to more information about the e-book or to your order page for a no-fuss sale.

7. Make it easy to read. I'm not talking about the way you write, I'm talking about the way you present your e-book. Make sure all of the hyper-links to Web pages work. Make sure that it is easy to navigate to different sections, via the contents and index.

It's important for non-Americans to write in U.S. English, since your largest market will most probably originate in North America. Also, make sure your e-book is set for U.S. letter paper, not international A4, for the same reason.

8. Consider getting an ISBN. This is an issue I raised recently in a couple of e-book forums. The International Standard Book Number is the 10-digit barcode printed on books to assist wholesalers, libraries, and retailers in ordering and organizing books. It is not required that e-books carry an ISBN. However, if you plan to sell your opus via one of the major online bookstores, like Amazon.com or BarnesandNoble.com, you will need to include your own ISBN. It could also be argued that an ISBN adds an extra air of credibility or professionalism to an e-book. You'll have to make that decision yourself. There are plenty of ISBN agencies online, such as Bowker.com.

Join the New Wave of Publishing

It's not an overstatement to say that e-books are revolutionizing the publishing industry. You just have to look at the big-name authors and publishers who already have a Web presence and distribute their books electronically.

E-books are currently enjoying their fastest growth ever, and industry commentators predict the market for e-books and other electronic documents will soon top two billion dollars. That's good news for all of us, and it's especially good news for the reported twenty-four million creative writers in the United States—95 percent of whom have never been published. Not to mention the 81 percent of U.S. adults who believe they have a book inside of them.[10]

We all have the same opportunity to see our words in cyber print. Our success online will, of course, be determined by the investment we make, not only in developing our craft, but also in understanding the needs of our potential customers and how the Internet can benefit both readers and writers.

CASE STUDY:
E-Books Open Publishers' Doors

Once I finished drafting my first e-book, *The Enterprising Writer*, I set to work on what's called in the business a "back-end product," a free e-book that I could give away as a method of promoting my primary e-book.

I decided the back-end e-book would contain a collection of quotes from writers, many of which I had gathered over the years. But, as I researched further, I realized the full breadth of the project and the depth of wisdom writers offered in quotes. I learned that the issues I had and the challenges I faced had also been encountered by wordsmiths throughout history. But, most importantly, they had discovered *solutions* and offered timeless advice I could apply in my own work. I knew immediately that this project had greater potential.

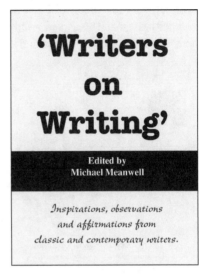

'Writers on Writing'

Edited by
Michael Meanwell

Inspirations, observations and affirmations from classic and contemporary writers.

The front cover of the e-book
Writers on Writing

Contents

Permission granted for single copy reproduction by rightful owner of this e-book.
http://www.meanwell.com

One of the advantages of PDF e-books is that you can include special features that make reading and checking information easier. For example, in *Writers on Writing*, you can click on any line in the contents and jump to the relevant section of the e-book.

So, once I had finished the free e-book, I set to work on a more grand edition that evolved into *Writers on Writing*, a compilation of more than 360 poignant quotations from 245 writers. Quotations were arranged into twenty-four chapters covering a wide range of writers' themes and issues, from the act and art of writing, igniting creativity, and developing technique to ensuring discipline, resolving writer's block, and the joy of accomplishment. In sharing writers' thoughts, my e-book shows today's writers they are not alone in their fears or frustrations any more than their desires or determination to excel in their craft.

What made this book of quotations different—dare I say, unique—was that it included more than 150 original affirmations, written by me, which support the quotations' messages and help inspire and motivate the reader in their own literary journey.

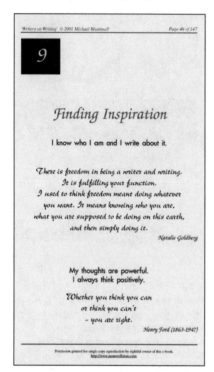
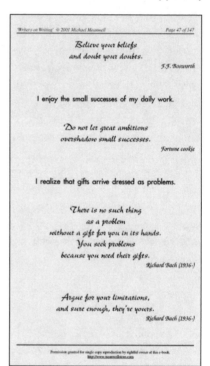

A typical two-page spread in *Writers on Writing*: When designing an e-book, use a simple graphic design to ensure pages are as easy to read on screen as they are on paper.

Writers on Writing joined *The Enterprising Writer* in e-bookstores in January 2001. Since then, it has attracted readers around the world, including the U.S., U.K., and Japan, as well as Australia and New Zealand.

This experience has taught me some valuable lessons about e-publishing: I have learned that it's a valid way to be published and to get your message out to readers around the globe, and it's also a valid method of attracting the attention of conventional print publishers and expanding your career as an author.

After all, you wouldn't be reading this book, in this format, if it wasn't for my e-books.

CHAPTER 10

Putting the PR Into "Professional Writer"

Don't tell the people how good you
make the goods, tell them how good your
goods make them.

Leo Burnett (1891–1971)

Think about a specific, large company. It may sell food, cars, or computers—it doesn't matter. Now, think about its image. How do you see its products or services? How does it differ from its competitors? When did you form this perception, and why?

Part of your perception is based on months, maybe years, of exposure to the company's advertising, part will be based on your personal experiences with the company, and another part will be the result of a pervasive public relations campaign. "Spin doctors," as PR practitioners are commonly called, are responsible for building a company's image or profile with its target audiences. In fact, up to 70 percent of what you see, hear, and read as news was initially developed by a PR practitioner.[11]

A positive profile, while not an easy concept to explain or pin down, is vital to the company's continuing success in business. In today's competitive environment, it's not enough to have good products or services; organizations need to promote them to the people who matter—their target audience of customers and prospective customers. And PR, in my view, remains the most cost-effective form of business communication.

PR wears various guises, and often the lines blur between what is considered the domain of PR and conventional advertising. Here are examples:

- Shopping center promotions and demonstrations
- Public seminars and workshops
- Sponsorship of public and sporting events
- Sales and marketing collateral
- Customer newsletters and magazines
- Media conferences and tours

That's just the beginning. There are plenty more ways of generating good PR. And in each case, there's a strong need for well-written information that reinforces the corporate message and its profile.

Shopping center and store promotions need accompanying literature for the general public and the media. Public seminars and workshops, which can be ideal sales and lead generators, need invitations to events and follow-up letters after events, as well as supporting material for attendees to take home.

Sponsors of public or sporting events have an even greater need for PR to raise their awareness with a number of audiences, including partners, customers, the general public, and the media. There are sponsors behind every major event, from car racing and musicals to opera and the Olympics—and if a sponsor wants to be remembered, it needs a well-oiled PR machine. And that machine needs, among other things, well-oiled press releases and marketing material.

While sponsoring big events is only within the reach of big business, there are other opportunities available to small traders. They can—and do—sponsor local fun runs, church events, and school and business functions, providing support in the form of funding as well as products or services. But if a business wants to stretch its promotion further, it will need to implement a targeted PR and communications campaign.

As you can see, there are plenty of opportunities available to a PR writer. For more than fifteen years, the bulk of my income has come from various PR (and to a lesser degree, advertising) tasks. I've worked with transnational corporations, government organizations, small and medium-sized businesses, and husband and wife teams. Whether you write PR directly for a company or through an agency, if you want sustained success, keep yourself open to accepting tasks beyond writing. Even though my PR activities focus on the written word, I've also handled tasks as diverse as event coordination, media relations, and media training, as well as strategic marketing advice.

Advertising is not the only way for a company to get its message out there. PR often offers companies a more cost-effective and credible form of promotion and communication. Not only is publicity free (apart from writing and syndication costs), it's also more believable because it is published as news. And, as we all know, if it's in print, it must be true!

Applying Classic Techniques in a New World

The popular view is that PR is a relatively new marketing tool that began to flourish in the 1960s. However, research by Dr. Kirk Hallahan, a journalism professor at Colorado State University, shows that the earliest PR material dates back almost four thousand years. Dr. Hallahan states that the Sumerians were responsible for producing the oldest existing example of PR—a farm bulletin showing farmers how to increase crop yields.[12]

These days, it's not unusual to return to your parked car and find a brochure or flyer on the windshield. This idea dates back more than half a millennium. England's first printer, William Caxton, printed the earliest advertising flyer in 1470.

Even today's modern publicity techniques have been used by big business for more than a century. Westinghouse established the first corporate PR center in 1889. Ford Motor Company was the first to implement media product previews in 1895 and motor racing events in 1903 to promote its products. Chicago Edison pioneered the use of an external magazine, films, and brochures inserted in customer bills in the early 1900s.

If nothing else, these examples show the power of PR and its proven techniques. They have helped to build and sustain the growth of these and many other organizations. And behind each of these techniques is the need for well-written words.

Multiply Your Income by Making News

Arguably the most viable form of PR is the press release. Why? Because this tool is used by a wide range of organizations on an ongoing basis. In fact, my business was built on the recommendation that each client commit to a regular publicity campaign, including one to four or more press releases per month. Every business that uses PR successfully knows it is most effective

---

in an ongoing media campaign or as part of a major marketing strategy involving other disciplines, like advertising and direct mail. If a company is new to PR and needs convincing, use advertising as an analogy. No business would promote itself or its products with a single ad. It would commit to a campaign with various messages spanning a number of publications and, budget permitting, select radio and television programs. The same approach applies to PR. One PR release isn't going to make a great difference to an organization's profile or profitability, but it will benefit from consistent exposure in the media. And, with just a handful of clients committed to PR, your business will also benefit from consistent work.

No matter what size company you're working with, there's a wealth of information stored within it that is worthy of the title "news"—or at least it will be, once you've been involved. Here's a sample:

- New product announcements or upgrades
- New services
- Innovative use of technology or processes to improve business or the environment
- Changes in company policy
- Publication of surveys, studies, and research
- Customer testimonials
- Industry applications (for the client's product or service)
- Changes in pricing (especially if prices have been lowered)
- New strategic and marketing alliances
- Senior staff and management appointments
- Winning of awards (by the company and/or its employees)
- Major domestic and export sales
- Upcoming industry/public workshops and seminars
- New industry certification
- Event sponsorship
- Addressing industry issues and trends

This is not a complete list by any means, but it shows you what gold lies within each organization, just waiting to be mined by a good PR writer.

Four Types of Press Releases for All Occasions

Just as there are many topics that make good press releases, there are many ways to present that information to the media.

1. The news release. This is the most common media announcement written for and accepted by both print and electronic media. A standard news release weighs in at between 250 and 500 words or one to two pages, double-spaced. Any of the topics in the list above can be fashioned into a news release as long as it is presented as a timely, newsworthy item. The news release can be published in part or in its entirety by the media. Alternatively, it can be used as background material for a forthcoming in-depth piece or interview.

2. The backgrounder. Backgrounders are supportive material for a news release or press kit. For example, if you are writing material for the announcement of a new product range, the news release could make the announcement and feature quotes from the CEO or managing director. It could cover the major product features and benefits as well as the company's commitment to customer service.

In addition to issuing the news release, you could also write one or more background releases, depending on the magnitude of the announcement. You could produce, for example, a backgrounder on each of the new products, detailing its technical specifications and other information. It's not uncommon to have four or five two-page releases in a press kit.

3. The filler. Fillers can be one to several paragraphs in length but no more than one page, double-spaced. They can be a brief company announcement, such as a staff appointment or a change in policy or pricing. Fillers are useful to the media in that, as the term suggests, they are ideal for filling a small space on a page.

4. The feature. The feature is the opposite. It can take the form of a detailed analysis of a trend or industry issue, comprising two, three, or four pages. Features can be used as backgrounders in a press kit to give the media more information. They can also be purpose-written for columns or regular industry features that run in metropolitan newspapers, trade publications, and business journals. Features can be written as an objective third-person piece or they can carry a byline (it's best to substitute the client spokesperson's name instead of yours, since the purpose is to generate publicity for them, not you).

Writing Stories Editors Print and Customers Read

If you've spent time as a journalist, you're in good company in the world of PR. Many in the industry are ex-journalists, because who knows the media's needs better than one of their own? I became a freelance journalist when I was seventeen and joined a newspaper at nineteen. Even though today I wear various literary, marketing, and business hats, I owe a great deal to the skills developed in those first few years.

Think like a reporter

If you haven't done time as a reporter, you can still learn how to write like one, while keeping your client happy.

As a PR writer, you need to wear two hats—a journalist delivering a strong newsworthy story and a PR/marketing consultant making sure your client gains good publicity and value for money. The key is wearing both hats simultaneously, so that you can please both audiences—your client and the journalist who will decide whether to print your story. That's why a large proportion of press releases fail, because the PR writer has failed to cater to both audiences.

You must understand that a busy journalist on a daily newspaper may receive anything from twenty to fifty releases a day. They haven't got all day to read them, so you have to attract their interest with your headline or lead, otherwise your release will be filed in the trash. It's also important to remember that any journalist who has been in the business more than a few months has become jaded by teaser campaigns, cagey copy, flattery, bribery, and every other trick in the book. The best—no, the *only*—technique that will work is to deliver clean, clear, straight copy. Anything else and you are wasting your time, their time, and your client's money.

Write like a journalist

We have already covered the "inverted pyramid." Put simply, if you want to see your PR in print, you will need to adopt this style of writing. As the name suggests, this style presents information in order of importance. It has the dual purpose of capturing the reader's attention and enabling the editor to cut the story from the bottom up to suit space requirements.

Your introductory sentence, or lead, should summarize the major points. All of the "who, what, when, where, how, and why" of the story should be contained within the first two or three sentences of your release. Begin with the "who"—your client if it's a company announcement, or one of their customers if it's a testimonial. Then follow with the "what"—your client's product, service, or solution to a business or consumer issue. The "when" should be as immediate as possible, preferably relating to today or some time in the immediate future (if you're announcing a forthcoming event).

In the second paragraph, the "why" explains the features and benefits of the story's focus (the product, service, or solution). This is followed by "where" (the locale) and the "how," which gives a greater explanation of the story's focus including further features and benefits.

You can alter the order, depending on the story, but it's vital that all are addressed in the first few lines. Beyond this, you can add supporting information that provides greater detail or elaborates on the main points. To get a better idea, read the first few sentences of stories in your newspaper. You'll discover that you know all of the essential information. The following paragraphs merely build on the framework. As you are fleshing out the body of the story, add relevant quotations. Quotes contain active language and, because they provide a direct connection to the people in the story, we are drawn to them. They also add an extra layer of credibility to whomever is being quoted.

Use your PR license to sell.

One of the distinctions between journalism and PR copy is a little thing called "license." Your goal is to satisfy three audiences: your client, since they're paying your bills, the editorial staff at the paper or magazine, since they're the gatekeepers to publication, and their readers.

To achieve this goal, you may need to add some PR license to the stories you are writing. If, for example, your client gives you a one-line brief regarding a new widget being released, and your task is to gather information from the product manager and quote the CEO (this is not unusual), then you can have some license with the quotes. Conversely, if you have interviewed a client's customer and some of the quotes are a little uninspiring, you can apply some license in enhancing words, as long as they remain true to the spirit of the interview and you obtain formal approval from the customer.

In fact, every PR story, brochure, or project you undertake should be formally approved by all relevant parties before it is sent to the media.

That means sending the finished draft to all people who have been interviewed or have been involved in the project, including an approval form so that corrections can be made and the form signed. This will not only ensure quality but will also protect you from any legal issues if you have misquoted someone. (See chapter eighteen for approval forms.)

Things to Remember When Drafting a Press Release

1. Grab interest with the headline. This is the first thing the journalist will see, so make it count with a short, clear, attention-getting one-liner. Study headlines that work in print, and be sure your headline is not misleading and relates to the enclosed information. Give your headline a larger type size (14-18 point) and highlight it in bold.

2. Write your lead to be read. Your lead is the second most important device, after the headline. If you've developed sufficient interest with your headline, the journalist will read your first paragraph. If your lead is well structured and includes the fundamentals (who, what, when, where, why, and how), the reader will continue. Make no mistake—the lead is critical to the future of your release. If it's ill conceived, your release is doomed. Keep your lead to eighteen to twenty-one words. Write it directly, simply, and in the present tense.

3. Use different leads for different stories. More often than not, your lead will be written in a reporter style, documenting what has happened (e.g., a product launch, a major sale, a new strategy). You can, however, use different approaches to make your story stand out from the pack. Your lead could be a controversial or thought-provoking quotation from a speaker at a convention. If so, this should be supported immediately with background information on the convention, including the fundamentals. Alternatively, you could begin with a bold statement presented in the third person, which could be a startling statistic or fact that has been released.

4. Create excitement. Your release should walk the fine line between offering journalists enough information to print, and also creating enough interest for them to chase you for more information or an interview. The more excitement you create, the better the chance of publication.

5. Include background information. The final paragraph of your story should be a short summary of background information on the company. This may include its reputation, innovations, years of experience, or range of products. The point is to deliver a quick snapshot of information that positions the company in the reader's mind as an authority whose story is therefore worthy of publication.

6. Include contact information. Make it easy for the journalist to seek more information from you or set up an interview directly. Include contact details for yourself, your client, and any third party (if appropriate and with their permission). This should be placed at the end of the story, so as not to detract from the headline and the lead. Contact details should include appropriate phone and fax numbers (with the international prefix, if you syndicate internationally) as well as e-mail addresses and the Web site URL of your client.

7. Keep it short. Keep the release to a page or two at the most, preferably set in 11- or 12-point type with justified text. The key to effective release writing is providing the most information in the fewest words (250 to 500).

8. Make it readable. Your story must flow. Each paragraph should follow the context and expand upon the preceding one. Your second paragraph should expand upon the information in your lead, the third should expand upon the information in the second, and so on. Remember to begin with the most important information and follow this with supporting but less vital information (in other words, use the "inverted pyramid" style of journalism).

9. Be objective. There's another fine line you need to walk: writing your release to satisfy both your client's need for publicity and the media's need for news. Write objectively. Any opinions or subjective comments should be attributed to someone, either indirectly or in quotations. The most objective and credible client stories will have a third party, such as a customer, praising your client or their product, rather than the company praising itself.

10. Turn new into news. Most PR writers are flogging a new product, service, or innovation. The press sees new releases all the time, but doesn't consider them news until the announcement promises to solve a problem or provide a profit. This gets back to the "What's in it for me?" question. How will this product benefit its customers? If it's a strong benefit, say so. If it's not, find one that is, and make that the focus of your story.

11. Bring your story alive with quotes. Quotes are the lifeblood of any PR story. They provide colorful contrast to straight narrative. They also legitimize more dynamic language to sell key points. As a rule of thumb, frame 25 to 50 percent of your copy in quotes.

12. Make an impression with your presentation. Always submit your release as hard copy, even if you're also sending it via e-mail. Double-space the text so there's room for editing if they choose to edit manually on the hard copy. This also makes the copy more readable if it is faxed. The headline should be written in upper and lower case, not capitals, which are harder to read. Keep headlines to one line and a maximum of ten words.

Issue client stories on client letterhead. This looks more professional and is standard operating procedure. (If your client does not have a letterhead, create a simple template, gain approval, and use this for releases.) Print stories on standard white stock, not colored paper. Color won't impress journalists; it will only telegraph your amateur status.

Include "For Immediate Release" at the top of your page before the headline. This tells the journalist that the news is available for publication. If, however, the story is not to be published until a certain time, substitute "Embargoed Until (relevant time and date)." Stories are generally only embargoed if they relate to a forthcoming speech or event.

Include the date of release. This can be presented as a dateline preceding the lead (e.g., "BOSTON, Mass.—August 25, 2004"), or the date can be included at the end of the release, accompanying the contact information.

13. Think before you syndicate. Once the story has been written and the media database compiled (and checked), you're ready to send your creation out to the world. But how will you syndicate it?

Research shows that large newsrooms prefer receiving faxes and e-mail; however, freelance and home-based journalists prefer e-mail and conventional mail. Where possible, ascertain the best mode of delivery for individual recipients or make that decision based on the urgency of the story.

Allowing for personal preferences, I generally issue stories via e-mail and fax if they are news stories, or via e-mail and snail mail if they are less urgent. E-mail gets your story into the journalists' hands more quickly; it also saves them precious time keying in the information. If you choose to e-mail stories, however, incorporate the copy into the message field, not as an attachment.

Check before attaching graphics or photo files. Some media organizations have firewalls in place that prohibit attachments, and some journalists prefer not to receive unsolicited attachments (for fear of viruses).

When sending press releases via e-mail to more than one recipient, always choose the "BCC" (blind carbon copy) field, never the "To" or "CC" (carbon copy) fields. The last thing journalists need to know—or you would want them to know—is who else received the same announcement. Also, remember that journalists no doubt receive a lot of e-mail, so make yours stand out with a compelling subject header that stimulates attention and also reflects the contents.

Take Advantage of All Communication Tools

With today's communications, there's a wealth of tools you can use to convey your message to the media in your city, your country, or around the world. You can arrange cyber interviews, conduct virtual press conferences, present media tours, and produce video news releases—all without the need for anyone to leave his or her desk. You can also set up an archive of material, from background papers to press announcements, on a media-friendly Web site. This gives the media the opportunity to collect what they want, when they want it. It also gives you another bite at the PR cherry, which you wouldn't ordinarily have.

Elements of a Media-Friendly Web Site

Easy navigation

Include a direct link in all media communications so journalists can simply click on the link and go to the correct Web page. Also include links from major pages, including the home page, on the Web site.

Background information

Never assume the media know your client as well as you do. Include sections for company history, brief biographies of the board of directors and management, the suite of products and services, customer testimonials and case studies, and up-to-date announcements.

Opt-in e-mail

You can invite journalists to submit their e-mail addresses and other contact details to receive regular announcements. This keeps your database updated and gives you another opportunity to keep your client top of mind with the media.

Pictures or video

If you have the budget and the skills available, high resolution pictures, or streaming video or audio, provide a visual element that both adds interest and gives journalists more information for their story. It's often smarter to let individual journalists choose whether to download photos, rather than sending them as part of an e-mailed press kit, as some may be irritated by the slow download time.

Newsworthy Stories or PR Fodder

It doesn't matter how much money your client throws at a media campaign; it will mean little to the media unless it's newsworthy. Judge a project by its newsworthiness, otherwise you're wasting everyone's time. I have rejected many stories that clients have thought were newsworthy simply because they weren't. On other occasions, I've developed new angles to transform just another ho-hum tale into something that entices the press.

Discovering what's newsworthy means thinking like a journalist. And you should think like one before you begin writing any announcement. Just for a moment, be a journalist and ask yourself these questions about the story:

- So what? (How will the story's focus benefit people or fulfil their needs?)
- Can you prove it? (Is it possible to back up the claims with hard facts, figures, authoritative statements, and quotes?)

If you haven't got convincing answers to the above two questions, you had better find them or ditch the story.

So what is news? What's news is something that neither you nor your client can dictate; it's something the media decides. On my first day as a cadet journalist many moons ago, I recall being told by my Chief of Staff the same story every journalist has heard: A dog biting a man is not news, but a man biting a dog *is* news.

There's a variation on this old guideline: When a dog bites a man, it's not news, but when a dog bites the President, it *is* news. Think about it. An important action makes news. But even a mundane action, which is not newsworthy in itself, can also make news if it involves someone newsworthy.

To see the light of day, your press release has to satisfy one or more of these three criteria. It has to:

- Contain news
- Make news
- Relate to existing news

For the story to *contain news,* your client must be doing something new or different in the market. For a new product or service to be newsworthy, it must provide a strong benefit to business or consumers, such as solving a problem, revolutionizing a process, or fulfilling desires for greater productivity, better lifestyle, increased profitability, or something else.

To *make news,* your story must create something new, for example by announcing a major event that's either open to the public or available to captains of industry. It could also be an open day at an institution or a celebrity tour.

To *relate to existing news,* your story must respond to a current issue or activity. Your release must position your client as an authority who can add value to the running story.

There's an old reporter's saying: *When in doubt, leave out.* If you cannot verify facts or statements, don't include them in your release.

There's also an old editor's saying: *When in doubt, find out.* Your stories need to be not only well conceived but also well researched. Don't expect a journalist to do your homework for you. Consider all angles to the story and cover all bases. That also involves verifying unsubstantiated claims, replacing cliché comments with compelling quotes, and checking all phone and fax numbers, as well as Web URLs, listed in the release.

One last thing—always be accurate and truthful. You won't impress anyone with bloated hyperbole that disappears under scrutiny. Dishonesty will only earn you a bad reputation with the press. When journalists "talk shop," sometimes they talk about PR people, and you want to be remembered for doing things right, don't you?

Five Steps to Building a Media Database

So, you've produced your press release. Now whom do you target? You should target the publications that your target audiences read. These may include newspapers, trade and business publications, and specific radio and television programs.

When inviting television media to an event, remember that it must have visual appeal, and with all media, there must be a spokesperson available for comment.

1. List what customers read. Once you know who your client's customers and prospects are, you can make a list of the kinds of publications that appeal to them. If the customers are at the CEO and Managing Director level, include business publications. If they are at technical or product management level, include trade and technical journals.

To get started, get a copy of a media directory that lists all print and electronic media as well as wire services and Internet publications across the country in all industries. This will form the foundation of your database. Once you begin issuing stories and following them up, you will begin to hone this list and know which outlets and which journalists will best suit the individual stories you are placing.

2. Include media specialists. From the beginning, think big. Include all relevant media outlets—big and small, close and distant. Larger newspapers and magazines will have a number of journalists who will suit your "media target audience." They may go by the titles of Chief of Staff, News Editor, Contributing Editor, Product Reviewer, or Section Editor. It's wise to include more than one journalist from a media outlet. That's not to say that a dozen journalists from one outlet should receive your releases. But you shouldn't assume that all journalists on a publication talk to each other and share stories.

When dealing with radio and television programs, it's best to target News Directors and Producers, not presenters, as they are the main decision-makers regarding content.

3. Customize each release list. Once you have developed your database, customize it to suit each announcement. You will save yourself time, your client money, and the media frustration by targeting your communications correctly and individually.

4. Know your media market. There's only one way to know the media and that's to read their publications and watch and listen to their shows. This should become a regular part of your media relationship.

5. Stay up-to-date. I've found that almost as soon as a media directory has been published, many of the entries are out of date. Journalists are one of the most transient groups of workers on the planet. So, keep on top of departures and arrivals. Find out where your good contacts have gone—if you've done your job right, they'll remember you and will be happy to continue working with you in their new position. Make a point of introducing yourself on the phone to a contact's replacement as soon as possible so you can get a feel for his or her style and preferences, and begin cementing your new relationship.

The Dos and Don'ts of Media Liaison

Ask any working journalist. The two most hated questions are, "When are you going to print my press release?" and "What page will it be on?"

Unfortunately for everyone concerned, these are generally the first two questions novice PR practitioners ask journalists. It's no wonder that PR people, as a rule, don't have a good rapport with the media. Here are some common-sense rules that are not commonly followed in the field.

Treat a contact like a client

I treat all media contacts like clients. Having been on the other side of the phone, I'm very conscious of their requirements, deadlines, and other issues. The media are the lifeblood of my business as a PR practitioner, so I do my best to meet their needs with timely information.

Don't follow up every release

Resist the temptation to follow up every story you issue by telephoning journalists. A deluge of news releases is issued every day. Journalists are expected to read all material they receive (although much of it hits the trash at the first glance), follow up regular contacts on their beat, chase stories, interview people, and file copy—all before their deadline. The last thing they need is one, two, or a dozen calls about insignificant stories. Think before you dial, and follow up only those of greatest importance.

Be timely

Like comedy, PR is all about timing. If you plan to follow up a release, call the media the day they receive your release, not a few days or a week later. By then, it's "old news" and a waste of time. They are more likely to remember your story if you call the day they receive it.

Be brief

Make your call brief and to the point. Before you dial, write down succinctly what you are going to say, and have key information handy for reference, including the release and contact details.

Be mindful of deadlines

If you plan to have an ongoing relationship with the media, determine which days (or times) journalists have deadlines. Never contact a journalist on a deadline day—he will have neither the time nor the inclination to talk to you. Remember, you and the journalist are part of a team (or should be), so respect their job function by respecting their deadlines.

Be courteous

Make sure your query is nonconfrontational, since mail can be lost or releases overlooked in a busy newsroom. A good way to start the call is: "This is (your name) and I'm calling to confirm that you received our (news release) on (subject)." You can refresh the person's memory by stating the main focus of the story and mention when the release was sent or should have reached their office. Once you have gained acknowledgment, you can ask if the person requires any more information or wishes you to arrange an interview with a relevant contact. By then, you can gauge their level of interest and whether they intend to run the story.

Stay up-to-date

If you are working with a new client or a new industry, it's wise to ask industry journalists a few questions so you can best meet their news needs and your client's publicity needs. If you are not familiar with specific journalists' needs, ask them what they require (for example, in addition to news releases, ask if they have a need for case studies, customer testimonials, industry features, or product reviews). It's also worthwhile contacting the publication's advertising representative to obtain a list of forthcoming advertising features. This gives you the opportunity to submit editorial features, and your client advertising opportunities. You'll find that most respectable publications do not seek advertising in return for editorial content, nor do their publication decisions regarding PR stories have anything to do with whether your client is an advertiser.

Confirm each journalist's fax number and e-mail address (many have a habit of changing e-mail addresses more often than they do jobs), and update your database with their personal preferences: what stories they wish to receive in the future, and whether they prefer to receive them via mail, fax, and/or e-mail.

Differentiate between journalists. Keep a list of who has been cooperative and who hasn't. Next time you make follow-up calls, you can choose which journalists to follow up with and which to avoid.

Be friendly

Contrary to popular belief, journalists are people, too. You should always act professionally in your dealings, but that shouldn't stop you from being courteous. If possible, get on a first-name basis with members of the press, since your goal should be to develop a comfortable, ongoing relationship with them.

Be positive

Media follow-up is arguably one of the most frustrating and disheartening tasks in the PR field, yet it is a necessary evil. We need to phone the media to develop relationships, determine the effectiveness of a campaign, and act with due diligence for our clients.

Timing Your Release Is Just as Important as Writing It

You may have written the best release, but if your timing is off, it's a wasted effort. Keep in mind different deadlines apply to different media. General news and business reporters working for daily newspapers or television and radio news have the tightest deadlines: twenty-four to forty-eight hours. Journalists working for magazine-style television and radio programs can be working a week or more ahead of airing; feature writers for newspapers can be working on stories one or more weeks ahead of publication; and feature writers for magazines can be working on stories one week, one month, or an entire quarter ahead of the publication date. Now you can see why it's vital to know the publications you are targeting.

When presenting stories that relate to special events or seasons (e.g., Christmas) to a newspaper or online news service, you will need to make contact a month or more ahead to allow the reporter time to research, write, and place the feature. If you're presenting information for a newspaper's advertising supplement, the deadlines may be different from those applying to regular editorial features. Check with the appropriate editor or the advertising department regarding requirements and deadlines.

Magazines will, of course, vary depending on their frequency of publication. For weekly magazines, you will need to present material one week prior to publication. For monthlies, two months in advance; bimonthlies (published every two months) three months ahead; and quarterlies, four or more months prior to publication. Fortunately for PR writers, quarterly publications and biannuals are becoming more of a rarity these days.

When dealing with broadcast media, you may get a response to a release the same day or later that week, depending on how urgent they perceive the story. If, for example, you are announcing an upcoming event or inviting electronic media to it, it's wise to give them a week's notice and a reminder the day before or, with television news particularly, first thing in the morning. News Directors and Chiefs of Staff do not plan very far ahead because of the fickle nature of news. They will log the initial communiqué in the news diary, but a reminder closer to the date will help improve its chances of coverage.

Good PR Begins and Ends With You

In summary, whether you're promoting a new product, launching a new company, or publicizing a major change or expansion of a company's mission, your media communications should incorporate the following points.

Choose the right medium for communication

If I had a dollar for every time a client wanted to hold a major launch or press conference . . . well, I'd be retired now. Companies that are new to the world of PR often feel that spending a lot of money on an event is the best way to achieve publicity. This is an approach that worked well in the late 1980s and early 1990s, when journalists had more free time and alcohol flowed more freely. Today's reporters generally have fewer resources and fewer hours to cover more ground than their predecessors. Long gone are the days when a PR person could invite media to a lavish lunch funded by the client and declaim at length. Today's journalist just wants the facts.

Certainly, creating a major event can create excitement, and it can produce positive response in terms of publicity. But you should determine up front whether it is the most efficient and cost-effective method of communicating. A lot of effort and expense is required to arrange an event or even just a news conference. Often, the same or better results can be achieved with one-on-one interviews and low-key press briefings, or even just the issue and follow-up of a well-conceived news release or press kit.

If you do decide to arrange a media event, call some of your buddies in the press beforehand to make sure there is nothing else set for that day.

Impress the media, don't bribe them

I loved my days in journalism, especially when I became an entertainment critic. I was invited to all of the celebrity parties and was showered with expensive and unique gifts. And I wrote exactly what I would have written if I'd received nothing but a press kit. This is another mistake PR people and their clients make. They feel all that's needed to obtain favorable press coverage is some kind of gimmick, gift, or memorable event. This may work with some, but most journalists value their integrity as much as the right to report news the way they see it.

The best way to impress the media is to present them with the information they need to report accurately and easily. If your lead is located on page six of a nine-page press release, if your story leaves many questions unanswered, or if your spokesperson is ill-equipped to handle media queries, these are the things journalists will remember, not the friendly chat afterwards.

The Future Looks Bright for PR Writers

As you've seen, there are many writing opportunities in PR—even if you have just a few clients, you can be kept busy. In addition to fruitful work, PR delivers fruitful rates. I have remained primarily in this industry for two main reasons: I honestly enjoy writing for the corporates, and I definitely enjoy the money it attracts. PR may be the poor cousin of advertising, but it pays better than most writing projects. And you can certainly make a healthy living pushing the corporate cause.

CASE STUDIES:
Kenworth Australia Keeps Moving With the Media

There are many different types of press releases you can produce for clients. In addition to issuing them to well-known publications, you can also take advantage of the myriad of trade and specialist publications, which are eager to hear from you.

Kenworth Trucks Australia, which is part of the worldwide PACCAR Inc., has gained the bulk of its publicity not from the mainstream press but from trade and niche media. Some companies consider these publications poor cousins to metropolitan newspapers and respected business periodicals. But, before you make that judgment, it's important to consider your client's target audience.

In Kenworth Australia's case, its target audiences are avid readers of the various magazines and newspapers of the trucking industry, so it makes good sense to focus on these publications. I also target transport features and truck columns in the metropolitan media. In addition, I regularly send releases to regional newspapers throughout the country.

As a general rule, trade media accept a wider range of PR releases, and stories can go into greater depth and detail. As we've discussed, customer testimonials and case studies can be a credible form of PR for a client. Case studies are widely used, particularly in trade media. The key, of course, is to make them as newsworthy as possible. The following are a small selection of the types of PR stories I've produced for the truck company.

Sample Release

The Bottom Line Isn't Always the Bottom Line for Findlay

Getting the lowest price in trucking isn't always the most cost-effective way of doing business, according to leading bulk dry freight hauler, Findlay Bulk Services.

Established twenty-five years ago, the company transports a variety of protein meals, grains, and coal throughout southeast Queensland and northern NSW. But it's not just well known on the highways of New England and the Darling Downs, it's also well regarded in the business sector.

Findlay Bulk Services has been recognized with a plethora of awards for corporate achievement, including back-to-back Telstra/Queensland Government Small Business Regional Awards, the Global NATRoad National Excellence Awards, and state and national training awards.

Managing Director Neil Findlay puts his company's ongoing success down to a combination of strong customer focus, service, and reliability.

"Our business is shipping products that are both time sensitive and weight sensitive. To remain competitive, we need to be reliable, and that means we need reliable tools of our trade—our trucks. And that's why we've stuck with Kenworth over the years," he said.

Neil says that one of the cornerstones of his company's viability has been the philosophy of rationalizing his supplier base, so that they use one brand of brakes, chassis, engines, and axles.

"It doesn't pay long-term to mix and match. That's one reason why we have standardized on Kenworth Trucks, but it's not the only reason," he said.

"Kenworth trucks are built in Australia, and that's important to us, not just from a patriotic viewpoint, but from a performance and maintenance viewpoint. They are built for Australian conditions, so we know they'll go the distance, year after year," he explained.

Findlay Bulk Services' mechanics have preferred Kenworths since their first new prime mover was purchased in 1974, simply because the Australian-designed trucks are built with ease of service and maintenance in mind, and consequently spend less time off the road.

The company, which over the years has purchased forty new Kenworths and today runs an exclusively Kenworth fleet of twenty-five trucks, has used other U.S. and European models in the past. Neil says they do not compare to Kenworth, especially in terms of robustness, reliability, and overall longevity.

"Kenworths generally cost a bit more. But that extra investment is well and truly returned over the life of the truck through less wear and tear on the drivers, better reliability and performance on the road, and less downtime. That's critical with time-sensitive freight, like grains.

"Another advantage Kenworth has over the competition is tare weight. They're generally pretty light, which means we can transport more freight—and that's also a major benefit with the weight-sensitive products we haul," he observed.

Findlay Bulk Services' trucks travel an average of 200,000 km a year throughout eastern Australia. The company has just committed to a further seven T604s fitted with B-Double configurations, which they will take possession of from January 2000.

Kenworth trucks are designed and manufactured in Australia to meet the world's toughest applications. Kenworth, a division of PACCAR Australia, is the market leader in heavy-duty trucks in Australia. Its trucks are also exported to Papua New Guinea and New Zealand. PACCAR Inc is a worldwide manufacturer of heavy and medium duty trucks under the Kenworth, Peterbilt, DAF, Leyland, and Foden nameplates. It also provides financial services and distributes truck parts related to its principal business.

RELEASE ENDS

The following release portrays Kenworth Australia as a good corporate citizen, which the company is, by supporting yet another worthy industry initiative:

Kenworth Australia Backs Program to Improve Forestry Operations

The Kenworth/Dealer Industry Fund has committed $10,000 dollars for an initial twelve-month period to the Forestry Technology Program (FTP) which is run under the auspices of the Australian Logging Council.

The aim of this program will be to reduce the operational impact of logging and wood stockpiles, while helping reduce the costs to operators and end users further down the line.

The program is jointly administered by Melbourne University's Institute of Food and Land Resources, CSIRO, the Australian Logging Council and the Australian National University. Funds will be used to improve industry skills and technology involved in harvesting, transport, forest establishment and cultivation, road construction and maintenance, which account for 60 to 80 percent of the cost of wood and are the main source of community concern over forestry.

Kenworth Australia's General Marketing and Sales Manager, Joe Rizzo, says the company is committed not only to its customers' business but also to protecting the environment.

"The Forestry Technology Program affects one of our most important markets, which is also a major contributor to the Australian economy. It's important for us to support an initiative that improves our customers' productivity and reduces operational costs while safeguarding the environment and reducing the price of wood products," he said.

FTP Director, Bill Kerruish, says it is vital that key industry organizations are involved in the program to ensure its research remains relevant.

"FTP is a progressive and responsible approach to addressing cost and environmental issues that have so strongly impacted on this industry.

"Much of our research concerns transport with the focus on improving road networks and fleet movement. This will lead to a more accurate definition of truck specifications, better fleet management as well as improved road systems," he explained.

Mr. Kerruish said satellite-based global positioning (GPS) technology was being used to track logging equipment in space and time, for the study of operational impacts and productivity. He said this approach may soon be applied to trucking and road network management.

"One of our latest projects is the development of a road network model for the East Gippsland region of Victoria. The model, which will be linked to a Geographical Information System (GIS), will provide both road information and estimated truck travel time to provide a basis for future planning," he added.

Kenworth Australia is the first truck manufacturer to support the program. Other major sponsors include fuel, logging equipment, and logging associations.

Established in 1994, the Kenworth and Dealer Industry Fund is a cooperative effort between Kenworth and its dealers throughout Australia. It has supported a number of industry initiatives, including the Road Transport Forum and the long distance road and freight users association, NAT.

Kenworth trucks are designed and manufactured in Australia to meet the world's toughest applications. Kenworth, a division of PACCAR Australia, is the market leader in heavy-duty trucks in Australia. Its trucks are also exported to Papua New Guinea and New Zealand. PACCAR Inc is a worldwide manufacturer of heavy and medium duty trucks under the Kenworth, Peterbilt, DAF, Leyland, and Foden nameplates. It also provides financial services and distributes truck parts related to its principal business.

RELEASE ENDS

Here's another customer testimonial. As you'll see, the story enables the customer to highlight the benefits of working with the company. It also gives the customer free publicity and demonstrates how both organizations are using the latest innovative technology or solutions to improve business.

Sample
Release

Lamattina Delivers Fresh to Market With Kenworth Australia

When you're in the business of fresh produce, choosing the right transport is paramount to your continuing success.

One of Australia's largest fresh food producers, A&G Lamattina & Sons, supplies fresh vegetables to produce markets as well as Woolworths and Safeway supermarkets throughout Australia.

For almost half a century, Lamattina has grown its business by implementing the latest technology to ensure it continues to meet the highest quality standards and demands of its customers.

Russell Lamattina, Managing Director and son of the founder, says transport plays an integral role in the company's growing success.

"Our product is perishable foods, so we need to rely on our trucks to get our produce to our customers on time, every time. That's why we've been using Kenworth trucks solely for the past twenty years. Their trucks are robust, reliable, and economical," he said.

The Lamattina group maintains two farming properties: 320 hectares at Rosebud on Victoria's Mornington Peninsula and 3,200 hectares at Robinvale, north of Mildura. The two properties grow carrots, broccoli, parsnips, cabbage, lettuce, and celery.

Lamattina prides itself in being able to produce consistent and high-quality vegetables. All produce is harvested, packed, and cooled without delay, under the strictest supervision, to maintain freshness and ultimate quality. It is then transported in state-of-the-art refrigerated units to pre-serve the cool-chain and prevent unnecessary strain on the produce, so it arrives in peak condition.

The group currently operates four Kenworth K104 Aerodyne cab-over trucks—a 500 hp model purchased in 1997 and three 600 hp models pur-chased in 1999. Each truck is equipped with a refrigerated B-Double trailer.

Between them, the trucks work around the clock, travelling one million kilometers a year. Each vehicle makes two trips daily between the two properties to collect produce, which is carted daily to various Melbourne outlets and occasionally Sydney markets. Lamattina produce is also trans-ported throughout Australia by other suppliers.

"The K104s are perfect for our operation. Their short wheel base and B-Double configuration give us great driveability and a good distribution of weight," he said.

"We work our trucks hard and we also turn them over every four or five years to keep up with the latest advances. That's another advantage of buying Kenworth—their trucks can go the distance and still have a great resale value," Russell added.

One of Kenworth Australia's most popular models, the K104 provides the best of both worlds for driver and owner with a powerful engine, comfortable cabin, excellent fuel economy, and the Kenworth Airglide suspension for superb handling and ride. This combination of features makes this model ideal for long intrastate or national distribution.

Kenworth trucks are designed and manufactured in Australia to meet the world's toughest applications. Kenworth, a division of PACCAR Australia, is the market leader in heavy-duty trucks in Australia. Its trucks are also exported to Papua New Guinea and New Zealand. PACCAR Inc is a world-wide manufacturer of heavy and medium duty trucks under the Kenworth, Peterbilt, DAF, Leyland, and Foden nameplates. It also provides financial services and distributes truck parts related to its principal business.

RELEASE ENDS

CHAPTER 11

Writing Speeches That Magnetize Audiences

> If I am to speak for ten minutes, I need a
> week for preparation; if fifteen minutes, three
> days; if half an hour, two days; if an hour, I
> am ready now.
>
> *Woodrow Wilson (1856–1924)*

Remember Winston Churchill's stirring "We shall fight them on the beaches" speech in World War II? And John F. Kennedy's patriotic "Ask not what your country can do for you" inaugural address? And how about Martin Luther King's inspirational "I have a dream" proclamation?

Of course you do.

From the beginning of recorded civilization, speeches have altered our thinking, stirred our actions, and often changed the course of history. Great speeches capture the essence of a situation. They inspire. They motivate. They memorialize events, define eras, and measure people.

And that's the irony. Despite the power and the potential of speeches, they are generally considered the poor cousin in marketing communications. Too often speeches are overlooked or regarded as an afterthought rather than as an integral part of marketing initiatives.

Speechwriting may not be the hottest freelance market (yet), but it's one area that's begging for attention from organizations and corporate communicators. Like all other commercial writing, you can introduce your speechwriting skills to prospective clients or offer them as a value-added service to your existing clients. If, for example, you are responsible for assembling all of the media material for a major announcement, it makes sense that you should be involved with the speeches on the day. In addition to knowledge of the project, you will also bring to the task your professional writing skills as well as a level of objectivity that the presenter may not possess.

Beyond traditional public relations functions, there is a growing need for competent speechwriting skills in other areas—everything from sales and marketing events, seminars, and training programs to trade shows, exhibitions, and even audio, video, and multimedia products. Once you have mastered the elements of speechwriting, they can be adapted to suit a range of media. But before you can do this, you need to alleviate any attitudes you may have about speeches and writing them. It's been said that making a speech in public is the number one fear in people's minds. Curiously, the prospect of writing a speech seems to have a similar effect on many writers. (Incidentally, after public speaking, death rates second and jumping out of a plane comes in a close third.)

To fully understand the mechanics of speechwriting, I recommend you read chapter seventeen on how to deliver a dynamic presentation. This will help put you in your speaker's shoes—an important place to be if you want to reach an audience with your words.

Think Before You Write

As with any piece of writing, you need to invest time not only in researching the topic but also deciding on the best way to present it. I've written speeches for politicians, executives, and regular people. While the subject matter, presentation, and end result may be completely different, each speechwriting assignment begins by taking into consideration four elements. Before you begin, you must:

1. **Know the occasion.** This will determine what is presented and how it is presented.
2. **Know the purpose.** What is the objective and what is the speech intended to accomplish?
3. **Know the audience.** Who will be hearing the speech and what are their expectations?
4. **Know the speaker.** Who is presenting the speech and what are his or her requirements?

Once you know these four things, you'll know what to write, how to write it, and how the speaker can deliver it. Let's look at each of them:

1. Know the occasion. The occasion sets the scene for your production. Whether it's a product launch, public safety announcement, or eulogy, the occasion sets the tone, content, and length of the speech as well as the attitudes, beliefs, and expectations of the audience. It provides a framework for your words and will determine the use of humor, quotations, audio/visual aids, or other devices. The occasion also reminds you that your speech is part of a bigger picture, so it's important to ensure that your piece complements other speeches and/or the entire event.

2. Know the purpose. Just as there are many different occasions, there are many different kinds of speeches. Before you write one word, you must know the purpose of your speech. Is it designed to inform, persuade, or entertain?

Defining the goal or purpose of your speech in a single sentence does more than just allow you to stay focused throughout the research and writing process. It also enables you to decide what material to include or remove when editing the speech and to check its quality at the end of the process by measuring it against that goal.

3. Know the audience. Once you know the occasion and the purpose of your speech, you need to determine the needs, background, beliefs, and expectations of your audience.

Your speech must be written as a personal address to each of the people. It must be stimulating and engaging, and it must motivate them, according to the goal of your speech. Tailor your message by presenting it in language appropriate to the audience and a suitable style (e.g., formal for a business presentation, friendly for a social occasion).

4. Know the speaker. Your speech will live or die depending on the way it is presented. Body language experts tell us that the words you choose account for only 10 percent of what you communicate to others. The rest relates to mannerisms and the physical method of delivery. It's important to have an understanding of the speaker's physical presentation and speaking style, and the way he or she interacts with others, so you can mesh the speaker's personality and vernacular with your message. Also, by meeting with the person prior to writing, you will get a better picture of what to write as well as how to write it.

Five Steps to Preparing a Successful Speech

Now that you have an understanding of what's involved in producing a speech, let's get specific. Here are five basic steps to preparing a successful presentation:

Step One: Establish your purpose.

As discussed, the first step is to establish the purpose (to inform, persuade, or entertain—or maybe all three).

Speeches fall into one of three main categories:

- *Informative*: Announce a new topic or new facts about a familiar topic. This covers a variety of talks, ranging from media briefings and business reports to demonstrations and skills training.
- *Persuasive*: Introduce new information, pricing, or benefits designed to influence an audience's attitudes, beliefs, or behavior. This category covers various corporate communications, including sales announcements (for example, product, service, and policy pitches) and shareholders' meetings.
- *Entertaining*: Provide short and casual entertainment, suitable for motivational and team building exercises as well as awards presentations, official openings, and other social events.

    Think about your audience, their needs, and the distinct message you wish to convey. Now distill this to a single statement. This represents the central theme of your presentation. By continually focusing on this as you prepare your speech, you will be able to determine which ideas to include and which to discard. Also keep it in mind as you fine-tune your speech and present it—it will ensure you stay on track. For example, the overall purpose of this book condensed into a single statement is: *To show freelance writers how to earn a sustainable living from their craft.*

Always keep the audience in mind as you develop ideas. Think about the presentation from your listeners' viewpoint and answer these questions:

- What are the occasion and the setting?

- What types of people will you be addressing (for example, occupation, education background)?
- What will they know and what do they need to gain from the speech?
- What inspires these people to attend?
- What are their needs, desires, and beliefs?

Continue to think about these questions as you develop ideas for your presentation.

Step Two: Brainstorm ideas.

The next step is to develop the contents of your talk, which is essentially a series of ideas in a logical sequence. Begin by focusing on your central theme and brainstorming related ideas. The easiest way to do this is to create what Tony Buzan termed a 'Mind Map.'[13] The Mind Map is essentially a road map, graphically showing all of your creative ideas, and enabling you to quickly determine the best concepts and the ideal order to get you from A to B or, in this case, the introduction of a presentation through to its conclusion.

Buzan's books offer a variety of advanced techniques for using Mind Maps. I tend to take a simplistic approach to his principle. First, get a large piece of paper or use a whiteboard, if you have one. Reduce your talk's theme to a key word written in the center of a page and allow thoughts to flow freely. Think about concepts relating to the theme and write them down, branching out from the central theme. Don't judge, just write whatever comes to mind. Sometimes a "silly" notion can sponsor a brilliant one.

Once you have filled the page with ten or more key words, you can continue the process on a fresh page or you can take your brainstorming to another level. Get a new page and focus on those primary ideas and draw a number of secondary ideas from each of them. Flesh out each concept by considering points, issues, problems, and solutions relating to the idea. You can continue this process, drilling further down into the detail of each thought, until you have enough information and inspiration to begin writing your presentation.

The great thing about Mind Mapping is that it can be used for virtually any creative endeavor. I have used it to prepare for media interviews (for anticipating questions and detailing answers), marketing copy (for listing features and benefits), and even writing a novel (determining character traits and plot points). In fact, before I began writing this book, I sat down and Mind Mapped the contents. The Mind Map is a wonderful tool for anyone. Its uses, as the saying goes, are only limited by your imagination. So think about Mind Mapping before you begin writing.

Sometimes you can get things moving quicker if you set a time limit. This is something I used to do in staff meetings. If the ideas weren't flowing, we'd set a time limit of one or two minutes to get down all the ideas we could for a promotion. By attaching urgency to a project, ideas flow faster and there's no time to judge.

Step Three: Write with heart.

Now you're ready to judge what you've brainstormed. Go through each of the ideas and their related points, either developing them further on paper or discarding them.

Once you know the substance of your talk, you need to organize your points sequentially, each building on the previous and moving you closer to a logical conclusion. Again, the best way to do this is on paper, arranging the key words of your talk until you get a logical sequence that gives you a natural progression from beginning to end.

Now research and write your presentation. When writing the speech, visualize your audience and their backgrounds. This will help you choose the best way of conveying the message. Avoid jargon and technicalities— keep it simple.

Step Four: Illustrate your points.

You can make any talk more interesting, memorable, or credible by backing your claims with supporting material.

You can make it more memorable and interesting with real-life examples from historical figures and events or experiences from your own life. You can add credibility with hard-hitting facts, figures, and statistics. And you can add authority by quoting experts.

Anecdotes and other supporting points empower your presentation. They enable you to remember key points and also enable the audience to understand and relate to your presentation better. Always look for power-ful examples to illustrate points. You have probably noticed that I have taken that approach throughout this book by recalling events that have happened to me. It not only personalizes the points I am making, it also illustrates what could happen to you and how to deal with it.

Step Five: Make sure your speech is purpose-built.

Once you've finished your presentation, run through it with your overall purpose in mind. Check that all of the points complement the central theme of your talk and finish by summarizing the purpose. This will reinforce the benefits of your speech and ensure a good reception from your listeners.

Make sure that the speech is worded so it focuses attention on the audience not the speaker. A simple way to do this is to take note of how many times the word "I" is used compared with "you." If the speech refers to the speaker more often than to the audience, you should rewrite it. Otherwise, you run the risk of losing your listeners' attention.

Now is a good time to conceive an appropriate title for your talk. It's important to develop an attention-grabbing title, not only if the talk will be advertised but also as a way of further motivating you to stay focused on the purpose of the presentation. For inspiration, take a look at some enticing magazine headlines or advertising material.

The best way to edit and polish the speech is to read it aloud. That way you will get a better feel for the flow and rhythm of the speech as well as its length. On that point, if you have to write a speech to length, use as a guideline 120 to 150 words per minute. This is the average rate of speech.

Because a speech is not read but heard by the audience, you may be thinking that presentation on paper doesn't mean much. But it does—for the speaker. Make sure the text is double-spaced and that specific points are emphasized in bold. Also, include any references to illustrations or other visual aids to be used during the presentation. Careful attention to the presentation on paper will ensure a flawless delivery.

By following this five-step system you will be able to conceive, prepare, and deliver a range of dynamic presentations to suit various occasions and audiences. In fact, you can even adapt this method to develop a variety of communications, including an instructional book like this.

How to Add Impact to Any Speech

Once you have your talk down on paper, you can fine-tune some of the elements for maximum impact.

Open with a bang

The opening is arguably the most crucial part of your speech. You have less than a minute to set the tone, stimulate interest, and build excitement.

How will you introduce the speaker and the presentation to the audience? Remember, a good talk is as much about presenting the person as it is presenting the message. And the key to opening is to do it dramatically.

Don't *tell* people what you are going to talk about—"Today, I'm going to speak about the rising numbers of car thefts in our city." *Show* them why they should listen to you—"In the time it takes to drink your coffee, your car could have been stolen."

You can grab the listeners' attention by opening in one of a number of ways, such as with:

- **Drama.** The speaker can wear a costume, act out a part, or demonstrate a product in a dramatic fashion (for example, slam a shock-proof watch on a desk or throw it onto the floor).
- **A question.** A rhetorical question makes the audience think ("Have you ever thought about . . ."); a regular question makes them participate ("Hands up if you have . . ."). Some people can be a little shy to raise their hands, so raise yours as you ask the question.
- **An amazing announcement.** Open with a statement or promise that relates to the theme of your talk ("By the end of this talk you will know how to set up and run a successful writing business.").
- **An unsettling statement.** Try a shock tactic. If, for example, your client is speaking to a group about improving their dietary choices, you will get their attention if you start with, "Eleven people in this room will die before their fortieth birthday."

Close on a high note

As British politician Lord Mancroft, no stranger to public speaking, said, "A speech is like a love affair. Any fool can start it, but to end it requires considerable skill."

The key to closing a speech is to do it quickly, strongly, and profoundly. Finish on a positive note, leaving your audience satisfied. In short, your close should also achieve one or more of the following:

1. Summarize the main points or argument of the speech.
2. Meet the listeners' expectations.
3. Motivate the listeners to action (to purchase or seek more information, if appropriate).

When you're on the final leg of your talk, let the audience know that the finish line is in sight by saying, "Finally, I'd like to . . .", "To sum up, let's review . . .", or "In closing, let me say . . .".

Your close can be inspirational, motivational, thoughtful, or entertaining; you can use humor, drama, or a stirring quotation, but make sure it summarizes or relates to your overall purpose. The last thing you say may be the most remembered, so make it count.

Make the transition

Whatever the length of your speech, you will most probably make a number of points that will require transitions to lead the audience from one point to the next.

You can do this by instructing the speaker to pick up a prop relating to the next point, handing out notes or using visual aids (all of these devices are covered in chapter seventeen). You can also add verbal transitions, which smoothly link points and move your talk forward. Another way to transition is by recapping material before starting a new point. Transition by asking questions (or ask the audience if they have any questions) or adding bridging phrases to link the two points. A bridging phrase is just a simple sentence that links two points, such as:

- "Let's examine how this . . ."
- "Now that we've covered step one, let's look at step two . . ."
- "Another way of looking at this issue is . . ."
- "I suppose you're thinking, how did this . . ."

Consider the time

When planning a speech, take into consideration the time of day it will be delivered. This can have a major impact on how the audience will respond, and consequently what material or delivery is ideally suited.

Morning sessions are best for presenting hard information. Audiences are fresh and most able to deal with seminar-style presentations. But it's not a good time for humor. People usually are not in the right frame of mind for laughter, especially at breakfast meetings.

Afternoon sessions are better suited for coupling humor with information. Listeners can be a little fatigued and less likely to respond to the same depth of information, so humor helps lighten the load, maintain interest, and support points you are making.

Evening sessions should be the shortest and lightest addresses of all. By this time, people are generally tired and less likely to respond to factual information. It's best to keep presentations to a minimum with a good mix of humor and any other entertainment devices.

In addition to the time of day, also consider what time of the week the speech will be heard. Mondays, more than other days, generally require more hard-hitting details or emotive illustrations to make a point. Some people are still recovering from the weekend and need an extra jolt of reality. Conversely, Fridays generally require a more direct approach, keeping people's minds focused on the details and not on what will be happening over the weekend.

Weekend addresses should be the most relaxed. It's best to present material in a short, lively manner with good use of humor and audience participation to maintain interest.

Markets for Writing Speeches

Speeches can appeal to the widest spectrum of emotions. Great speeches can incite violence or promote peace, but always they will stimulate action. And that's why experienced speechwriters can—and do—command healthy fees.

In addition to approaching your existing clients, there's a wealth of speechwriting markets you can tap. In fact, opportunities are as close as your local community.

Every area has high-profile people who have a need for speechwriting services, usually because they don't have the skills or the time to draft them. These include local politicians, business figures, and community leaders in your town. In addition, there are community organizations, such as churches, business groups, chambers of commerce, and larger businesses, all of which make regular presentations in public.

You can easily identify personalities and potential clients from your local newspapers. Send them a modified direct mail letter explaining the benefits of your speechwriting services or your complete marketing communications services.

Once you have handled some speeches for your local community, you are in a good position to handle more of a company's marketing requirements and to cast your net further afield.

CASE STUDY:
Two Ways to Get the Telstra Message Across

There are many ways to publicly launch a company, product, or service. Whether you put on a big show or settle for a straight media briefing, a well-conceived speech should play an integral role.

Over the years, I have written all kinds of speeches, from full-blown, hour-long, multimedia presentations to technical briefings and sales pep talks.

High-profile companies, like Telstra, are used to making high-powered presentations. But when the telecommunications carrier decided to launch one of Australia's first e-communities in 1999 on the island state of Tasmania, it wanted a relatively low-key affair. That meant a small media event, including brief speeches from the major stakeholders.

As you'll see, there are two basic speech writing formats—full speeches, which are read verbatim, and speech notes for those who prefer to fly by the seat of their pants.

On the day of the launch, we had three guest speakers. I've included sample speeches for two of them here. The first was Chris Rowles from Telstra's management. His role was to officially launch the new e-community and to give an overview of the highlights of its three-year development as well as what people could expect in the future. The following is the short but full speech I prepared for him:

Sample Speech

Understanding Your Needs

Thank you and welcome to the launch of eLaunceston.

This is an exciting time for Telstra Research Laboratories and, may I say, for the people of Launceston.

It represents the culmination of two years of research, development, and consultation with the community at large as well as many local businesses and residents in particular.

It also represents another part of Telstra's "big picture"—our evolution into what Managing Director Ziggy Switkowski calls "a next-century leader in multimedia communications."

We are committed to evolving into a high-tech, multimedia provider. The Internet will continue to be a key area in which we will invest heavily, from developing the latest enabling technologies to producing quality content.

Both of which are integral to the eLaunceston regional portal project.

An integral part of our corporate philosophy is to understand *and* act on our customers' requirements.

That's why we are investing a further three years in studying the needs of the people of Launceston so we can continue to meet the public's demand with this groundbreaking regional portal that provides streamlined information, facilitates better communication, and engenders true community spirit over the Internet.

The Internet—A Way of Life

For some, the Internet is still a mystery, but for most people today, it's more than a fascination—it's a way of life.

The Internet reminds me of a beige box that the world fell in love with just twenty-five years ago—the personal computer. Today, the PC has become an indispensable tool in our business and personal lives. In just over a decade, the fax machine has also reached this status as well as the mobile phone.

We can't imagine life without them—and for many people, the same applies to the Internet. In just a few short years, the Internet has opened our eyes to a new electronic world of information, shopping, banking and, more importantly, communication.

The Web offers a whole new marketplace for companies to attract customers to their products and services. And residents are using the Net for education, telecommuting, entertainment, and to stay in touch.

Just like the humble PC, fax, and mobile phone, the new breed of regional portals, like eLaunceston, may change the way we communicate forever.

And Telstra sees that as a plus.

We see eLaunceston offering the community a simple and safe haven for communication, information and commerce.

eLaunceston Nuts & Bolts

One of the first concerns people have when they surf the Net is the enormity of cyberspace. You can spend hours bouncing from one Web site to the next before you find information that should otherwise be at your fingertips.

So how does a regional portal change all that?

The regional portal acts like a focal point for information and resources of interest to its users.

In our case, the eLaunceston regional portal aims to be an online mecca for all things Launceston—from what's happening locally in the news, weather, and future events to who's who on the Internet, accessible via hyperlinks, to local Web sites.

But that's not the whole story.

eLaunceston will provide communication and commerce services that are relevant to the community. It will also provide Telstra Research Laboratories with valuable information that is necessary for us to continue to meet industry demands and customer needs.

Who is TRL?

So, who is Telstra Research Laboratories?

TRL is one of Australia's largest industrial R&D organizations, with more than seventy-five years of experience, expertise, and dedication to Australian innovation.

Today, we play a preeminent role in information technology and telecommunications research in the Asia Pacific region.

eLaunceston is one of our most ambitious projects.

That's because it's not a typical R&D project but an interactive pilot that will enable us to better understand the factors that motivate people to use, and continue using, the Internet.

eLaunceston is testament to the catchphrase, "think globally, act locally." It will provide a focal point for important, local information. It will also bring local people together by stimulating online communications, discussions and later online shopping, banking, and other electronic services.

eLaunceston Benefits

The eLaunceston regional portal is both entertaining and informative.

It will appeal to both existing users of the Internet as well as first-time users. There is a whole suite of free online services to get people up and running from day one. You can e-mail friends, colleagues, and family. You can participate in live chat sessions or discussion groups. And you can also develop your own homepage with eLaunceston's easy-to-use Web page templates. We'll even host the home page for you.

In addition, people can also check out links to local business and community organizations on the Net and discover other information using its search engines.

Our aim is to make this the premier Web site to visit for anyone wishing to know anything about Launceston with links to almost every local organization online. We've got a way to go, but already we've been overwhelmed with support from the community.

And we're sure that in time, you will be overwhelmed by the information available online about your city. And the beauty is that all of this is available to anyone, anywhere, who is hooked into the World Wide Web. It's not hard to imagine the level of tourism Launceston is likely to attract with this new global presence.

We expect that the eLaunceston initiative will help put Launceston on the global map. Because today, Launceston joins a small group of innovative online communities around the globe. We also expect the regional portal will position Launceston as a leading electronic community in Australia.

This project is not only significant for Tasmania, it is vital for the whole of Australia's online development.

eLaunceston is the nation's first Internet research trial. We are examining the way people interact in an electronic marketplace so we build the next generation Internet landscape over the next few years.

Win-Win for Everyone

And the good news is that everyone wins.

For organizations, eLaunceston provides another "doorway" into their existing Web site and electronic business services. It also provides the local IT industry with the potential to use the portal as a place to test new Internet-based products and services.

For consumers, it offers instant information about a wide range of local issues and areas of interest. It also offers people choices. Those who don't currently use the Internet can now experiment with a new information resource. Old Internet hands can also benefit from gaining faster access to local information and also road-testing emerging technology.

Put simply: If a Launceston business' customers are online, they can now find that business by visiting the eLaunceston site. Likewise, if consumers want the latest information on what's happening in the area, eLaunceston has it at their fingertips.

Consultation

The key to our success of this project so far, and our progress in the future, is close consultation with the Launceston community.

We have been fortunate to have Launceston's complete support since day one.

Even though this is the first official day in the life of eLaunceston, it has been in Telstra's life for more than two years.

In July 1998, TRL began work to develop the concept. In December 1998 Launceston was chosen to be the site of the project, and we've been working with the community to refine the regional portal project ever since.

The strategic alliance between Telstra and the Tasmanian State Government ensured that Tasmania was an excellent location. In particular, the Tasmanian Community Network process has energized the community around information technology.

So why Launceston?

To begin with, you have an innovative city council, headed by John Lees. The Launceston Council is open to new ideas, and it has been proactive in its support of this project. We have had their full cooperation and assistance every step of the way.

Second, Launceston is large enough to provide the project with demographic diversity, but not so large that the project will be overwhelmed by other activities.

And third, Telstra has a strong local presence in Launceston. We also have a solid commitment to the technology development of the region and Tasmania as a whole.

Cisco Networking Academy

Our commitment to Tasmania is multifaceted.

In February this year, we announced our involvement with another technology provider, Cisco Systems, in developing its Cisco Networking Academy—an education program designed to provide a range of IT skills for tomorrow's workforce.

Telstra and Cisco have been working very closely together over the last eight months with the Tasmanian Government and Education sector to encourage students in Year 11 and 12 to take advantage of this excellent skills program.

Telstra has added value to the Academy with our own Schools_2_Net Working initiative—a work experience pilot program that we launched in Tasmania last year, and have since implemented throughout Australia.

This is just one more example of the good work we are doing in this state. This program, like eLaunceston, was a pilot that started in Tasmania and now flourishes around the country.

We hope to see similar results with this regional portal.

Launceston Broadband Program

Another area where Telstra is helping change the communications landscape is the Launceston Broadband project. This is a joint Telstra-Federal Government initiative, which will see the progressive rollout of high-speed digital access for several thousand homes and businesses in Launceston.

It will also involve the establishment of a Telstra Multimedia Development Laboratory, which will provide commercial support for new Internet-based services and jobs for twenty-five people.

Essentially, the laboratory will provide five million dollars funding and support for high-tech businesses in the region. That means opportunities for local technology providers to benefit from high-tech industry development as well as product development support and training.

Local Employment

And what's the by-product of all of these initiatives?

Employment.

Our programs create jobs by skilling people, and our new services also employ Tasmanians so they can help Tasmania progress.

Another example of this is Telstra's National Service Assurance Center, which we opened in Hobart earlier this year.

This is a fault-reporting system, which greatly improves our communications service to the state. It also employs more than two hundred Tasmanians.

Skills Shortage

These kinds of initiatives are vital for the continuation of not only Tasmania's but the whole of Australia's evolvement as an online economy.

Right now, Australia is in dire need of thousands more IT professionals—and that's just to cope with current demand, not future demand, which is expected to rise at around 9 percent per annum over the next five years.

A survey conducted in August highlighted Australia's skills crisis in the information technology and telecommunications industry. The survey found that employers will be looking for more than thirty thousand people in the current financial year, and that most businesses are already having difficulty finding the skilled people they need.

Not surprisingly, the skills in greatest demand include those required to drive the Internet into the next century. Interestingly, we hope that Launceston will play a role in fuelling that drive, as other regions follow your lead and benefit from an online e-community like eLaunceston.

So, we hope that the work Telstra is doing in skilling young Tasmanians while at the same time developing local, leading edge technology complements the next Internet wave—something all Australians will be proud of.

Electronic Marketplace

In closing, let me remind you that the phone is no longer the only means for finding out about local and council services. People are now curious to experiment with online delivery of information, shopping, banking, and other services.

After spending a century ensuring that most Australians have access to a phone, Telstra is now mapping out plans for what the electronic marketplace might look like in the next few years. The eLaunceston trial will give Telstra the knowledge and the impetus to fulfill our promise of delivering communications solutions and technology products and services that meet their needs and exceed their expectations.

Today, Launceston is making history with the launch of eLaunceston. It represents the first Internet research trial in Australia. It also represents the most ambitious regional portal ever developed in this country.

Telstra—Serving Australia

For Telstra, it's all part of being 100 percent Australian. We look after our own.

And today we are helping Launceston look after its own by building this innovative facility.

Making Life Easier

Remember, eLaunceston is *your* regional portal. It will evolve in close consultation with *your* community, *your* local businesses and *your* residents—all so that Telstra can continue to serve you best.

Like everything we do, eLaunceston has been designed to make life easier for *you*.

Thank you . . .

The next speaker was David Llewellyn, the then State Minister for Primary Industries, Water, and the Environment. David only wanted speech points because he enjoyed ad-libbing, so I put together the following for him:

Sample Speech

- Thank you, Chris, for sharing Telstra's vision of eLaunceston. The Tasmanian State Government is indeed fortunate to have Telstra as a partner in our development.

- The success of any project depends on the cooperation of the parties, and that seems to be the linchpin in the success of eLaunceston. Just as the initiative is designed to bring the community together, the project has also rallied enormous support within the community. Community organizations, small businesses, and hundreds of residents have joined forces to provide eLaunceston with honest input, participation, and expertise.

- It's vital, not only for Launceston, but for the whole of Tasmania, that we get behind this initiative. It is part of a brave, new online world. It is part of our future.

- Launceston is an ideal location for Telstra's initiative. It has a reputation for innovation and leadership. It also has the right attitude of developing solutions that are good for the city, the region, the state, and beyond.

- The important thing to remember about eLaunceston is that it is transferable. Other cities and other communities around Australia will be able to take advantage of the innovations made here, making us a more competitive and creative country.

- History is in the making today. Tasmania will be remembered for playing a pivotal role in the dawning of a new era of online community networks.

- eLaunceston perfectly complements Tasmania's environmental stance. The Internet is a clean industry that neither harms nor destroys natural resources. It is also the world's fastest-growing industry. This means the region and, indeed, the state could become a test case as well as an innovator in this burgeoning industry.

- The State of Tasmania benefits from a strategic alliance with Telstra. As Chris outlined, this has seen the development of many initiatives this year alone.

- eLaunceston offers the city and the state a bright future. Individuals will benefit from smarter communications; businesses will benefit from more cost-effective services; and Australia will ultimately benefit from asserting itself as the creative country in information technology.

The final speaker on the day was the then Launceston Mayor, John Lees, who also was content to work from speech notes.

As you can see, the content of each speech must complement the preceding presentation, providing the audience with a strong and complete picture of the activity and how it will benefit them.

CHAPTER 12

Cracking the Corporate Communications Market

In your writing, be strong, defiant,
forbearing. Have a point to make and write
to it. Dare to say what you want most to say,
and say it as plainly as you can. Whether or
not you write well, write bravely.

Bill Stout

For me, one of the easiest and most enjoyable transitions from the objective world of journalism to the subjective world of PR was corporate communications: newsletters, custom magazines, annual reports, and prospectuses.

Any company of note has a newsletter, and some major organizations publish full-fledged glossy magazines. Some of these do more than promote products; they also address the information needs of the customer and the industry. Their aim is to present an info-product that is objective, credible, and just as valuable to the reader as any magazine on the stand. That's a major challenge for any publication, and it's only achieved by a select group of custom magazines.

The company newsletter or magazine represents a cross between the two genres of journalism and PR. If you have had experience in either discipline, you should have a smoother transition to the role of corporate communicator.

The Newsletter: Four Hundred Years in the Making

It would be a mistake to think that the newsletter burst on to the scene with the proliferation of PCs in the 1980s. It's true that the newsletter gained renewed vigor with the introduction of desktop publishing, but newsletters have been around for more than four hundred years.

The most successful early examples were *The Continuation of Our Weekly News,* first published in 1631 by Forraine Press and distributed regularly throughout England. *The Boston News-Letter* in 1704 became the first U.S. newsletter, and it paved the way for the country's first newspapers. Public newsletters enjoyed a great deal of popularity throughout the 1700s, but the 1800s belonged to their successor, the newspaper. By the early 1900s, however, newsletters were back in favor, providing business and industry with specialized information. The first investment newsletter, *Babson's Report,* appeared in 1904. The most long-lived newsletter, *The Kiplinger Letter,* first came off the presses in 1923 and continues publication to this day. Corporate newsletters continued to gain in popularity, especially from the 1930s onward, as they addressed an increasingly wide range of topics.

Today, there are newsletters for every industry, published by private and public companies, large and small. Newsletters appear in all shapes and sizes. They can be mailed, faxed, e-mailed, downloaded from the Internet, or available on a secure Intranet site.

Today's newsletters must work harder to be more successful than their precursors because readers are more sophisticated, more time-conscious, and wary of promotional gimmicks. More than two million newsletters are published annually around the world. And, with the rise in popularity of e-zines, there's just as much competition online as offline.

Marketing Objectives and Reader Satisfaction

As an external publication for customers and prospects, the newsletter can:

- Promote new products and services
- Showcase achievements
- Develop a brand's identity
- Improve or maintain a company's image
- Establish credibility
- Attract sales leads
- Qualify prospects
- Generate sales

As an internal publication for employees, the newsletter can:

- Educate regarding new procedures
- Communicate revised schedules
- Inform regarding new policies
- Praise personal achievements
- Improve productivity and quality
- Engender team spirit

Whether you are producing a free newsletter or a subscription-based publication, its success will be determined by its content. For a newsletter to be seen as credible, it must include specialist information that benefits the reader, not self-promotion that only benefits the company publishing it.

As the newsletter writer and/or publisher, you must satisfy the needs of both your client and the readers. If you succeed, the newsletter will be held in high esteem. Readers may keep it as a reference tool and even look forward to receiving future issues. Fail, and your prized publication will be deemed "junk mail" and "filed" accordingly.

Planning for Success

For many companies, the newsletter is seen as an inexpensive way of building and maintaining relationships. But it's easier to create a newsletter than to sustain it. Whether you are publishing an employee/member or a nonprofit newsletter, an issue-based advocacy publication, or one for a company's customers, it will ultimately fail without proper planning and ongoing evaluation. Many companies launch a newsletter with a grand vision only to see it grind to a halt after the first few issues. You need to research and plan a few issues ahead to ensure that you don't run out of ideas. You also need to seek early feedback from your target audience to make sure the newsletter meets their needs.

Not only does the publication need to satisfy your client's objectives, it also must give the readers the information they're seeking. While you must know what's going on in their industry, and how your client's products, services, and expertise can best serve the readers' needs, you also need to understand your readers. Many newsletters fail because they misjudge what the readers will find interesting. What you find interesting may not be as interesting to your audience.

Before picking up a pen, research your target market's needs and your objectives as you would for any other marketing campaign. Survey your readers. Offer them various options that are achievable by your company, and ask for feedback on what they'd like to see in your newsletter. Then plan before you implement and, finally, evaluate the printed newsletter.

Research begins with questions

If you are planning a newsletter or have an existing one, it is important to ask yourself:

- Who is the target audience?
- What is the objective in publishing the newsletter?
- What are the benefits to the readers?
- What are the evaluation techniques you will use to ensure that your message hits the mark?

To identify the target audience, you need to develop a reader profile. This will determine whether you will have to introduce the readers to the company's products and services or just add to existing information. Either by phone or e-mail, survey your readers to find answers to the following questions:

- Who are your readers? Determine demographic information based on your type of publication. (For example, for a company newsletter you might want to know job title and education level, but probably not sex, marital status, or political party.)
- What do they know about the topics or issues to be covered in the newsletter?
- What publications do your readers already receive?
- How do your readers feel about your subject?
- What is the audience attitude to the organization publishing the newsletter?
- How do you plan to affect your target audience through the newsletter?

Objectives and evaluation techniques

To make sure your newsletter is read, every article should contribute to its overall goal. For example, if it's a customer newsletter, your goal or mission statement may be "to add value to other marketing activities while promoting (the organization) to customers and prospects." Evaluate each story against the mission statement. If it doesn't complement it, you should rethink the story or rethink your goal.

Each story should be written for the specific needs and interests of the target audience. It should deliver what you think they need to know. Finally, each story should motivate your readers to action and encourage response. You can do this by including a toll-free number, a "more information" coupon to complete and return, a Web URL, or some other "call to action" device.

Budget

One of the most critical components of any publication is the budget. This will determine the various parameters that comprise a newsletter, including paper quality, format, frequency, design, and content. Once this is ratified, decisions regarding each of the following elements should be based on the needs of your target audience as well as the budget and resources committed to the project.

Paper quality

Your budget and the style of your newsletter will dictate the kind of paper stock you use. You can choose from a wide range of coated and uncoated paper, including colored varieties, recycled papers, and textured stock, available in various weights and thicknesses.

As a general rule, business-to-business newsletters are printed on a thicker paper, while disposable newsletters can be produced on thinner, cheaper stock. Coated gloss or matte stocks generally suit both types of newsletters as well as brochures, flyers, and other promotional material. Gloss stock has a shiny, reflective finish that highlights full-color photos and printing. Matte stock has a dull finish that is more suited to reading large blocks of text and viewing illustrations and black and white photos. Talk to printers and look at samples to see which stock work best for you.

Color

Like paper stock, how many colors you use will depend on your budget and the look you're trying to achieve with your newsletter. These days, full-color printing (referred to by the industry as "four-color process") is not prohibitive in cost. And, with the short-run technology now available

---

at quick printers, you can produce a relatively small number of copies at a reasonable cost, straight from your computer file. These days, there's no excuse for not printing four-color and every reason to do so. Research shows that readers respond more positively and have greater retention of four-color publications compared with two-color publications (that is, generally speaking, a single color for headlines plus black for the text, and black and white photos).

Whatever you choose, use color wisely. Don't go overboard with rainbow-like headlines and highlighted text, which is the look of an amateur's publication. It's best to standardize one or two colors for headlines and highlighted text, plus a common color for body text, and reproduce photos and illustrations in full, living color.

Format

The standard size newsletter is from four to sixteen pages. Anything bigger is generally considered a magazine; anything smaller is generally regarded as a flyer. Whatever you decide, maintain a consistent number of pages in each issue.

Frequency

This will depend on your budget, content, and readership. Ask your readers how often they would like to see a newsletter from your company.

Publishing a newsletter every one, two, or three months is the norm. Less often would be a waste of time for your readers in terms of consistency, but more frequently would be a drain on resources for many businesses. You need to maintain regular contact with your target audience (e.g., customers or employees), and the newsletter remains one of the most cost-effective methods of building relationships—but *only* if it's produced regularly.

Design

Design and layout are similar to the packaging of products. These elements perform the vital function of attracting the reader's attention, but then it's up to the product—the words—to do their job in selling the information.

Whether you will be briefing a graphic designer for the initial design only, working with a team, or doing all of the design and layout work yourself, your newsletter will need a consistent "look" to it so readers will recognize it and know what to expect from its appearance, structure, and sequence.

The layout should feature quality photos, strong headings and, if appropriate, illustrations to enhance the impact. It should also follow a modular layout: Stories should fit into columns and have a rectangular shape, not spread across a series of uneven columns. We will discuss design elements in greater detail later in this chapter.

Content

Every story needs to be relevant and worthwhile to the reader. The key to success is to involve people. Write about real people; invite readers to participate. People are most interested in reading about themselves or benefiting from the real-life experiences of others.

When interviewing people, do your homework by collecting background on the topic that will be discussed. This will help you formulate the right questions to ask and save time in both the interview process and the writing process.

Depending on the size of your company, ideas for stories can come from various divisions (for example, customer activities from branch managers and new technologies from research and development). Stories can also be based on prepared press releases, or they can form the basis of future media announcements. You can even establish an "idea bank" and stockpile stories for future issues.

Implementing your research

I can't stress enough the value of research and planning. It will save you time in the long run and ensure that your publication remains relevant to your audience. Once the research and planning are complete, you're ready to start producing the newsletter. The implementation process should include:

- Setting an editorial meeting with decision-makers to determine areas of interest
- Researching potential stories
- Drafting stories
- Editing stories
- Gaining story approvals from internal and external customers

- Writing headlines
- Taking or sourcing photos, and getting permission from the sources to reproduce them if necessary
- Design and layout
- Prepress preparation (including scanning of pictures, color separations, and proofs)
- Approval of proof
- Printing
- Distribution (from an internal database or commercial lists)

How long it takes

Production cycles will vary, but as a general guideline, an eight-page newsletter should be completed in a month. That's allowing two weeks for research and drafting of stories, one week for design, and one week for prepress preparation and printing. It may take a little longer, depending on your client and their customers' approval process.

Evaluating the success of the newsletter

Your newsletter should be treated like any other marketing program. It should be evaluated regularly to determine whether it is reaching the right people and whether they are actually reading the information—and, more importantly, whether they have been motivated to act on it.

What Makes a Newsletter Worth Reading?

Now let's look at how to create informative and interesting stories that hold the readers' attention. Let's take the example of a customer newsletter, since it is one of the most popular forms of corporate communications in use today. There are many types of stories that will both interest customers and also benefit companies. These include:

New product announcements

Announcements of new products or improved products can be made more appealing if, instead of just setting out the features, you concentrate on how those features will *benefit* the reader. For example, you might show how a product will benefit a client's business by increasing their productivity, saving them money, or improving the quality of service to their own customers.

Customer testimonials

This is one of the most effective ways of demonstrating the benefits of your client's product or service. Rather than promoting the company's virtues, ask your customers what *they* find most valuable about working with your client. Case studies are not only more interesting to read, they're also considered more credible. They give customers an opportunity to see a company's products and services in use in the "real world." To make them even more beneficial, focus on a customer's unique insights and methods of using your client's products. This will stimulate more interest and enable your readers to apply this wisdom to their own business.

Industry issues

This type of writing can take the form of "how-to" stories or comment on controversial issues affecting the industry and your client. By discussing issues in an authoritative manner, you are not only providing a value-added service to readers, you are also positioning the client as an industry expert. Once you achieve that, it's easy to work out whom they'll call when they need advice. These stories can quote a staff member or executive, or they can be presented as a byline piece from an expert within the company.

Company announcements and other news

Company news stories can be quite varied, ranging from appointments of sales staff and management to announcing upcoming events, such as sales conferences, exhibitions, and policy changes (for example, price changes or statutory/regulation changes). They also may include news briefs, regular columns, or a calendar of upcoming events of interest.

To sum up, all stories should:

- Inform, not sell
- Offer advice that interests or assists the reader
- Identify issues or problems and provide solutions
- Provide exclusive editorial information readers cannot find elsewhere
- Avoid jargon

Quotations and formal approvals

People like to read quotes from people, rather than slabs of impersonal text. And direct quotations make the language more active and interesting.

If you are going to quote customers in your newsletter, for example in customer testimonials, it is important to gain prior approval. This will help protect you legally if there is any problem with the story after it's published. It will ensure that the customer is satisfied with what's been said and can reinforce your client's quality approach to service.

In fact, this approach should be applied to all stories. All information provided to you should be signed off by those people within the organization who have been quoted or who are responsible for the information, so that everyone is clear about what is being produced in the client's name.

Story lengths

How long should you write your newsletter stories? The short answer is—how long is a piece of string? It varies. An eight-page newsletter contains approximately four thousand words, or five hundred words per page. The trend today is to write shorter stories, with each issue of the newsletter covering three or four topics. This structure enables you to cover a range of information and offer variety to your readers.

Stories can vary in length depending on the complexity of the subject and its likely importance to the reader. A story can be as brief as fifty words, such as a reminder about an upcoming event, or as long as five hundred words on a topical industry issue or a customer interview.

In special cases, you can even break a story into two or more parts and run it as a continuing series over several issues. In this case, each article should be self-contained. It should also summarize what was written in previous issues and what can be expected in the following issues.

Inject "News" Into Your Newsletter

Most newsletters are journalistic in style. They usually include straight news and feature stories. I would suggest putting your strongest, newsworthy story on the front page and continuing it toward the back of the issue, much like a newspaper. By "spilling a story," you have the opportunity to run other stories closer to the beginning of the newsletter to maintain reader interest. You can also include a contents box or pointers to entice readers to turn the page.

Feature stories can be placed further back in the newsletter. These are written in a more relaxed tone and can afford to be longer, taking up a center spread, for example, with supporting photos. But they have a lower priority than the shorter news stories that generally command the first few pages of a newsletter.

If appropriate, include a call to action at the end of each story so people can call to place an order or request further information. You can also include a "more information" coupon for those who may not like to phone and would prefer to have a brochure mailed.

Creating Words and Pictures by Design

The success of your newsletter will depend as much on the layout as any other element. First, however, you will need a text design. While of course there will be different stories and different pictures in each issue—and therefore the exact layout may vary a little. There are some things that should be kept consistent. This includes the fonts and type sizes, column width, margin, and gutter size, and where certain regular features can be found. For example, announcements about staff promotions or departures might always be on page two.

Desktop publishing software and many word processing programs can be used to create a template for your newsletter, with certain elements that will be repeated in all issues. These include:

- A nameplate or the title of the publication, which is usually designed as a separate graphic at the top of the first page
- A table of contents, which is especially useful for larger newsletters
- A masthead or information box that features company information (phone, fax, e-mail, and a physical address)
- Section headings for regular features (e.g., the MD's address, new products)

Keep it simple. You can spend a lot of time trying to be fancy by using a variety of fonts and visual aids, but too many can distract or confuse the reader.

Choosing typefaces

Choose two distinctly different typefaces—one for headlines and one for body copy. It's best to pair sans serif headlines and subheads with serif body copy. Sans serif fonts (such as Helvetica, Avant Garde, or Arial) have clean, modern, straight lines and a geometric appearance that makes them distinctive in larger type. That's why they are the popular choice in newsletter headlines as well as posters and display advertising. Serif fonts (such as Times, Garamond, or Baskerville) have short lines or hooks at the ends of the letter strokes. This type is most readable in smaller type or large blocks of text and enables readers to read quickly and decipher your message. That's why these typefaces are the popular choice in newspaper text as well as books and reports.

Working with photos and illustrations

People are visual creatures. They generally understand concepts more quickly when they can see pictures in addition to reading words. If you are responsible for the illustrative material in your newsletter, as well as the words, choose striking or informative pictures that complement your stories. A photo—and consequently the story it accompanies—will have greater impact if it is cropped to accentuate its main feature. Alternatively, you can include a head-and-shoulders photo of the person being quoted in the story. Include captions with all photos, and make sure they explain the picture as well as its relevance to the story.

In addition to photos, you can also enhance the look of your layout with relevant illustrations and clip art. For example, a technical drawing such as a cutaway illustration of the inside of a ship, or a graph or chart, may be more effective than a photo.

Never sacrifice the size of photos or illustrations if your stories are too long to fit. Chances are they won't be read in their entirety if the page is filled with slabs of text and few or no pictures.

Choosing the right printer

Choosing the right printer is as important as any other component in the production of a publication. Ironically, when it comes to printing, many people simply settle for the cheapest quote rather than properly researching what they need and what they can expect from specific printers.

Essentially, there are two types of printers—quick printers and commercial printers. Quick printers are generally more competitive on simpler, shorter print runs (from a few hundred to a few thousand copies). Commercial printers, using large-format presses and high-resolution drum scanners, offer a higher quality service at a higher price. They are better suited to more complex publications and larger runs (upwards of several thousand copies), which they can produce faster and more cost effectively than quick printers. (In fact, many quick printers outsource large, multi-color runs to commercial printers.)

I have used both. I tend to go with quick printers for stock standard publications on a strict budget, and commercial printers for bigger, quality publications for higher-profile clients. In this instance, I find using commercial printers is a little like taking out insurance—I am assured of quality work, with less chance of anything going wrong. I know it's subjective to say, but I find good commercial printers tend to take more responsibility for the process than quick printers who are more concerned with turnover. As I said, this is subjective. I have worked with some excellent quick printers as well. So, as you can see, it's a matter of getting out there and meeting prospective printers, getting a feel for their work, and making sure the relationship will work for you.

Here are some questions you should ask printers:

- How long have you been in operation?
- What clients do you have? (It's a bonus if your printer handles clients in the same industry as yours; it also gives you a sense of confidence when you see that a printer works for some big names.)
- What print jobs do you specialize in? (Don't settle for "everything"; ask the printer to be specific, especially in terms of their color capabilities.)
- What other services do you offer? (Many printers offer a complete range of services, from graphic design, scanning, and separations to printing and distribution. Know what they offer and determine if it's worthwhile doing the whole production under one roof.)
- What PC technology do you use? (Some printers are set up for Windows PCs, some for Apple Macs; others can handle both. Also find out what storage devices are used, such as Zip disks, CDs, and DVDs, and determine if your software files are compatible.)
- What proofs do you provide? (You must receive a proof before you print. This can range from a simple paper proof to a chemical proof, which is my preference.)
- What is your turnaround time for specific jobs? (You need to know how long the printer will take to handle each phase of the process.)

- What are your payment terms? (This can vary from seven to thirty days; try to negotiate for the longest period to ensure your client pays you before you must pay the printer.)

The ultimate test for a printer is the quality of their finished product. Take a good look at samples of their work, especially those similar to what your publication. Checking through samples is also a good way to stimulate ideas. You may find that a different size, shape, or paper stock gives you the distinct look and feel you're after.

Tips for Producing a Professional-Looking Publication

This checklist will ensure a quality newsletter:

Five ways to a readable newsletter:
1. Use simple words to convey your message.
2. Don't print headlines in CAPITALS.
3. Have a healthy sprinkling of direct quotes in all stories.
4. Avoid two spaces between sentences.
5. Balance layouts with a good mix of photos and words.

Five ways to use color effectively:
1. Nameplates and logos
2. Borders around graphics
3. Bar charts and pie charts
4. Pull quotes and subheads
5. Color the background of select stories

Five ways to smarter layouts:
1. Add white space between headings, photos, and body copy.
2. Use subheads, pull quotes, and raised caps as attention grabbers.
3. Place select stories in colored boxes.
4. Design in consideration of two matching pages.
5. Make template layouts for future issues.

Distribution: Getting It Out There

Distribution begins with good database management, which starts by having an up-to-date mailing list of customers and prospects. If you don't have a mailing list, create one and continually maintain it by deleting return-to-sender mail, updating business contacts, and adding new prospect or customer information. Talk to your local postal service about registering your publication so that you can receive postal discounts for bulk mailings.

Evaluate for Ongoing Success

As we discussed earlier, newsletters need constant evaluation to make sure they are reaching the target audience and meeting the company's objectives.

The evaluation process should include:

- Evaluating the editorial content during and after distribution (in addition to surveying readers, you can include a coupon in each issue with check boxes for more information on your products/services).
- Measuring the newsletter against other marketing initiatives. Determine what percentage of leads and sales are generated by it, compared with advertising, PR, and direct marketing.
- Checking the newsletter's profile among the readership. Ask customer service and sales staff whether customers mention it or remember it.

This process is how you keep the communication lines open and ensure that you have a newsletter worth publishing. And you'll soon be reaping the benefits: generating new business from prospects and building loyalty with your existing customers.

What's in a Name? Everything!

Naming your newsletter is an important consideration. Branding a newsletter is similar to branding products and services. The name will be around for a long time (we hope), so give some thought to a title that will be immediately understood, readily recognizable, and memorable.

Since it's an industry-specific publication, you can name it after an industry-specific term that people in the know will be familiar with. When I created a newsletter for Australia Post's direct marketing division, I thought a little about their target audience—direct marketing agencies and professionals within small, medium, and large organizations.

Some of the titles I suggested were a play on the company's name, the industry, and/or the marketing profession. These included:

Post Mark	Post Power
Postscript	Director
Marketeer	Direct
Market Force	Direct Hit
Marketing Work	Direct Result
Marketplace	Post Effect
Marketing Mixes	Post Works
In the Post	Direct Action
Direct Express	Pushing the Envelope
Go Direct	Direct Forces

In the end, the client went with *Post Review*—their choice, not mine. The other approach you can take is to include the company name or the industry it represents with a generic word, phrase or term, such as:

Agenda	Monitor
Alert	Monthly
Briefings	Newsline
Briefs	Outlook
Bulletin	Outreach
Communicator	Post
Connection	Profile
Courier	Times
Digest	Today
Eye	Trends
File	Update
Focus	Views
Forum	Voice
Guide	Weekly
Insider	What's News
Journal	World
Letter	

This is probably the most common approach to settling on a newsletter name. If I had a dollar for every publication I've seen entitled *(Company) News,* I'd be—well, just think of the tax I'd be paying!

Mining the Corporate Gold

Whether you see the newsletter as the "company rag" or an exciting marketing medium, there are plenty of opportunities to make money writing and producing newsletters. This is particularly true now, as many companies have downsized and outsourced this activity to agencies and freelancers.

As discussed, like most writing projects, you have two ways of quoting and billing the client: on an hourly basis and on a per-job basis. Most companies prefer a flat fee so they can budget on a per-project and annual basis. Once you have produced a few newsletters, you will know generally how much time you need to commit so you can quote accurately. Also, if you're a fast worker, you can afford to increase your hourly rate.

Unlike other freelance projects, the advantage of writing a newsletter is that it represents ongoing work. You've just put one issue to bed, and it's time to begin working on the next.

As we discussed earlier, company newsletters remain one of the most popular forms of corporate communications.

Over the years, I have taken a variety of editorial approaches for a variety of clients. These include staff newsletters for large companies, marketing and technical publications for executives and specialist staff, and generalist newsletters for the general public. Each newsletter is written with a different style and a different focus, depending on the company I am representing and the audience the client is targeting.

Océ promotes corporate solutions

My firm managed a variety of marketing communications for Océ, an international manufacturer of engineering and office automation products such as plotters and highspeed photocopiers. We handled a wide range of marketing communications including direct mail packs, telemarketing campaigns and brochures as well as public relations, product launches, and media conferences. But it all began with the launch of a sixteen-page, four-color newsletter for the company's two major product ranges, which can be seen in the images above.

In Print was distributed to dealers (who would send it to their customers as a value-added communication) and to large customers that dealt directly with Océ. The publication soon became the company's premier communications tool, conveying a variety of information, such as:

- Large, unique, and new customer applications
- Major staff appointments and promotions (we only featured senior staff and management who were directly involved with customers)
- Product announcements (products were being released on a continual basis—of course, our stories covered the major features and benefits)
- New services (the company also introduced new services which helped make life easier for its customers)
- Technology innovations (Océ is known throughout the world as an innovator and, because part of the target audience was technically minded, we included information regarding major achievements and innovations by the company)
- Technical tips (this area, although small, included helpful information for resolving problems. While the information was technical, it was delivered in layperson's terms, since the job of fixing problems was often left to a junior or nontechnical person)

In Print could be classed as a conventional customer newsletter, given the content; however, my company always made the effort to distinguish it from competing communications.

Most major stories featured a call to action, including a 1-800 number for more information. Each issue also included a coupon to gain more details, demonstrations, and extra newsletter issues (see images on page 153). We were so confident in the text that we included relevant media on our mailings. And to prove the quality of our stories, it was not uncommon to receive several calls from the press seeking more information or to arrange interviews.

The humble newsletter can serve several purposes—promotional vehicle, information resource, PR prompter—it's all in the way you choose to write it.

Kodak Reaches the Teen Market

The newsletter I wrote for Kodak, *SnapShots*, is a prime example of writing for a specific audience and can be seen in the images above. In this instance, the audience was composed of pharmacy assistants aged around seventeen to twenty-one. Obviously, writing for this audience required a major cerebral shift from the standard target audience of senior management.

My task was to keep pharmacy assistants informed of new Kodak products and promotions as well as to provide tips on how to manage difficult customer queries and handle any technical issues. It would have been easy to fall into "tech mode" and produce a dry, uninteresting dissertation. But it was more fun to write (and read) a newsletter that really *spoke* to the audience.

SnapShots' design complemented its message. It featured big, bold photographs and colorful pages. Each story was written in a light, conversational style to make the newsletter interesting as well as informative. A typical selection of stories in one issue can be seen in image below.

- **Competitions:** In each issue, we would ask readers to answer a few questions about a product or promotion, and they were entered in the running for a premium product or an island vacation. This is a simple way to keep readers interested from issue to issue. It also helped Kodak make sure its young sales people were getting the marketing message.
- **Customer service tips:** Commonsense hints showed employees how to handle difficult customers.
- **New products:** The stories didn't just list the features and benefits; they also made comparisons with other products and showed why Kodak's were superior.
- **Promotions:** These young people are part of Kodak's sales force, so it was important for them to know which new promotions were running in the media, and when.
- **Q&A:** Each issue featured a guest column from an expert photographer who explained in plain English different films for specific occasions, as well as other photographic tips to share with customers.
- **Bright Ideas:** We also encouraged readers to write in with innovative ideas they were using in their store. Each person whose idea was published won two movie passes.

It was a lot of fun putting together the newsletter, and clearly it was considered fun to read, judging by the amount of mail Kodak received for each issue.

Simplot Serves Up a Tantalizing Newsletter

Simplot is the parent company to a dozen well-known food brands. The company publishes regular newsletters for its three target markets, which are take-out shops, fast food outlets, and cafeterias. Each edition contains a mix of customer features, industry news, how-to information, and menus prepared by in-house chefs.

The following article was written for the regular column on French fries, titled *Talking Chips* (Australians refer to French fries as chips) as seen below. It is designed to show operators how to save time, money, and improve product quality and customer service—and that's all by cooking French fries properly.

Whatever marketing communication you are writing, whether you're talking chips or talking profits, always think of your reader—their interests, their knowledge, and their information needs.

The point to keep in mind is that this article—and, in fact, this column—preaches to the converted. Cooks believe they know how to cook French fries already. Let's face it, you and I know how to do it at home, so how hard can it be with the right equipment? Well, according to Simplot, a lot of product is wasted through poor handling, cooking, and presentation.

I have included this article to show you an approach you can take when you are writing for an informed audience:

8 Easy Steps to Increasing Your Profits

How would you like to make an extra $4,000 in net profit each year? Every business would. But what you may find surprising is that you can achieve these savings simply by employing better product management principles.

Market research conducted by our Foodservice Division found that the average operator wastes up to 7 percent of their chips through poor handling. Over a 12-month period, this cost accumulates to a figure that erodes profit levels and sales margins. Yet by improving your work practices and training your staff to be mindful of waste, you can reduce your costs and improve the bottom line.

With this in mind, here are some ideas to help you along:

1. **Avoid overfilling your chip baskets:** Many business owners find they achieve the best cooking results, and serve great tasting chips, simply by controlling the amount of product that gets placed into the chip basket. The lesson they have learned is simple—don't overload your chip basket. Another tip they have learned is to check the manufacturer's cooking instructions. You may find you are under- or over-cooking your chips, simply by ignoring the instructions provided. The instructions can often help you get maximum value from your frozen chip product, so it is worthwhile checking them before cooking.

2. **Take the guesswork out of frying:** Invest in a timer. This simple device will help you cook chips to perfection each and every time. Timers are great for staff that are new to your business because they take the guesswork out of cooking.

3. **Use a chip scoop:** Chip scoops are a great way to minimize product damage and manage your portion control. Some of our successful takeaway customers have found serving equipment, like metal or plastic tongs, ineffective for portion control. They also found the tongs would damage the cooked product (make impressions in the chip, or cut larger chips into smaller pieces).

4. **Cups or bags?:** Some operators find chip cups a great way to maintain portion control, while others prefer serving their chips in a paper bag. Both options have merit, but you need to experiment to determine which one is best for your business.

5. **Use the right product:** The old saying, "You get what you pay for" is appropriate to consider when buying cheaper chip grades. This decision will effect the quality and appearance of your chips and ultimately have an impact on your sales. So always compare brands and grades to find the one that best suits your business. Don't fall victim to the "chip is a chip" mentality. Remember, customers don't buy chips simply because they are the cheapest, they buy for quality and taste. So ask yourself, how do your chips compare in this regard?

---

6. **Cook to order:** Avoid having an abundance of precooked product in your bain marie. Try to cook what you need, when you need it. A properly filled basket takes just over three minutes to cook, and cooking to order will help maximize your product portions and ensure you serve better tasting chips to your customers. From a customer's perspective, freshly cooked chips are the best chips.

7. **Learn from the success of others:** The major fast food outlets realize that chips are their greatest profit source. They also understand that customers expect to receive a good-quality product at an affordable price. Their philosophy is that "quality sells; cost cutting kills." If you deliver quality, you will attract more sales. But if you continually cut your costs by using lower-grade product, you risk compromising the quality of your product to a point where customers will stop buying from you. And this can be a bad move for your business.

8. **Talk to your Simplot representatives:** Why not tap into the market and product knowledge afforded by your Simplot representatives? They can assist you with pricing information, effective portion control, chip yield tests, and in-store promotions. To find out how they can add value to your business, simply call and make an appointment. After all, they know the market because they service the market.

So far we have presented some logical techniques to help you improve your bottom line and maximize your chip product usage. But how did we arrive at the magical $4,000-a-year saving?

Our research found that the average take-out operator buys ten cartons of chips a week. The average portion weight is 180 to 200 grams, of which 7 percent (14 grams) is wasted. That means from a 1-kg yield, you receive four to five serves (depending on the cut and size), with up to 70 grams per 1 kg of product wasted. Using this principle, the average take-out wastes around 800 grams to 1 kg, or five serves per carton.

The average gross profit per serve is $1.45, equating to $7.60 wasted per carton. At ten cartons per week, it means that $76 is lost through poor product management.

Multiply this by fifty-two weeks and it adds up to almost $4,000!

Even if you undertake the ideas we've presented, but only reduce your waste by half, you will still achieve savings of around $2,000, direct to your bottom line. Not only will you save money, you'll also see an increase in business and customer satisfaction, simply by serving great tasting chips.

Other great profit improvements, using Simplot's extensive range of products, are also available. To discuss how we can help your business, simply call your local Simplot Representative or State Office (contact details can be found on the back cover). Remember, in foodservice Simplot's solutions work!

CHAPTER 13

What You Must Know to Make It in Advertising

Advertising says to people,
"Here's what we've got.
Here's what it will do for you.
Here's how to get it."

Leo Burnett (1891–1971)

Being a freelance writer allows you to cover a number of marketing disciplines, both directly for businesses and indirectly via their creative agencies. We've discussed opportunities for writing public relations; now let's look at PR's rich cousin, advertising.

Advertising, PR, and direct mail, which we'll look at in chapter fourteen, fall under the one umbrella of marketing. There are an enormous number of agencies that specialize in each discipline, but there's also a growing number that actively promote all marketing communications as "integrated marketing" solutions. As a well-rounded freelance writer, you can do the same thing—write convincing copy for ad, PR, and DM projects.

For the purposes of this book, let's stick with the traditional boundaries, as we've done in the previous chapters. Even within this confined space, advertising, also known as "above the line" marketing, takes in a broad spectrum of communications worth more than $400 billion a year in the U.S. alone. Here are a handful of the types of advertising that require your skills:

- Handouts
- Displays
- Posters

- Coupons
- Print advertisements
- Packaging
- Point-of-sale signage
- Television commercials
- Classifieds
- Radio commercials
- Flyers
- Data sheets
- Menus
- Demonstrations

Whatever the medium, your job is to promote, persuade, inform, influence, and *sell* people on a company and its products and services.

If you're a literary purist who has never written advertising copy, you're in for a rude awakening. To begin with, you can put aside your copy of Strunk and White's *The Elements of Style*. The traditional rules of writing don't really apply to advertising. But, having said that, it pays to *know* the rules before you begin *breaking* them. Then at least you'll know what you're breaking and what effect you're creating by doing so.

In essence, copywriting places a great emphasis on the choice of words rather than adherence to good grammar. Also, good copywriting means simple copywriting. You don't win any prizes for exercising your vocabulary, only for connecting with the reader, your potential customer. So, simplicity sells.

As you know, copywriting is just one component in developing an advertising message. Other professionals, including a graphic designer, photographer, art director, and creative director, also play a part in the product.

The Formula That Works

No matter what your intention or the advertising medium you're using, to communicate successfully, your copy must follow a proven formula.

There's no room for fat in any writing, and this is especially so in advertising messages. So get off to a good start with an emotionally charged statement. This could be a controversial or thought-provoking headline or opening sentence that grabs attention and compels the reader to read on.

Once you have the reader's interest, you need to build on it. You can do this by following your opening statement with supporting information, or you can cut straight to the point by making the reader a promise. And that promise is to make his or her life better by delivering some kind of benefit. Depending on the length of the piece, you can add supplemental information in the form of brief customer testimonials, more facts, and benefits.

By now, you not only have the reader's interest, you also have his or her unconscious consent to be taken to the final stage. So now's the time to take action.

The weaker your offer and the more complex the call to action, the less chance you have of making the sale. Remember, your call to action will be the last thing on the reader's mind, so it has to be a powerful statement to succeed. It can take various forms, from inviting the reader to call, fax, or e-mail the order to filling out a coupon for more information. To be effective, the call to action has to be powerful, compelling, and easy for the reader to initiate.

Copywriting Rules to Live By

Cutting through the advertising clutter is a constant challenge for copywriters. It's no wonder, considering the fact that every day the average person is exposed to more than 3,500 messages. With so many messages bombarding our senses, we have become experts at blocking out unwanted "noise" Your copy has to work hard to get through these defense mechanisms, known as the "sheltered ear" and the "filtered eye," in order to have any impact on the consumer. Your words will have a greater chance of survival if they follow these principles:

Read what works

To write great copy, you should read great copy. Examine ads that win *you* over. Pull them apart and analyze why the headline drew you in. Discover the magic words in the copy, the compelling statements that led you to the conclusion, "I've got to have this."

Read books by the all-time advertising greats—Claude Hopkins, Albert Lasker, Maxwell Sackheim, and my hero, David Ogilvy. Take note of today's top guns like Joe Vitale and Bob Bly. They're on the cutting edge, and their words are wisdom.

Remember the basics

The best approach is a simple, credible, and conversational approach. Before you write a word, you must identify the target audience. Knowing who will be reading your copy will dictate the writing style you use. Remember, you're not here to win awards or impress the reader. Your entire mission is to connect with the customers and influence them.

Be salesperson first, a copywriter second

Whether you like it or not, advertising is selling. To be a good copywriter, you need to be both a good writer and a good salesperson. You need to exude enthusiasm about the product. See it from the customer's viewpoint, consider all of the advantages, and then you can write about all the benefits it offers the customer. Don't be timid. Ask for the order. Guide the reader to the action you want—to call you with that order.

Make advertorials read like news

U.S. marketing consultant Joe Vitale says advertorials can attract 80 percent more attention than other advertising styles.[14] The reason is simple. We buy newspapers and magazines to read the news, not the ads. But when an ad is presented in a news style, equipped with headline, photo, and caption, and maybe also quoting a spokesperson, the average reader can't help but be drawn to it.

In addition to catching the eye, this style of advertisement can often have a stronger pull than conventional approaches for the same reason. It is presenting information in what appears to be a more objective manner than regular display ads. Not all products, services, or even messages can be conveyed in this manner. Advertorials are best suited to testimonials and products that require a lot of copy to convince the reader. This approach is closer to PR or direct marketing than standard advertising copywriting.

Interact with your prospect

None of us likes to be talked down to or spoken at; we want to speak with someone. We prefer to have a meaningful dialogue rather than endure a monologue, and the same applies in writing. If you want to gain your reader's trust, think and write as if you are having a two-way conversation. Taking this approach will ensure that your presentation is warmer and that your message addresses the reader's problems and also answers his or her questions before they're even asked.

Put simply, you must focus on benefits that are relevant to the prospect. After you have spelled them out, you need to build credibility in your company (for example, years of industry experience or success in the marketplace). Then follow this with proof of the success of your product (for example, customer testimonials). And finally, give them a real reason to buy it (a time-limited offer, a strong money-back guarantee).

To succeed with interactive writing, you need to stay one step ahead of the reader. Reread your copy. Look for holes and fill them with more compelling benefits, stronger statements, and an enticing offer.

Grab attention with a stimulating, relevant headline

Whether it's news or ads, we are drawn first to the headline. Readers put their toe in the water with the headline. If they like what they read, they'll wade deeper. Headlines not only sell the copy; they also go a long way toward selling the product. It's well known in the industry that a good headline can pull up to nineteen times more response than a poor one.

Be the customer—remember "What's in it for me?"

Benefits rule over features. When writing, always have the customer in the front of your mind. Continue asking yourself, "Why would the customers care? What's in it for them?" Asking yourself these questions will keep your work grounded, relevant, and appealing to the reader.

Tell more to sell more

Advertising experts agree that long copy sells better than short copy, but *only* if it interests the reader. The optimal approach is to present as much detail and information as is required to convince the reader but also allow for those readers who are ready to buy after the first paragraph. Show them a clear path to a coupon, a toll-free number, or some other device that makes the buying process quick and simple.

Be specific

When you've got facts, state them. When you've got statements, attribute them. Replace "they say" with "John Frost said." Turn wishy-washy copy into bold statements that engage and convince the reader.

Answer every objection

Vitale lists the five biggest copy killers, which you need to demolish in order to win over your reader. They are:

- I don't have enough time.
- I don't have enough money.
- It won't work for me.
- I don't believe you.
- I don't need it.

Think of these common objections as you write. Answer these and you're well on the way to converting a reader into an enthusiastic customer.

Maintain interest throughout the message

It's easy for any of us to get distracted, so try to keep your readers interested with attention-getting devices, such as benefit-laden subheads (every few paragraphs), pullout quotes, bullet points, and other copy tactics. This will keep both the stayers and the skimmers on the same page.

Use customer testimonials to sell prospects

Even in this enlightened advertising age, nothing sells better than word of mouth. We are more inclined to take the word of a friend or a fellow customer than that of a copywriter. Include compelling testimonials that support your copy. The more the better, and the shorter the better. Sprinkle these throughout your message so they validate all of your claims.

Reverse the risk

When you guarantee your product, you put the reader at ease. Many businesses are frightened to offer a guarantee for fear that they will be inundated with returns. But, in actual fact, the rate of returned merchandise is generally 2 percent or less.

So why not try a longer guarantee? Instead of offering thirty days, offer one year or maybe even a lifetime guarantee. That will impress your reader. Experience indicates that longer guarantees not only get a better response rate, they also have a lower return rate. That's because inertia kicks in. Instead of having a month to evaluate the product, the customer now has all year or more, so there's no rush. And after a while, the customer either is convinced of its value or has forgotten about the guarantee.

Keep it short

The KISS principle should be amended for copywriters to "Keep It Short and Simple," As stated, there are countless messages clamoring for your reader's attention, so you had better make your point well, and make it now. Longer sentences are less read than shorter ones, and the same applies to paragraphs. Readers get lost in a sea of gray text. Keep your communications on target by writing short words, short sentences, and short paragraphs. Write only as much as required to make your point and make the sale.

Identify specific advantages

One of the questions I used to ask prospective employees was, "Why should I hire you?" Needless to say, it's the most feared question you could ask most people at a job interview. But it's also a question you should think about when writing an ad—and answer it before your reader does.

There are a lot of products out there that customers can choose. What's so special about yours? What distinguishes it from the competition? If it's faster, how much faster? If it's better, how and why? If it's cheaper, how much and why? Quantify your claims as much as possible in terms of percentages of speed (for example, "50 percent faster"), dollars saved, or some other measure of comparison.

Build rapport with your reader

You can't write a successful ad, or any other communication, unless you have developed rapport with your reader. One effective technique, as explained by Bob Bly, is to tell the readers something they already know. This proves that you, the advertiser, know the readers' industry and its applications, and that you understand their problems. So it stands to reason that you would be the best person to offer them the right advice and the right product.

Ask for the order

Remember, your copy is a silent salesperson, and the best way to sell is to *ask for the order*. It sounds simple, but a significant percentage of ad copy fails to follow this simple rule.

Your copy must not only outline the benefits of buying, it must also ask the person to buy. Include a coupon, a toll-free number, a fax number, an e-mail address, or a Web URL—and most importantly, ask people to place their order now. You can entice them further by offering a free gift or a special price if they order within a specified period.

Make it available now

When you want something, how long are you prepared to wait for it? I can't remember the last time I put something on layaway. Most of us want instant gratification. When we have been sold something, we want to buy it now. Make the order process as simple and as quick as possible.

Rewrite and test your copy

You know as well as I do that it's rare to get the words right with the first draft. This is especially true in the frenetic world of advertising, where so many factors play a vital role in the success of the copy.

Research your audience's needs and your product's benefits. Write it, rewrite it, remove jargon and difficult-sounding words until the copy *sings*. Then comes the best part: Test it. Test your headline and your copy. You can either just wait and see how well the ad works, or go a step further by using surveys to get feedback. Rework it until you get a better response rate. Something as simple as changing a headline or changing some choice words can—and often does—make the difference between success and failure.

Tell the truth

It's easy to get overexcited when you're writing advertising copy. In fact, it's a prerequisite for writing good copy. But don't let your words get ahead of the truth. Never over-hype, mislead, or abuse the trust your reader places in you. If you do, you may win the sale, but you'll lose the customer for life. Always tell the truth, and always tell it in the most interesting, exciting, and beneficial manner possible.

Sell dreams, not products

We've discussed the value of benefits many times, but the point is worth making once more. Selling benefits rather than features is probably the single most important thing to remember when copywriting. It's also one of the most overlooked principles.

So, before you write a word of your next ad, think about this. Your customer is not buying a product or service from you. They are buying a *benefit* from you. You are not selling a software program, you are selling an improvement in productivity. You are not selling a sports car, you are selling excitement. You are not selling vitamins, you are selling good health. You are not selling shoes, you are selling comfortable feet. You are not selling film, you are selling happy memories. Well-crafted words are a catalyst: They attract, entice, and motivate the customer to satisfy his or her desire.

Think about the end results your product can achieve, and tell the readers how much better they will feel, look, work, or live. Show them how they will benefit, and your copy will benefit your client with improved sales.

Make a strong offer

Every ad should feature a strong offer. This achieves two things: It motivates the reader to take the next step (to buy or to contact the company) and elicits an *immediate* response. And both are essential to the success of your ad.

Whatever the offer, especially if it's a free one, give it a high perceived value. "Call now and we'll send you this FREE book, *Write Well*, valued at $19.95." "Buy now" or "Call us today" gives your ad a sense of urgency, but the strong offer itself is the necessary ingredient in the call to action.

Choose a call to action

We've used this term a lot, but what kinds of calls to action are there? Here's a list of the most popular tactics you can use. Try one alone or combine two for added impact:

- A free gift
- A free sample
- A time-limited offer
- A pending price rise
- A special trial or introductory period
- A "buy now, pay later" deal
- An "unadvertised special"
- An upgrade
- A "no-risk" trial

It's best to first discuss call to action options with your client. You will be limited to what products the company has available or what promises it is willing to make.

Just when you thought you'd finished . . .

Okay, you've finally finished your ad, and you're happy with the way it looks and reads. Now it's time to check that the following elements work properly:

- Does the headline grab the reader's attention?
- Do the subheads cover all the major selling points for the skimmers?
- Does the copy include all the major customer benefits?
- Are the benefits presented in the most convincing manner?
- Does the closing statement bring the message to a logical conclusion?
- Does the call to action compel the reader to take positive action?

If you would answer "no" to any of these, you know what to do.

Breaking Into the Industry

As mentioned at the start of this chapter, you have two options when working in advertising copywriting or other marketing disciplines: freelancing for agencies or working directly for companies. When starting out, it's far easier to freelance for agencies, which offer piecemeal and overload work. Established agencies have a number of clients in various industries, so potentially there are plenty of opportunities and variety, too. You'll learn at their expense and have the safety net of being part of a larger, professional team. Also, you do not have to know every facet of the business (e.g., art direction, production, media buying, and account service), just hone your skills as a copywriter by working across a range of projects.

But, let's not forget one of the reasons you chose to be a freelance writer—freedom. The freedom to choose your clients and projects, the freedom to run your business your way. You will lose some of that freedom if you freelance strictly for agencies. It's okay in the start-up phase, but when you're ready, spread your wings, win your own clients, and take your business to the next level.

Finding work

There are two approaches you can take in finding work with agencies and companies: You can visit various online employment and freelance

---

Web sites as well as check ads in industry publications, or you can take the more proactive route by approaching agencies and businesses directly. Both methods are covered in greater detail in chapter fifteen.

Are You Cut Out for Advertising?

If you're new to advertising copywriting, you may need to make an attitudinal adjustment. But, once you're in, you can expect this to become an exciting and lucrative avenue of writing. A few years back, I wrote a series of short radio scripts for Telstra, Australia's largest telecommunications provider. The scripts were essentially discussions between a radio announcer and a famous Australian Rules football player at the time. Each script introduced a new service that the company was bringing to market. The scripts were written for sixty-second slots. Apart from some initial research and a brief from the product manager, I managed to write half a dozen radio commercials in a lazy Sunday afternoon. To this day, it's the most money I've earned for an afternoon's work.

Advertising is, and always has been, the big brother of marketing. It commands the largest portion of revenue because it pulls customers in better than any other medium. There's a lot of competition in ad copywriting, but if you can crack this market, you can write your own ticket. It's always good to remember the old copywriter's ode:

> When the client moans and sighs
> Make his logo twice the size.
> If he still should prove refractory,
> Show a picture of his factory.
> Only in the gravest cases
> Should you show the clients' faces.

CASE STUDY
Labels That Sell Themselves

This is one of the more unusual copywriting projects I've handled over the years: writing copy for alcohol labels. I must say it was a little challenging coming up with something interesting to say about spirits I'd never sampled. While I enjoy a good drop, I was not familiar with each of these drinks, so I needed to apply a little license.

If nothing else, these examples of copywriting, shown below and on page 171, should demonstrate the wide range of work available. Every product you pick up at a store needs words to promote and sell it. And there's a professional writer behind each message—or there should be. Why not you?

Sample Copy

BJR Gin

Crisp, bright, and bracing.

BJR Gin is a pure spirit that is smooth in character and aromatic in flavor. With fresh juniper berries, orange peel, coriander seeds, and angelica, *BJR Gin* is distilled using the traditional pot still method to retain all the natural citrus and herbal flavors and balance demanded of the highest quality "London Dry" style gins.

This product is proudly made in Australia, using only the finest natural Australian and select imported ingredients. BJR Distilleries is a 100 percent Australian-owned family business, with more than thirty-five years experience in the fine art of liquor production. And, because we're Australian, you know you can trust the products we make and the fact that every dollar you spend stays here, benefiting all of us.

BJR—the new taste in gin.

The Wealthy Writer

BJR Ouzo

BJR Ouzo is the Ouzo of choice for the discerning drinker.

Blended from the highest quality spirit using star anise, aniseed, and several herbs and spices, *BJR Ouzo* is double distilled using the traditional pot still method to retain its sweet-dry character and balanced aromatic flavor.

This product is proudly made in Australia, using only the finest natural Australian and select imported ingredients. BJR Distilleries is a 100 percent Australian-owned family business, with more than thirty-five years experience in the fine art of liquor production. And, because we're Australian, you know you can trust the products we make and the fact that every dollar you spend stays here, benefiting all of us.

BJR—the new taste in Ouzo.

CHAPTER 14

The Direct Mail Dozen: Essential Ingredients for Power Writers

> The consumer isn't a moron; she is your wife.
> You insult her intelligence if you assume that
> a mere slogan and a few vapid adjectives will
> persuade her to buy anything. She wants all
> the information you can give her.
>
> *David Ogilvy (1911–1999)*

A s discussed in earlier chapters, direct mail, or DM, is one of the major disciplines of marketing today, and it offers a hive of opportunities for the smart writer.

Direct mail is actually a subset of direct marketing, which encompasses telemarketing, mail order, and other direct-response techniques. The major difference between direct marketing and other marketing disciplines is that it is a personal medium. It communicates on a one-to-one basis with individuals and elicits a direct response from them.

DM communications can be as simple as a single, personalized letter or as comprehensive as an information pack with an involvement device, brochure, and reply coupon. You can use DM to reach literally any target audience in any geographic area and any demographic segment. You can use DM to introduce new offerings, sell products, promote services, communicate with prospects, follow-up with previous customers, inform shareholders, educate a sales force, conduct surveys, distribute sales literature, and respond to queries. You can also use DM to support other marketing efforts by reinforcing marketing messages and sending further information, a mail-order product, a free gift, or a free sample.

As you can see, DM can be used for a wide range of marketing purposes, but there are three key elements common to every DM communication:

- An offer (it motivates the recipient to do something, such as buy a product or request more information)
- A response device (it includes a reply coupon, phone number, fax, e-mail address, or URL)
- A tracked response (you can determine the buying habits of market segments and individuals over a number of campaigns and measure the effectiveness of specific mailings, including the cost per response)

Before we get started, it's a good idea to look over chapter thirteen again. Much of what we've already covered applies equally to DM. When you're ready, take note of the techniques below.

Writing Memorable and Marketable Direct Mail

1. AIDA spells DM. Direct marketers will tell you that the key to success, especially when it comes to writing letters, can be summed up as AIDA:

- Attention
- Interest
- Demand
- Action

This translates to:

- Get attention with an arresting headline and strong opening statement.
- Arouse interest by identifying or acknowledging the reader's problems, needs, or wants.
- Create demand by making the reader a promise or an offer of some benefit.
- Prompt action by asking for the order.

2. Start with a bang and build on it. You've got only ten seconds to make the right impression on your reader, so start off with your strongest argument and make sure it's what the reader wants to hear, not what you want to sell.

3. Keep it short. Contrary to what we said about advertising, short letters are better than long letters. Many marketing experts suggest that you write

---

as much as you need to write (I have received sales letters of more than a dozen pages—I said *received*, not *read*). For some, writing lengthy letters is a license to be verbose, and it risks losing the reader. Remember, readers' time is limited and their attention span is even more limited. So be brief and to the point, and keep your letter to one or two pages in length. If you need more room, include a brochure.

4. Get personal. Direct mail should be personal mail. Wherever possible, address a letter to the person who will be reading it. "Dear Sir or Madam" no longer cuts it (if it ever did). Also, getting personal means writing personally. Be friendly, build rapport, and you'll win over more customers.

5. Know your reader and write accordingly. The simple approach to writing DM is to write simply. That works fine when you're appealing to general consumers, but if you're addressing business professionals, you must write at their level of knowledge and vocabulary. Write below it and you will lose their interest and their respect.

6. Keep the mail pack simple. Just as you need to keep your communication simple, you should also keep your mail pack simple. It's best to keep the items down to a personalized letter, a brochure or catalog, and a reply card. Any more and you risk diluting the reader's interest and, consequently, your response rate.

7. Find out more about your prospects. If you include a reply coupon, also include questions that tell you more about your prospects and your market. This is essentially a brief questionnaire or survey, but it can become a vital component of your marketing arsenal.

8. Offer more choices and get a better response. Research indicates that the more choices you give a prospect, the better the response rate. Your reply card can include a number of options, from buying or trying a product to requesting a brochure or a sales call.

9. Treat your repeat customers like gold. The Pareto Principle, also referred to as the 80-20 rule of disproportion, applies in DM: 80 percent of repeat business comes from 20 percent of customers. In addition, as DM specialist Richard Benson observes, the most important order is the second one, because a two-time buyer is at least twice as likely to buy again as a one-time buyer.[15] That's why it's important to recognize and acknowledge your loyal customers in your communications. Consider developing a loyalty program that benefits repeat buyers, which could be as simple as sending them an exclusive mailing with special offers and information.

10. P.S.—don't forget to add one. The postscript is the most-read element in a DM letter after the headline and opening sentence, so don't forget to include one, and make sure it features a strong statement. It's the ideal place to emphasize a key point, offer, or benefit. It's also an ideal place to repeat your call to action in a slightly different manner. You will obtain an even greater response if you neatly hand write the postscript or present it in a different color.

11. Rewrite until you get it right. As with all forms of promotion, presentation must be of the highest order. Your letter must read simply, using short, emotive words that capture the imagination. Hemingway admitted to rewriting every sentence up to five times before he would hand a novel to his publisher. I'm not saying you have to commit to that degree of revision, but a first draft should never be your final draft. A large part of my business involves words, and I never let anything go out without reading over it and redrafting and redrafting until the copy is as good as I can make it.

12. Think about the packaging. Experience indicates that a neatly handwritten envelope addressed to an identified individual will be opened and read, particularly if the envelope carries a colorful postage stamp rather than an anonymous franked stamp. While it may not be feasible to hand write mass mailings, you can compromise by printing directly onto the envelopes rather than using mailing labels. Experience shows this personal approach gains a better response.

Direct Mail Opportunities

Direct mail, like other major marketing mediums, is a competitive industry, but there are plenty of opportunities for savvy writers.

As mentioned in the previous chapter, there are two roads you can take to gain DM work: Dealing directly with companies or via their agencies.

The same advice that I mentioned regarding advertising opportunities also applies to DM. You can seek opportunities via various online employment sites and offline advertisements, or you can be more proactive by going directly to the source. Target relevant companies and agencies, and demonstrate your abilities as a DM writer with a well-conceived letter and brochure detailing the benefits of working with you. Chapter fifteen covers everything you need to know to promote yourself and track down opportunities.

The Final Word on Direct Mail

You could sum up DM, advertising, PR, and most communications with this old ditty:

Tell me quick
And tell me true
Or else, my friend,
To hell with you.
Not how this product
Came to be,
But what the damn thing
Does for me.

What else is there to say?

CASE STUDIES:
Getting Personal With Direct Mail

There are many ways to write to prospects and customers. Most DM experts will tell you length is not critical, and that it's better to write a longer letter than a shorter one. I agree that you need to write as much as you need to get your message across. But your message doesn't have to be restricted to a letter. Make your point as quickly as possible. If you need to say more, include a brochure.

Here's my golden rule with DM: When writing, always be conscious of your readers' time, keeping in mind that they may be sorting mail over the wastebasket.

Pin Point Tele Marketing Targets Prospects

Here's an example of a short letter written for a local telemarketing company:

Sample DM Letter

«Date»

«First_Name» «Surname»

«Title»

«Company»

«Street»

«City» «State» «ZIP code»

Dear «First_Name»,

Are you having trouble finding the right prospects? Do your promotional campaigns need a shot in the arm?

Whether you sell products or provide services, you need pinpoint accuracy in reaching the decision-makers. That's why other companies call Pin Point Telemarketing. We handle a wide range of projects for small and large businesses that need professional support without adding to the payroll.

Telemarketing is one of the most cost-effective forms of sales and marketing. We can cover more ground with a telephone than a representative on the road. And because our staff is made up of highly motivated sales professionals, we ask the right questions and gain the right answers for our clients.

Pin Point Telemarketing offers a wide range of services including:

- Sales Assistance
- Consumer Feedback
- Independent Surveys
- Market Research

Pin Point Telemarketing is available for short and long-term projects. We also work well with management and can enhance internal marketing efforts. So call me today and let's discuss how we can assist you with your next promotion.

Burgundy Lunch Box Rewards Loyal Customers

While there are plenty of opportunities for writers working with large organizations, there is also a variety of work with small to medium-sized businesses. And the emphasis is on the word "variety."

Here's one example of a small promotion I undertook for a local food outlet. The business had been running for a number of years and, during that time, had gained a good reputation because of quality foods and service. The problem, as for many businesses, was gaining an ongoing stream of customers.

The following "customer loyalty program" was designed to bring satisfied customers back to the shop more often, and to reward them.

The marketing process was simple: Draft and issue a personalized letter to customers (the business had already developed its own database of customers) and send it out with a VIP customer loyalty card (see image below). All customers had to do was present the card when they next visited the store, at which time it would be stamped and, after ten visits, their next meal was free.

A VIP card can be a simple-looking but powerful loyalty tool that keeps customers happy and cash registers ringing.

It's a simple approach but an effective one for both small and large businesses. Here is the personalized letter I wrote:

Dear «First_Name»,

Have We Got a Deal for You!

We value your business, so we are now offering—for a limited time—a special VIP Customer Card.

This offer is available to regular customers of *Burgundy Lunch Box*. It's our way of saying thanks for your support—and we hope to continue being of service to you.

We invite you, your colleagues, and business associates to lunch with us on a regular basis and we will reward you with a free meal* on your eleventh visit in a month.

Who said there's no free lunch? There is at *Burgundy Lunch Box* for our VIP Customers!

You can choose from our full menu including:

- Gourmet Sandwiches
- Roast of the Day
- Hot & Cold Dishes
- Fruit Smoothies
- Garden & Fruit Salads

We also offer fresh sandwich and fruit platters as well as full catering for special events. And, you can even phone or fax your lunchtime orders by 11 A.M., and we'll deliver them to your office free. How's that for service!

It's our pledge to offer you not only great discounts on your lunches but the highest level of service and food in the quickest possible time.

Enclosed you will find a special VIP Customer Card, which will be stamped each lunchtime you dine with us.

We hope you like the new offerings at the *Burgundy Lunch Box*.

Hope to see you for lunch soon.

GETTING DOWN TO BUSINESS

By now you have a clear understanding not only of the hottest-selling areas of writing but of which avenues best suit you. Now it's time to get down to the business side of writing.

The vast majority of writers who fail in business do so primarily because they fail to plan. Many PR and marketing writers have the skills and the knack for marketing a client's enterprise, but they fail to apply these principles in their own commercial lives. For small operators, this exacerbates the "feast or famine" phenomenon, where they're waiting for the phone to ring or it's ringing off the hook.

In this part we'll examine strategies you can apply to attract new revenue, improve your work style, and handle slow-paying and no-paying clients.

CHAPTER 15

Marketing Your Business

There is no such thing as "soft sell"
and "hard sell." There is only
"smart sell" and "stupid sell."

Charles Browder

For many business professionals, marketing is something they neither fully understand nor fully utilize. They "haven't got the time" to understand how to win new business and keep it, or they "haven't got the skills" to achieve it.

Fortunately, you're already ahead of the pack. You possess one of the most important skills a marketer needs: the ability to communicate. And, if you apply the many marketing strategies we've already discussed to your own as well as your clients' business, you're well on the way to running a successful freelance writing enterprise.

Working on Your Business

Most experts agree that self-employed people should invest 20 percent of their time in marketing and corporate development. Most freelancers I know don't even get close to a fraction of that figure. But it's important to make that investment for your business today and for your growth tomorrow.

You should divide your working time into two categories: working *in* the business and working *on* the business. A good portion of this book is about working *in* the business. These next few chapters are about working *on* your business. The key, like everything in commerce, is to develop discipline. Plan what times or what days you'll work on developing your enterprise, investigating new markets, approaching prospects, and keeping existing clients satisfied.

Let's discuss ways you can put this into action.

Diversify your markets

There are two reasons why I've branched out into different writing markets. The first is the obvious one: to "spread the risk," as investors say. Some believe it's better to be a "niche writer" because you can command a higher rate and will be recognized as an expert. That may be so, but what if a number of other "experts" are all competing for your piece of the pie? Or what if the market dries up?

I've worked a broad spectrum of writing markets. I've enjoyed the good times when clients just couldn't get enough of me, and I've also suffered the bad times when clients were restructuring and were instituting a "change in policy" or a "change in direction" or a "change in management." If this happens, you may as well have a change in your phone number, because the phone won't ring anyway. The sad part is that when these times come, it's usually too late to shift gears and go after new markets. Unless, of course, you already have contacts and clients in other markets.

The second reason I've diversified is to maintain mental health! One of the great advantages of being a freelancer is that you can choose your own markets and the clients within them. Having said that, there's nothing worse than being stuck in a rut, writing on the same subject for the same clients, month after month. So, in addition to having a variety of clients, I find it's better for my sanity to service a variety of markets. This way, when I've had enough of one writing area, I can switch to another.

Having skills in diverse markets also assists my existing clients. I can and do, for example, offer a variety of writing services to some of my corporate clients—everything from PR, advertising, and DM writing to drafting speeches, brochures, newsletters, and Web content.

Developing a Nose for Business

As I've shown, there's plenty of corporate work out there for freelancers. But how can you sniff it out? Keeping up with the news is a good start. You need to know what's happening, not only in the community and business sections of your daily newspaper but also in the employment section. When you see tempting opportunities for copywriters, PR consultants, marketers, and even sales managers, why not respond with a unique application?

Do a little digging beforehand to determine the size of the company and its needs. Maybe the company has just been launched or it's expanding rapidly or opening new markets. Whatever the case, how is it supporting this move with marketing? Is there a marketing manager or sales manager responsible for marketing communications? If so, is there an opportunity for you to handle their overload or to manage all of their marketing support activities?

There's only one way to find out. Pitch your proposition to them, and follow through with a timely phone call. Remember, 70 percent of jobs are not advertised, and a sizeable portion of work is available to freelancers that most never know about, including the client. That is, until some bright person brings it to their attention.

Mining your database

One of the current buzzwords of marketing is "data mining." This refers to mining your existing database of customers in order to gain new commercial opportunities. The buzzword may be new, but the principle isn't, and you can apply it to your advantage.

Go through all of your useful contacts: old clients, prospects, and even colleagues. Send each a letter, updating them on your new business direction, the markets you offer, and the benefits you can provide to them. Depending on the nature of your relationship, apply the various principles discussed in chapters thirteen and fourteen, then follow-up the letter with a friendly phone call to determine their level of interest and the future direction of your relationship. If the person shows sufficient interest but is not ready to work with you, ask if it is all right for you to call in the near future and log the task in your calendar.

If you haven't already developed a database of hot and cool prospects and clients, then do so now. The sooner you establish this resource, the sooner you can profit from it.

Joining or developing a network

Whatever markets you are interested in pursuing, there are a number of professional organizations that serve them, and these organizations provide the perfect place for you to develop a network of both potential clients and potential colleagues, such as graphic designers, photographers, filmmakers, or any other professionals who are aligned to your target markets. Why do you need these people? Well, for one thing, you can develop your own network or consortium and pitch for business that benefits all parties. I've pitched for a number of corporate and government tenders over the years. That's business I couldn't handle by myself but could manage with a team. This networking approach gave me an edge over other freelancers and put me on a level playing field with large agencies. Try it yourself. You may have another advantage over the larger agencies, and that is overhead. Because your consortium isn't paying for high street offices or for several layers of bureaucracy, you can effectively undercut the big guys and still make a handsome profit.

Another advantage of networking is, of course, meeting potential clients. By attending meetings, presenting free talks, or becoming more community minded, you expose yourself to a wealth of business opportunities with people you otherwise may never have had the chance to meet. In addition, getting involved in professional groups gives you the chance to keep updated on new industry and market trends as well as new ways of improving your business.

Calculating your earnings

This is something I don't like doing, but it's still a necessary part of business if you want to stay in business. Whether you're working for clients on a project basis or an hourly rate, take note of how much time you invest in specific projects. Draw up a simple time sheet into quarterly increments and log the amount of time you spent on a project, from conceptualizing, researching, and writing to client liaison and any other associated tasks. Then calculate your hourly rate by dividing your project fee by the amount of time you have invested.

It's a good habit to get into, especially when working with new clients or new markets. You'll get an instant snapshot of what markets and clients are worth, and which are worth pursuing in the future. (I've found it's also a useful exercise when you're evaluating future dealings with a client. I feel more comfortable about letting go of a client once I've worked out that it's "costing me money" to continue working with them.)

Again, you will probably find that the Pareto Principle applies: 80 percent of your revenue will come from 20 percent of your clients—and similarly, 80 percent of your problems will stem from 20 percent of your contacts.

Getting your clients talking

Which do you more confidently accept: advertising or a personal recommendation? The latter, of course—so why not apply it in your own business? Many freelancers are shy about asking for a testimonial. If you do good work, others deserve to know, and who better to tell them that the people who know best—your clients.

It doesn't matter whether you've been working with a client for a short time or a long time; there's no better time to ask for a testimonial than now. I've received them from clients I've worked with for several years as well as clients for whom I completed a one-off project. By asking for a testimonial, you automatically reinforce your competence and confidence in the mind of your clients. Testimonials are the "proof" prospects are looking for. You can include original testimonials in your portfolio when presenting to clients. You can also include brief versions in any company or personal profile, brochure, or Web site.

Asking your clients for referrals

Now that you've got your clients thinking positively about you, why not ask them for referrals? Whether your client is a marketing manager, an editor, or an agency director, he has friends and colleagues in the business and in different industries. And these are potential clients who will be warmer to your inquiry following a personal recommendation.

Again, don't be shy in asking for referrals. Satisfied clients are only too willing to help spread the word for you—but only if you ask them.

I've generated a lot of business through referrals. In fact, I would say that referrals account for the majority of new business I have won. It's the cheapest form of marketing you can do; all it takes is providing exemplary customer service (which you should be doing anyway) and a few words in the right ear of the right client.

Don't forget to acknowledge your client's referral with a small gift, thank you card, or phone call—even if you don't gain any work from the prospect. Remember, if they have referred one potential client to you, they'll more than likely do it again. So encourage them by acknowledging them.

The Perfect Pitch

By now, you should know where to look for new business, but how do you handle that first contact?

Whether you have sent a direct mail pack or chosen to phone first, that initial contact can be difficult for some people. So do what you do best—write it down.

Write your own speech notes

Even after many years in business, I generally have a few notes handy when calling prospects for the first time. Maybe it's because of my training as a journalist, but I find that even if I don't refer to them (which is usually the case), just having that literary security blanket ensures a smooth presentation.

I am not suggesting you draft a rigid spiel, just a few points and a few questions about the person's business and marketing activities to engender a true conversation. Here are a few for starters:

- How do you promote your products and services?
- Have you tried PR or DM (or whatever service you wish to sell them)?
- Do you use internal staff or freelancers?

There are plenty of others you can add. Think about the company you have targeted and the questions will come. By creating a dialogue with your prospect, you:

- Establish rapport
- Gain a greater understanding of their business and marketing approach (and their needs)
- Discover areas where you can help them (and you can suggest these during the conversation to gauge interest and entice response)
- Demonstrate your skills and ability to understand their needs (How many of your competitors have taken the time to call the prospect and ask meaningful questions about their business? Not many, I bet.)

By the end of the conversation, you are in a prime position to gain a meeting with your prospect, and add a new name to your client list.

Present yourself in the best light

Once I get the meeting, I present my portfolio, which contains my best work over the years, ranging from corporate videos and radio commercials to press releases, the results from product launches and press conferences, as well as newsletters, brochures, and DM packs. The trick to presenting your work is not to bore the prospect with how brilliant you are but to show them how successful communications can be used to improve *their* business.

The point to make is that marketing is to some degree a science, or at least a formula, and that formula can be applied to any industry or business. So that's what you do—present your previous work in a way that shows the prospect how it can benefit them.

Yes, I'm back on that old chestnut—benefits! When the meeting is finished, I leave the client with a more extensive document on my company. This is a corporate profile, a bound document that includes:

- My company's industry experience and marketing know-how
- The list of services available and the benefits to the prospect
- Profiles of the team (remember, I have a staff of one, but I use a number of sub-contractors. I include their names, experience, and expertise in my profiles—with their permission, of course)
- Client case studies and testimonials

If, however, the meeting has gone according to plan, and the prospect wants to do business, then I leave nothing. I return a few days later with a formal proposal that includes the corporate profile.

Web Sites for Freelance Work

In addition to tracking down your own prospects, there are a growing number of Web sites promoting a variety of contract work and freelance opportunities. These include:

The Burry Man Writers Center (www.burryman.com/freelance.html) An exhaustive list of writer-specific job links. It also includes journalists and nonfiction organizations, and other industry-related resources, such as newsletters, forums, and prescriptive articles.

Craig's List (/www.craigslist.org) A range of jobs available throughout the U.S., as well as Canada and the U.K. You can search by region or job category and specify telecommute, contract, internship, part-time, or nonprofit. The site also features events listings, classified and personal ads, and forums.

Freelance Writing (www.freelancewriting.com) A variety of employment opportunities, including job banks for freelancing, full-time writing, agency, and writer/publisher opportunities. In addition, the site features industry news, interviews and articles, and networking opportunities.

Creative Freelancers (www.freelancers.com) Various creative positions for freelance, part-time, temp and full-time work. It includes a "talent search" for showcasing your skills and experience.

Journalism Jobs (www.journalismjobs.com) Journalism jobs at newspapers and wires, magazines, TV and radio, and online. Includes industry news, interviews, and information on internships, fellowships, and awards.

MediaBistro (www.mediabistro.com/joblistings) Register to access postings on various creative positions. It also includes free articles, forums, and a job alert e-mail service.

NewsJobs Network (www.newsjobs.net) An A-Z list of links to hundreds of writer-related employment sites, including those in Canada and the U.K. Narrow your search by specifying freelance, new, or super sites.

Sun Oasis (www.sunoasis.com) Search a range of writing jobs by region or category, including freelance, telecommute, and online. Also includes other resources, such as industry news, media links, and pay rates.

Worldwide Freelance (www.worldwidefreelance.com/markets.htm) Register to access international writing markets covering disparate topics including Christian, technology, and travel. It also includes links to writing sites, working from home, and writers' references.

Writer's Weekly (www.writersweekly.com/payingmarkets.htm) The site features the latest writing markets and jobs as well as warnings on unscrupulous publishers and editors, a list of articles, and a discussion forum. Stay up-to-date with the free weekly e-zine.

Putting Your Skills Into Practice

We've talked at length about the rudiments of good PR, DM, and ad writing. Now you have the perfect opportunity to road test what you've learned—in your own business.

DM vs. ads

Okay, before you run off and produce your first television commercial, let's look at what you're trying to achieve and how much money you have to accomplish it.

I believe the best form of advertising available to small businesses, like ours, is the telephone directory. You should be in the directory, even if it's with a free listing. I've tried free listings, bold listings, and display ads. The more costly ads do pull better responses, but not enough to justify the added cost. I've found that a bold listing gives me the best value. It's enough to distinguish my company from the majority, and it's not too much of my marketing budget blown in one hit. Beyond this, I only advertise when I am recruiting.

This isn't just because of the exorbitant cost of conducting an ad campaign; it's also a matter of considering the market needs. In a business such as ours, promotion is better served through information—and that's where DM and PR have it over conventional advertising. There's room to explain what you do and how you do it while you build rapport with the prospect. In my view, advertising can't match that.

If you read chapter fourteen on DM, you saw that most of it applies to your own marketing efforts. In addition, I suggest you do the following:

- Keep your DM letter to prospective clients short and to the point.
- Include a company brochure and/or relevant clips. (See what I have to say about this in the next section.)
- Follow up the letter within a few days with a phone call, requesting a meeting.

This final point is very important. If you don't follow up your letter, chances are you've lost a good prospecting opportunity. Sure, you'll get rejections, but selling is a numbers game. There will be positive responses along with the negatives, so stick with it. And smile as you dial—remember that a cheerful mood is infectious.

Also, remember what I mentioned earlier: Have a few key points in front of you as you are talking with your prospects. This will help if you get stuck for words. Also, just as with your written communications, emphasize the benefits to your prospect. This phone call is about him or her, not you. You or your product is a catalyst, a means to the satisfaction of a want.

Making news with good PR

You can begin by writing a PR release that introduces your business to both the media and the marketplace. Put some thought into this, based

---

on what we've discussed about PR. Your story has to be newsworthy rather than merely promotional. It must have a hook.

You could write an article addressing a current issue that's been discussed in the media. You could identify a trend and comment on it. You could promote a unique service you're offering. There are plenty of ways of getting column inches, but the story must be newsworthy.

When I first started my consultancy in 1991, Australia, like the U.S. and many other countries, was in a recession. When I told my colleagues that I was starting my own PR firm, many expressed concern about my survival. I was confident that as budgets were cut and staff retrenched, there would be a greater need for freelance writers and PR practitioners, like me, to pick up outsourced work. So, when it came time to promote my fledgling business, I turned to the humble PR release to help me win new clients.

Sample PR releases

My first story was based on the premise that now was the time for business to be proactive, not reactive. History shows that forward-thinking companies, such as Westinghouse and Coca-Cola, dramatically improved their market share and profitability during economic downturns because they continued to use smart marketing. And, in my view, smart marketing means using cost-effective PR in addition to or as a substitute for expensive broad-based advertising.

Here is the main meat of the press release written way back in 1991:

Sample Release	**Companies Need to be Proactive, Says PR Man**

Companies Need to be Proactive, Says PR Man

Companies need to promote themselves during economic recessions in order to protect their market share and establish new business, says Michael Meanwell, managing director of PR firm, The Write Advice.

"Downsizing may offer a short term solution to a downturn, but organizations need to promote now in order to survive and position themselves for when business picks up," he advises.

"For all but the large organizations, a concentrated advertising campaign is too expensive to maintain—but businesses still need to get their name out in the marketplace."

He says companies generally switch their promotional funds to PR during market downturns, as was seen during the credit squeeze of the 1960s, the recession in the early 1980s, and now the early 1990s.

"Small business needs to create and maintain a profile, and companies realize that PR is the most cost-effective way of achieving this.

"Advertising can create immediate interest in a product or service, but PR creates and builds a level of awareness far beyond advertising. It is not only more cost effective; it is also more credible because the public perceives it as news. A large percentage of what you read in the newspaper, hear on the radio, and see on television is based on information supplied by a public relations practitioner," Mr. Meanwell says.

"But there's more to PR than simply promoting product. It's an entire ethos that should be reflected throughout the company structure, from the way the telephone is answered to the way goods and services are invoiced. Creating the right image serves as the foundation for any successful company, but its lifeblood is communications—with staff, customers, distributors, and prospects—and that's where PR can help," he added.

The Write Advice can meet a company's needs and budget with a full complement of services ranging from the preparation of news stories, direct mail, and media conferences to the design and publication of sales brochures, corporate profiles, and company newsletters.

Mr. Meanwell says that PR consultancies offer a distinct advantage to small business in that a company can employ a team of professionals on a short-term or part-time basis at a fraction of the cost of employing a full-time PR person. He said most larger organizations also sought the services of an external agency in addition to employing PR staff.

"Whatever the case is, it is important to choose an agency that employs trained journalists; they know how best to promote a company and its products and services in the media and the marketplace," he added.

The story was distributed to a select group of both metropolitan newspapers and business journals—the main media markets that I believed best served my target audience. In addition, I wrote a version for my local newspapers. That one story not only picked up good coverage, it also won me a number of inquiries, one of which turned into a long-term client.

Conduct a survey and create publicity

Another approach you can take is to conduct a survey or market research, and announce the results and discuss the new trends in print.

By the time I'd been in business a few years, my consultancy employed several full-time staff. One of our specialties was producing company newsletters and magazines. We wanted to gain a better understanding of people's attitudes to these publications, so we decided to conduct a small survey. It targeted a select group of small and large companies based in Australia's commercial capitals, Sydney and Melbourne. We prepared a questionnaire and surveyed key executives in these companies, none of whom were clients.

The results were interesting. They confirmed most of our beliefs and identified the buttons that turned readers on and off. Initially, the survey was conducted for our own edification. But it made sense to offer the information to the wider business community, via the media. It would help them, and probably would also help us, so a PR release was born. Here is what we issued:

Survey: Newsletters Hit the Mark

The majority of customer newsletters are considered by recipients to be of value and interest, according to a recent survey by Melbourne marketing communications consultancy, The Write Advice Pty Ltd.

The survey, conducted to measure the effectiveness of customer newsletters, was based on a poll of one hundred Melbourne and Sydney organizations ranging in size from large corporations to small businesses.

Based on the results of the survey, the term "junk mail" clearly does not apply to the vast majority of company newsletters received by metropolitan executives.

The Write Advice's Managing Director, Michael Meanwell, said that the results of the survey were very interesting and showed that, while there was value in newsletters, businesses needed to take care in whom they targeted and with which message.

"Newsletters can be one of the most cost effective means of communicating with customers. But they must be relevant or add value to the reader, otherwise they will be discarded," he said.

"Like any marketing program, you should begin with a clear understanding of your objectives as well as the needs of your customers. It's also important to continually evaluate the effectiveness of the newsletter by surveying readers and assessing other criteria, such as sales results," Mr. Meanwell added.

Eighty-five percent of managers surveyed claim to regularly receive unsolicited newsletters, and the vast majority found them to be of value and interest.

"Making sure that your database is correct so you are sending your message to the right person is the most critical factor, and that means making sure you understand the job that your target reader is doing, not just spelling the name and address correctly," Mr. Meanwell explained.

When it comes to the issues that make newsletters worthwhile reading, most of the companies surveyed stated that they needed to see what was going on in their industry, and that included using newsletters as a tool to determine their competitors' activities.

The survey also indicated that customer profiles and industry comments were highly valued, as was humor and a light-hearted approach. One of the interesting issues mentioned by 20 percent of respondents was the need for lifestyle matters to be addressed.

"While this appears to be contradictory to the claimed need for information to be relevant to the readers' jobs, I think what this really means is that the newsletter content needs to be relevant to the readers' lives— both work and play," Mr. Meanwell said.

"Of course, those businesses out there with psychographic as well as demographic databases are a step ahead. On the negative side, newsletters that are too self-centered, too cluttered, and too long-winded are on a fast track to the wastepaper bin," he added.

This story got a lot of coverage in daily newspapers, marketing magazines, and business journals. It also attracted a lot of business inquiries, including one from Australia Post.

At the time, Australia Post had recently hired a new DM manager who was responsible for heading up a new direct division of the company. He read an excerpt of the release in one of the marketing magazines and called me to ask for a copy of our results for a newsletter he was producing. That conversation resulted in an invitation to quote on producing the newsletter (see top image, page 194) and the start of an extended client relationship.

It wasn't long before the newsletter project grew in size and frequency, and it opened the door to other projects for the company (see bottom image page 194), including interviewing top marketing professionals from around the world, documenting local case studies, and producing a booklet that showed small businesses how to publish their own newsletters. Since then, the marketing manager has moved on to greener pastures and taken me along for the ride. I'm now working on other DM projects for his new employer.

In addition to regular PR stories, you can also build a profile with byline articles that position yourself as an expert in your field. Depending on the publication you choose, you can draft a series of prescriptive articles that show how businesses can use marketing communications to their advantage. This is something I did for a national small business magazine as well as a newsletter published by a local business network. This approach is more objective than straight PR stories, which means you may be able to negotiate payment, depending on how the publication views the story.

Whether you get paid or it's free publicity, you can gain business inquiries from readers of the publications. You can also clip published articles and feature them as part of a mail pack to prospects, in addition to showcasing them in your folio. Not only is writing press releases and articles a low-cost form of marketing, it can also be a highly effective and credible form of promotion.

Maintain a Professional Image

Whatever field you choose as a freelancer, it's important to your ongoing success that you project a professional image.

Busy people get business

Henry Ford once said, "If you want something done quickly, give it to a busy man." I've found that to be true in my dealings, and you'll find it's true when you're dealing with clients. Who would you choose to work with—a professional who is always busy or one who's got time on his hands? The busy one, of course. Busy people are busy because they're successful. And they're successful because they're doing things right. We're not so sure about the person twiddling his thumbs.

Whenever a business contact asks how busy you are, tell them about all the activities you're involved in, but *never* tell them what you're doing with your spare time—even if it's the highlight of your day. There's no doubt: Busy people get the business. I've found that when I appear busy, I soon become busy. It's not just a matter of what I'm projecting to my clients and prospects; it's also a matter of what I'm projecting to myself and to the world as a whole.

Courtesy counts

Some business people view creative folk as being difficult to work with. That's true of some in our profession, and they don't get much business.

First and foremost, you need to get along with your client and any third parties working on a project. There's nothing worse than spending days, weeks, or months working with people you don't like and who appear to block you at every turn. It slows the work, antagonizes everyone, and no one wins.

We are in the people business, so personality counts. If you have an affable nature, you will have a better than average chance of winning new clients and retaining them. We all like being around like-minded people, and it's no different in the workplace. However, there is a distinct difference between being a professional and being a pushover. Being friendly and approachable doesn't mean becoming a phony or a "yes man." You are hired as a professional, so act like one. If you have an opinion, voice it, but keep it professional and objective—never get personal.

Maintain professional ethics

In business, reputation is everything. Develop and maintain a standard of personal and commercial ethics. When handling corporate work, treat all client information as confidential. Never gossip about one client to another, even if their industries are unrelated. If you're talking so loosely, how can you be trusted with trade secrets? With many larger clients, you may be required to sign a nondisclosure agreement before commencing work. When I've contracted work to third parties, I've asked them to sign my nondisclosure agreement to protect my interests and those of my clients.

Never risk a conflict of interest by representing separate clients who are competitors. I have never handled competing accounts at the same time, and neither should you. The temptation may be there, but the payoff could be losing both accounts and tarnishing your image. If you are unsure about the competition, ask your existing client if they deem your prospect to be their competitor. Needless to say, you should be honest in all your professional dealings and all of your communications.

CASE STUDY
Marketing Communications for Your Business

Following is a series of direct mail letters I have sent out to prospects to gauge interest and hopefully gain an interview. Feel free to adapt these to suit your circumstances:

«Date»

«First_Name» «Surname»

«Title»

«Company»

«Address»

«City» «State» «ZIP code»

Dear «First_Name»,

Every business depends on communication. How well you communicate with your target markets and, indeed your customers, determines the success of your products and services.

No doubt, you know that already.

What you may not know is how Marketzing can help you achieve targeted communications that hit the mark with minimum fuss and maximum gain.

We are a marketing communications consultancy that has worked with well-known businesses like ANZ, Kodak, World Vision, Telstra, and Australia Post. We are experienced in delivering messages to potential customers, without wasting the sales pitch on the wrong market.

Marketzing comprises a team of professional marketers and experienced journalists who can assist «Company» with:

- Press releases promoting your products and services
- Brochures and newsletters for your potential and existing customers
- Direct marketing to target audiences
- Special events that are memorable and measurable

«First_Name», I will contact you in the next few days to discuss how Marketzing can help. Should you wish to talk sooner, please call me at 999-5555.

Yours faithfully,

MICHAEL MEANWELL

Managing Director.

That approach worked pretty well for me. Let's examine it briefly:

- We build rapport by recognizing that the reader understands the process of marketing (the target audience is sales and marketing managers or Managing Director or CEO).

- We introduce who we are and what we can do for them.
- We establish our credentials. Success breeds success, so it doesn't hurt to mention some of the better-known companies we've worked for. The client list can be adapted, depending on what company you're pitching to (for example, you might wish to include like-minded companies to demonstrate that you are industry savvy, or just stick with well-known companies).
- We go into greater detail regarding the services we can offer.
- We finish with a subtle call to action.

As I mentioned, that was the first approach I used to take with prospects. Later on, I tried the following:

Dear «First_Name»,

Are you looking for marketing communications that work? If so, read on.

Market*zing* got Kodak's new digital camera a spot on the top-rated TV shows *Hey Hey It's Saturday* and *Sale of the Century*—millions of people saw it and it didn't cost a cent in advertising.

This month one of our industrial clients achieved thousand of dollars worth of editorial space in industry magazines, with a press release that cost him just $500.

And, since the release was printed as a *news story* in a wide range of different industry publications, it had the added credibility a paid advertisement couldn't give.

Market*zing* is the Swiss Army knife of product promotion—we have a tool for every job:

- Press releases—we can establish a database of publications to suit your needs. You won't pay for copies to be scattered to publications you don't need, and we'll write them so editors will print them.

- Direct marketing—why advertise to millions when you can spend a lot less getting the message direct to the decision makers via telemarketing and direct mail?

- Brochures—attractive, easy-to-follow brochures for the customer at your front counter, the browser, the shop-around customer, and the one who has to take one back to the boss for a decision.

- Newsletters—our journalists and layout artists can blend your message into stories that customers, staff, and potential customers will *want* to read. We can present your products at their best and your company as a well-established authority in its field.

- Special events—maintain existing customers and impress potentials, while using old fashioned face-to-face contact in a relaxed outing or seminar environment to satisfy their needs and wants.

Market*zing* is an experienced company with marketing, public relations, and media relations professionals on tap. We are specialists in serving the small client with a tight budget and the big one who drives a hard bargain.

And we're very good at what we do. Who says so? ANZ, Kodak, World Vision, Telstra and Australia Post—they're all happy customers, just like the variety of small firms who use our services.

«First_Name», I will give you a call next week or, if you have any urgent needs, you can call me at 999-5555.

Regards,

MICHAEL MEANWELL

Managing Director.

As you can see, this is a more proactive approach to prospecting letters. It received mixed results, depending on the target audience. Let's examine it:

- We begin by asking a qualifying question: Does the prospect need our services?
- Rather than telling the prospect how great our services are, we show them by documenting our client successes with companies they know and probably admire.
- Then we explain how we can benefit the prospect's business.
- We back this with more details on our company and our record of achievement, including some of our big-name clients.
- The writing style is fast, efficient, and confident, and reflects a bold image.

This approach doesn't suit every writer or every prospect. That's why it was used selectively, depending on the companies I was approaching.

Okay, the pendulum has swung in both directions, so now it's time to look at a prospect letter that pitches somewhere in the middle:

Dear «First_Name»,

In days of old markets were places where you bought fish and cheese, margins were always on the left and ruled in red ink, and having a relationship with a customer was just not talked about in polite company.

How times change . . . today markets are in segments, margins are tight, and budgets are even tighter. Competition is global, and the players are aggressive. Customers are inundated with communications from a plethora of sources: there are over 1,800 different magazines and 670 newspapers printed in Australia, and then there are 300 radio stations and 96 TV stations. Imagine how many billboards, signs at arenas, on buses, trains, trams and taxis, ads on supermarket trolleys—not to mention the 80 newspapers and magazines that are printed in a language other than English.

Is it any wonder that the market has started to switch off? The fact is, many customers have stopped listening because it's getting too hard to hear.

Perhaps you too have noticed it's hard to get your customer communications heard?

Here at Market*zing* we specialize in making sure that your message hits the target on time, every time—for less. We employ a team of journalists, people who know the media and who know the people in the media, as well as marketing strategists, direct mail specialists, and ethnic language translators—experts in getting your message to your customers.

Market*zing* has worked with many businesses in the design and production of brochures, press releases, event management, and strategic marketing communications planning. We are happy to work with our customers' mainstream advertising agencies to ensure that real marketing integration occurs, maximizing your media exposure through unpaid media and special events, as well as through your advertising.

«First_Name», can Market*zing* assist «Company»?

I will call you in the next few days to see whether there is some task Market*zing* can complete for you—I hope that we can help get your messages heard.

Regards,

MICHAEL MEANWELL

Managing Director.

You may feel that letter was a "safer" approach. Let's take a closer look:

- We kick off by building rapport with a little humor—something missing from most DM today.
- Then we get serious about business and build interest by detailing markets and the challenge of being heard in a busy marketplace.
- We offer a solution to the problem—our services.
- We then explain how we can achieve results for the prospect.
- And we finish by asking if we can help them, and promising to call soon.

Each of these letters did its job by allowing me to get a foot in the door. But I gained the greatest response when I included the following, final paragraph:

Rather than tell you what we can do for you, I'd rather *show* you. I'm offering you a free, no-obligation marketing consultation, valued at $250. I will call you in the next few days to arrange a suitable time to speak with you. If you can't wait, feel free to call me at (212) 123-4567.

This final paragraph contains a stronger call to action—an offer many prospects cannot refuse, a free marketing consultation valued at $250. The figure is a "perceived value" I place on my time. Let's face it, the whole point of sending the letter is to gain an appointment with the prospect. During the meeting you will offer your time, free of charge. But when was the last time you actually told a prospect you will do this—and placed a value on your time? Placing a rather high value on my time does two things: It makes the offer worthwhile (wouldn't you like to receive something worth $250 for nothing?). It also demonstrates the value of my services.

CHAPTER 16

Dot-Communications: Essentials for Building Your Web Site

Put it before them briefly so they will read it,
clearly so they will appreciate it,
picturesquely so they will remember it and,
above all, accurately so they will be guided
by its light.

Joseph Pulitzer (1847–1911)

Before we begin, please understand that we don't have the space to explain all the ins and outs of building your own Web site. That would take one or more books to discuss properly. My intention here is to lay the foundation, to get you thinking about establishing a Web presence or improving an existing site so that you can maximize your exposure and opportunities for working online.

Whether you like the Internet or not, it's here to stay. The Internet has literally transformed the way we communicate. Today, it is commonplace to communicate and collaborate with editors, corporate clients, and others electronically. As discussed in an earlier chapter, the Net provides a variety of advantages over conventional communication, most notably:

- **Speed:** You can send and receive information in a matter of minutes rather than days or weeks.
- **Cost:** E-mail is virtually free.
- **Flexibility:** Living in a virtual world means you can communicate with people wherever they are and whenever you wish.

And, by having your own Web site, you have your own electronic shop front that's accessible by hundreds of millions of Web users worldwide, 24/7.

There are plenty of free tools to help novices establish a Web presence relatively easily and painlessly. Unfortunately, however, many people rush the process and the result is an ill-conceived site that's heavy on dazzling graphics and light on substance. Worse still, a site may have what Web visitors are looking for, but fail to hold their attention because of poor navigation or illogical links. So what's the measure of success online? To put it simply:

- **Traffic:** Attracting visitors to your site
- **Communication:** Establishing contact with site visitors, either directly through e-mail or via their response to an opt-in e-zine
- **Action:** Through online customer sales or gaining work from clients

As mentioned in chapter nine, whether you wish to promote yourself online or sell your own e-books, I suggest you flatten the learning curve by acquiring a few excellent books that cover the terrain extremely well. Read *eBook Secrets*, and also *Make Your Site SELL!* and *Make Your Words Sell!* The titles are self-explanatory, and they live up to their promises. They were among the first e-books I downloaded, and they have helped me enormously in my own e-publishing efforts.

Launching Your Site and Being a Cyber Success

Before you begin putting together your Web site, it's a good idea to look at chapter eight again to refresh your memory about online writing. Many of the principles we discussed there can be applied to your own work. Add to that the following quick tips:

1. Think in ink before printing in pixels. The more pages you add to your Web site, the greater the chance that your visitor will lose track of the information. Before you design your site on computer, design it on paper. Decide what information you want to present and what pages it will appear on, and assign links to other pages within the site as well as other links to other Web sites. Once you've mapped it out on paper, make sure there's a logical progression from the home page to the various categories/pages.

2. Check your content. As stated on earlier occasions, content is king, and copy is the king of content—even more so if you're promoting yourself as a professional writer. There is no room for typos or grammatical errors.

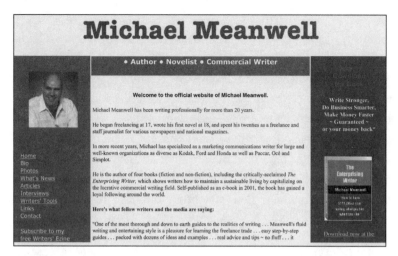

Michael Meanwell

• Author • Novelist • Commercial Writer

Welcome to the official website of Michael Meanwell.

Michael Meanwell has been writing professionally for more than 20 years.

He began freelancing at 17, wrote his first novel at 18, and spent his twenties as a freelance and staff journalist for various newspapers and national magazines.

In more recent years, Michael has specialized as a marketing communications writer for large and well-known organizations as diverse as Kodak, Ford and Honda as well as Paccar, Océ and Simplot.

He is the author of four books (fiction and non-fiction), including the critically-acclaimed *The Enterprising Writer*, which shows writers how to maintain a sustainable living by capitalizing on the lucrative commercial writing field. Self-published as an e-book in 2001, the book has gained a loyal following around the world.

Here's what fellow writers and the media are saying:

"One of the most thorough and down to earth guides to the realities of writing . . . Meanwell's fluid writing and entertaining style is a pleasure for learning the freelance trade . . . easy step-by-step guides . . . packed with dozens of ideas and examples . . . real advice and tips ~ no fluff . . . it

Write Stronger,
Do Business Smarter,
Make Money Faster
~ Guaranteed ~
or your money back"

A Web site can be both an electronic billboard and storefront. It is a smart, low-cost way of showcasing your work, demonstrating your writing skills and, if you offer e-books or other products, making sales around the clock and around the world.

Run a spellchecker over your copy, and then run another pair of eyes over it to catch bigger mistakes and ensure that the content makes sense. In addition to checking the text, also check your links to be sure they all work and that the navigation aids are simple and logical.

One of my web sites, EnterprisingWriter.com, is more than just a promotional vehicle; it also offers writers a range of helpful information, including free prescriptive articles and reviews of writers' books. The key to maintaining a site's momentum is to include beneficial material and update frequently.

3. Road test your Web site. When you're happy with the look and feel of your site, post it online and then trial it by testing links and checking load speeds for each page. In addition to testing it yourself, seek feedback from others. Where necessary, optimize speeds by reducing the size of pictures or graphics, or removing them.

4. Interact with your visitors. Your Web site is not a static billboard. It should be a living device that enables you not only to promote your books, information products, and freelance writing services but also to interact with your visitors. You should build interactivity into your site by regularly updating the information (e.g., news and future events) so it continues to project a fresh look.

In addition, encourage direct communication with your visitors by way of an opt-in e-zine (this is where you ask visitors for their e-mail address in exchange for offering to send them a regular online newsletter or updates). Other interactive methods you can employ include an online forum survey, or feedback form on your site to gain more information on users' needs, educational backgrounds, and other issues.

An online forum is one of the easiest and most effective ways of adding value to a Web site. Literally anyone can ask or answer questions, post comments, or provide information. This makes it not only a highly interactive tool but also an excellent way of maintaining interest in your Web site, year after year.

5. Create interest and build excitement. Remember that Web users have limited time and attention spans, so kick off your home page with a strong headline, followed by your unique selling proposition (USP), and support it with a summary of the benefits of working with you. Your USP should be designed to differentiate your business from the myriad of competitors that are just a click away. It should give visitors an instant snapshot of what your business means and how it can benefit them.

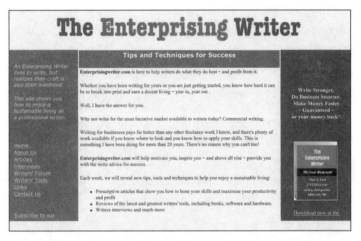

Your home page is most probably the first Web page visitors see, so make sure you make a good impression by telling them what to expect and how they will benefit.

If you're having trouble listing benefits, consider what you're promoting. Look at it from an objective customer viewpoint. Ask yourself: "What's in it for me (the customer)?" When you get an answer, refine your USP. Then strengthen the benefit by asking yourself: "So what?" Now reshape your USP again. If you still haven't got to the core of the benefit, then ask the question again: "So what?" Now, you should have a strong customer-oriented benefit.

Remember to start off on the right note with your USP backed by strong benefits. You never get a second chance to make a first impression, especially on the Net.

6. Make everything easy for the user. Everything on your Web site should be designed to make life easy for the Web visitor. It should be easy to:

- Obtain information
- Navigate around your site
- Contact you
- Request a quote regarding your services
- Purchase your goods

Consequently, every page should include links to other associated pages or provide a natural progression through the site. Also, you should include contact information and an e-mail address on each page. Copy should be presented in bite-sized pieces for easy digestion, with links to more info. Finally, there should be a "home" button on each page so the visitor can return to your introductory home page.

7. Tell them what your other clients think. As you know, the most credible form of promotion is what others say about you, so include written testimonials from them. If you haven't got any, request them. If appropriate (and if they consent), include the clients' e-mail addresses so the visitor has the opportunity to verify testimonials or seek further information from satisfied clients.

Most Web sites that feature testimonials are content to keep them all on one page, but I think you're missing an excellent opportunity if you take this route. My advice is to feature them as brief pullout quotes sprinkled throughout your copy. Testimonials should be used to reinforce your benefits and your guarantee, and provide reasons for ordering products or contacting you regarding your services.

8. Help your visitors help you. Tell your visitors what you want them to do, whether that is to subscribe to your e-zine or to purchase your information products and freelance services. Make sure you make it easy for them to do so, with simple follow-through links or navigation.

9. The sale is just the (new) beginning. As in the offline world, for many, the sale represents the end of the cycle with the customer. Some sales people are anxious to leave the scene of the crime or to go hunting for new prey.

In my view, the sale of an e-book or e-zine represents the start of a new cycle. First, you have just converted a prospect into a customer. The goal should now be to turn this customer into an advocate for your business. Once they have had a chance to review your product, there exists an excellent opportunity for you to seek further sales, referred customers, an enthusiastic testimonial—or all three.

Having made the sale, follow up immediately with a thank you and a restatement of the benefits of doing business together. This can be sent automatically through one of the auto-responders available online. I recommend and use GetResponse (www.getresponse.com). Second, send another e-mail within a few days of the sale as a courtesy to see how your customer is progressing. If appropriate, offer to discuss any issues personally, via e-mail.

The process will be a little different when a Web visitor inquires about your freelance services. In this case, you could e-mail a corporate document to the prospect stating the benefits of working with your company, as detailed in another chapter, plus a formal quotation relating to their inquiry. As with product sales, you can elect to e-mail the prospective customer of your services within a few days or you can call them directly, which would be my preference.

Once you have won the customer and completed the project, you can take the same tack as you would with a customer of one of your information products. Transform the customer into an advocate by asking him or her to identify friends or colleagues who would like to know about your products or services, or request a testimonial, which you can then use in future marketing and on your Web site. Why is this important? Because your obvious confidence reinforces the value of your product or service in the mind of the customer. Always ask with *enthusiasm*, because you are keen to help others, just as you have helped the new customer.

10. Define your goal. What do you wish to achieve with your Web site? Do you want to make sales or generate leads? No doubt there are other motivations for setting up a Web site, such as providing a free information service. But, if you are developing one to enhance your writing business, your goal should be either generating direct sales of your information products or generating leads in order to gain freelance work from clients.

If your goal is to develop a sales site, focus on your products and your ability to provide good service to your customers. Forget about trying to make your site a portal for the community or the industry. Forget about adding animated graphics, sound files or "me too" tools, such as a search engine. None of these devices will add value to your sales message; they will merely distract your visitors.

Just give your potential customers what they want: pure and simple information. If it is well written, it will stimulate interest, instill confidence, and motivate them to buy. Explain in detail the benefits and the features of each information product or freelance service so there's no misunderstanding or any reason to "think about it"—just every reason to buy *now* or hire *now*.

If your goal is to develop a lead generator, again, focus on the benefits of your solution—that is, your ability to provide customers with what they want. In addition, provide plenty of details about your offerings as well as supplementary information. This includes helpful hints, tips, and news. Your site should allow the visitor to take control, gather knowledge, and request more information from you via opt-in e-mail.

Your aim is to initiate contact with your customers, but it has to be on their terms. They will not want to volunteer an e-mail address if they suspect you will harass them. They are looking for quality communications and a benefit in exchange for an e-mail address; you can offer it in the form of a regular e-zine that they are able to unsubscribe to whenever they wish.

The goal of all sites should be to gain loyal, repeat visitors. The best way to achieve this is to continually offer them fresh content—new information, new products, and new benefits, so they come back again and again. And the best way to remind them to return is to mention the new additions in your regular subscriber e-zine. If you have posted new articles, include a hypertext link to the pages on your site. If you have a new product or service, include a link to the home page so they can experience the site in its entirety.

11. Design a consistent appearance. You should consider your Web site as a form of marketing collateral. Apart from consistent and convincing copy, it should have a uniform theme throughout.

Establish a color scheme, background, and fonts, and use these throughout your Web site. Use a consistent layout that incorporates a company or brand logo and slogan on each page and a corporate banner or other motif at the top or down the side of each page (see image on page 204).

What's in it for You and Your Customer

The three most important factors to remember when developing your Web site are:

- Your customer
- Your goal
- A mutually profitable outcome

Keep these three points in mind throughout each stage of your site's development. When you're reviewing graphics, site features or your content, ask yourself these two questions:

- Does this help or hinder the customer?
- Does this add or detract from the goal of my Web site?

Continue to ask these simple questions. Take an objective view of your work, and your site will remain on target and on the money with your customers.

CHAPTER 17

How to Deliver a Dynamic Presentation

I do not object to people looking at their
watches when I am speaking. But I strongly
object when they start shaking them to make
certain they are still going.

Lord Birkett (1883–1962)

Public speaking is not an area that all freelance writers will need or wish to know, but it's a valuable skill for all commercial writers to master. One day—sooner than you think—you will need to speak on your feet.

If you intend getting into PR, you will be responsible for communicating with the media, which means you may have to, at the very least, introduce a number of company representatives at a press conference or coordinate the entire affair. Other commercial work may also mean participating in sales presentations, team-building workshops, or other corporate events. Public speaking and interpersonal skills are also important in other business situations, such as pitching to prospects and presenting proposals to customers as well as general networking.

This chapter is best read in conjunction with chapter eleven on speech-writing. While it focuses on public speaking qualities and techniques, you will benefit most when you consider the big picture—how to develop *and* deliver a presentation.

As I've said earlier, it's not uncommon for people to have a fear of speaking in public. We've all seen someone struggle with a speech, and maybe you've experienced the fear first hand. I know I have. I recall many years ago being asked to say a few words at a friend's wedding. I was fine with that until the moment arrived. A spotlight fell upon me the same time a microphone was placed in my hand. Instantly my hands became moist, my throat dry and my mind went blank. That didn't stop me talking, but I wish it had—I could barely believe what was coming out of my mouth—especially when I saw the video of my performance a month later.

And so began the horror and mystique surrounding public speaking. I thought that it was something for polished businesspeople and politicians. Thankfully I have since learned differently. It's within the grasp of every one of us. If you can communicate in person, you can communicate effectively in public. To a large degree, it's a matter of adjusting your attitude—seeing it as a friendly conversation rather than a nerve-wracking presentation, which means having a central theme—a point—to your presentation, understanding what you want to achieve with your speech, and focusing on the needs of your audience. Speaking in public can be a lot of fun, if you allow it to be.

It's important to realize that when you speak publicly or personally, you are not just selling your views, products or services; you are selling yourself. The same applies to your chosen profession; as a writer, you are not just in the communication business but also in the *persuasion* business. Your job as a communicator is to persuade your audience to act a certain way, whether it's to buy a certain product, commit to a specific service, believe in an individual company, or subscribe to a way of thinking. In this sense, there's no difference between writing and speaking, especially when you craft and deliver the words. Consequently, public speaking should be a natural extension of your skills as a writer, and the moment it is a natural extension you will be in a unique position of authority.

Let's face it, speakers are leaders. Once you get to your feet and speak to an audience of ten or ten thousand, you are considered a leader, an authority. Whether your words are inspirational, educational, or just entertaining, they touch people and incite action, just as your written words do. And, of course, effective speaking begins with effective writing—so, with your skills, you're already ahead of most people.

How to Act Like a Star of Stage and Screen

We've all seen a speaker wander around aimlessly on stage or sway from side to side as if on a boat. That's the problem—we've seen that but generally not heard what they've said because their actions distract us from their message.

Body language is a critical component of any performance, including public speaking. What you say can be undermined by how you act on stage or screen if your performance is taped. The best presentation is one where your posture, body movements, and facial expressions complement your speech.

Let your body speak for itself

You should adapt your body language to suit your content, setting, and the size of your audience. If you are speaking to a large group, use slower and more deliberate hand gestures and movements. If you are addressing a small number of people or the presentation is being filmed, use smaller gestures and rely more on facial expressions.

Whatever the audience size, support your message with thoughtful body language. The most important areas that audiences focus on are the face and hands. When communicating, our facial expressions naturally telegraph our feelings, emotions, and attitudes. So don't try to stifle them; instead, use them to your best advantage. If you're making a serious point, look serious; if you're concerned, show it. But, where appropriate, smile. This is the simplest and most effective way to make your audience welcome, comfortable, and receptive to your presentation.

So, what should you do with those hands? Always keep hand movements between your waist and shoulders. Hold gestures for longer than you would in normal conversation, and make sure your gestures mirror your thoughts and support your words. Here are some positive things to do when talking with your hands:

- Use fingers (for counting)
- Switch gestures from hand to hand (for variety)
- Open your hands (to express integrity);
- Bring your hands together (to make a point)
- Move your hands in unison (to make a comparison)
- Move your hands in opposite directions (to show contrast)
- Clasp your hands together at chest level (to indicate harmony)

There are, however, some hand gestures to avoid, including:

- Fidgeting (signals distrust and distracts attention)
- Crossing your arms (suggests negativity or a lack of confidence)
- Hands in pockets (indicates disinterest or hiding something)

- Hands behind your back (projects detachment or superiority)
- Hands in front of your groin (defensive posture)
- Clenched fist (signals aggression)
- Pointing finger (suggests hostility)

There are exceptions to some of these body language rules: It is acceptable, for example, to place your hands behind your back during Q&A time. You can also clench a fist or hit your fist into your open palm to show strong emotion or make an important point. But, it's best to use these gestures sparingly. When in doubt, keep your hands by your sides—it may feel strange, but it looks natural and relaxed, and it's better than using the wrong gestures or abusing the right ones. You can also prompt your audience by showing them what you want: Clap, for example, if you want applause; raise your hand if you want a response to a question.

Exit, stage right

As we've discussed, your gestures and movements can either work for you or against you when speaking in public, especially when you are all alone on a big stage.

There is a real psychology to working the stage. Tom Antion, professional speaker and author of *Wake 'em Up!*, offers some tips on where to position yourself on stage for the right effect:

- Strongest position: Center stage. If you want to command greater attention, move three steps forward (closer to the audience).
- Weakest positions: Upstage left and right (toward the back of the stage, farthest from the audience). Ideal only when you wish to lessen attention on yourself, such as when the audience is involved in a group task.
- Crowd pleaser: If you really want to get the audience's attention, leave the stage and move among the audience. This is the best way to work a room but, like all effects, it should be used sparingly. Also, take note that you can lose visibility in the audience, especially in a large room filled with people. If you are taping the performance, it's wise to warn the production people ahead of time that you will be walking out into the audience so they are prepared and able to follow you.

Where possible, avoid speaking from upstage center (farthest from the audience). While this is a strong position, you are still some distance from the audience and it can make you appear aloof.

Control your audience

There's nothing worse than seeing a speaker lose control of an audience, either with people talking amongst themselves or continually asking questions throughout a presentation. It's distracting for both the speaker and those trying to hear him or her. To retain control of your audience:

1. Stop talking: One of the best ways to stop people talking before or during a speech is for the speaker to be silent. It won't take long before people notice and stop talking.

2. Keep talking: The reverse approach is also effective. Raise your voice so that you talk over those speaking in the audience. Soon enough, they will get the message and quiet down. If you are starting a speech after a break, you may like to give the audience a warning before you begin your talk ("We'll be starting in one minute . . .") and begin on time.

3. Ask for questions: It's a good idea to give yourself and your listeners a small break at the end of each section. Ask if there are any questions relating to the material just presented. This ensures everyone understands and is paying attention and also encourages audience participation. Make sure you answer questions briefly, saving more detailed responses for the end of the presentation.

4. Answer questions later: When asking for questions, be careful not to be trapped into giving long-winded answers that steer you off course. Too much Q&A during a speech can rob you of momentum and even audience interest. If people persist with questions, respectfully request that they hold them for the end of the talk.

For the best results, set the ground rules during the speech's opening. Let the audience know what you expect from them. You may, for example, invite people to ask questions or hold them until the end of a section or the presentation. Make it clear what you want and they will generally comply.

Improving Your Performance

There are usually three distinct times when a new speaker gets nervous. The first is when the realization sets in just after they agree to give a talk;

---

the second is when preparing for the talk; and the third is a few moments before standing up to talk.

The fear is different for everyone. Some fears relate to talking—a fear of not being able to physically speak or forgetting what to say. Other fears relate to the audience—a fear of being heckled, of walkouts, or of being generally scared at the size of the audience. But most fears center on the speaker's own performance and what people will say and think afterwards. Whatever the fear, you can make the butterflies in your stomach fly in formation by using simple but powerful techniques.

Focus on the positive

Fear is a natural defense mechanism. It's vital for our survival, but left unchecked, it can be detrimental to our performance. You need to realize that when you focus on the fear and imagine all of the awful things that could happen, you are feeding your mind negative thoughts. And thoughts manifest action. So, it's important to counter these fears with positive thoughts in the form of positive affirmations (for example, "I am a great speaker and an excellent communicator," "I love speaking in public and I am good at it") and visualization. Remember Napoleon Hill's timeless words: "If you can conceive it, and believe it, you can achieve it."

Relax your body and your mind

Before your speech, ease tension by doing some stretching exercises and taking some deep breaths. This will help loosen you up physically and settle you emotionally.

Prior to going on stage, program yourself. Tell yourself you are relaxed, that you will be relaxed throughout the talk, and that you will enjoy it as if you are having a friendly conversation. Remind yourself that the fear you are feeling is just that—fear of the unknown. It usually occurs just before you get on stage and disappears soon after you take the stage. So take comfort in that and know that it's just a temporary thing that will disappear when you begin talking. Keep in mind that many professional speakers get a bout of stage fright just before they perform. I can certainly vouch for it. I love public speaking but don't like starting—that's when the nerves usually hit, but thankfully they don't last. If you still have some nerves, accept it, and work with it. Use the excitement and the adrenaline to improve your performance.

Use humor

Humor is arguably the most effective element you can add to any presentation. Garnishing your speech with the right amount of humor offers numerous benefits to both the speaker and the audience. It allows you to relax and connect with your listeners, stimulate interest, and maintain attention. It enables you to illustrate points, lighten heavy material and, most importantly, make your presentation meaningful and memorable.

To use humor effectively, use it discriminately. Don't go overboard, otherwise you run the risk of making an entire joke of your presentation. Use humor to reinforce points and the overall theme of your presentation.

Scott Friedman, humorist and author of *Punchlines, Pitfalls, and Powerful Programs*, says the shortest distance between you and the audience is a good laugh. It's an effective tool for creating a bond with your audience. Friedman's "Ten Laws of Adding Humor to Your Presentations" states that the best style of humor is your own personal style: "You need to uncover the style you already have and use it, rather than someone else's style. Select material carefully so that it complements your style. If your humor is too much different from your own personality, it appears awkward and incongruent. Be yourself!"

The beauty of humor is that it's all around us. Virtually every facet of life is teeming with humor, depending on the way you view it or twist it to make it funny. Everything from the jobs we have and the way we act in situations to the broader issues of current affairs and world events. You can find an amusing take on most aspects, but some things are considered taboo. The general no-nos are politics and religion, although they can be handled by a deft touch. Remember that humor is intended to enhance your overall message, not distract attention from it. So, play it safe and use humor as a tool, not a weapon.

You don't have to be a naturally funny person to identify and deliver humor, but it helps if you know where to look. The best humor, in my view, is that which you experience or perceive. It's personal, so you're more than likely to deliver it better than secondhand humor you have found elsewhere. Start by observing life. Take notes and record your observations for future use. Another deep wellspring of humor resides in your own life. Think about past experiences—embarrassing situations, mistakes you made, and outdated perceptions you had. You've got enough material right there for several stand-up routines!

There are plenty of other sources of humor, including seeing professional comics in action, watching comedy videos, and listening to tapes, and also just enjoying the company of naturally funny people.

No matter how serious the subject matter, humor can play a role in improving your speech, but don't save it for the end. Closings should leave the audience with a powerful message. If you hit them with your only punchline, it may have the opposite effect. Use humor throughout your talk and your audience will love you for it.

Don't read a speech

I don't agree with reading a speech, unless you are delivering a legal argument or an important statement that must be precise. You will find that audiences prefer a speaker who speaks naturally rather than one who reads fluently. Speaking rather than reading demonstrates to listeners that the presenter is confident, credible, and authoritative and knows what she is talking about. Speaking unencumbered allows you to concentrate more on looking at and connecting with the audience. It allows you to work the stage or the room and give an animated performance.

If you have a lengthy presentation, you may like to keep your keywords handy. That's what I do when presenting half or full-day workshops. Often, my lectures require drawing various illustrations or even listing foreign terms. I work with a whiteboard and place in the left-hand corner a handful of keywords or points relating to the presentation. These are the only notes I have—or need—for a half-day or full-day course. I find they help keep me on track, if ever I lose the plot, and they also help guide the audience, giving them an indication of what's next on the agenda.

Alternatively, you can keep your key words on some small 4"×6" cards or a single sheet of paper. Another trick other speakers do is to write their keywords on a copy of the handout notes given to the audience. This way the speaker can naturally refer to their keywords, and listeners think they are being referred to the information in the handout. I personally don't like this approach for the same reason given earlier in this chapter: I prefer not to give handout notes until after the presentation; I find that audiences spend more time reading them than listening to and watching the presentation.

Whichever way you go, remember that the trick to being a good keynote speaker is to be a good "keyword" memorizer. Once you've got the key-words down, there's no need for notes, and there's no excuse for reading.

Top Ten Tips for Power Speeches

1. Know the room. Familiarize yourself with the room before you speak. Practice using the equipment, including the microphone and any audio/visual tools, an hour or more before.

2. Know your audience. A great way to break down barriers between you and the audience is to meet people at the door as they arrive for the presentation. This way you won't be speaking to strangers, but new friends, and you won't be giving a speech, but having a friendly conversation.

3. Involve your audience. Every great performer knows the key to success is audience participation. Get your listeners involved by asking them questions requiring a show of hands or brief comments, or dividing the audience into small groups for discussion—whatever is appropriate to the occasion and the theme of your talk.

4. Speak with enthusiasm. Enthusiasm is contagious. When you're excited about your speech, the audience will be, too. Remember, you're a performer, so perform with enthusiasm.

5. Get personal. Whether speaking to five people or five hundred, your audience will respond to someone who speaks *to* them, not *at* them. Make yourself and your speech more accessible. Speak to your listeners on a personal level by not only sharing information but also relevant experiences from your own life.

6. Keep the company of experts. Empower your arguments by quoting experts and industry leaders. When authorities in a field agree with you, your speech is seen as credible and valid.

7. Make a point until it's understood. Emphasize major points by re-phrasing them in consecutive sentences. Winston Churchill, said it best: "If you have an important point to make, don't try to be subtle or clever. Use a pile driver. Hit the point once. Then come back and hit it again. Then hit it a third time—a tremendous whack."

8. Don't worry about mistakes. Your audience doesn't know the material or the format of your speech, so don't worry when you omit some points or make minor mistakes. Just don't turn them into bigger issues by focusing on them. Also, don't apologize when you do make minor mistakes, which only draw your audience's attention to the issue and may exacerbate it.

9. Rehearse "live." Before you give a presentation, rehearse it in your mind. Don't just go through the words of your speech; visualize the entire event, including what you say, how you say it, and how the audience responds. See yourself in your mind's eye speaking loudly and clearly, performing confidently, and the audience responding with laughter and applause. Anticipate questions from the group and envision answering them correctly.

10. Practice, practice, practice. You will naturally get better at public speaking, like all things, the more times you physically practice. Consider joining a speakers' club, such as Toastmasters, where you will have plenty of opportunities to test your mettle.

Get the Most Out of Visual and Audio Aids

There are a variety of visual and audio aids you can try, and just as many reasons why you should use them to enhance your talk. They enhance communication, improve understanding, and increase retention. They also enable you to emphasize and reinforce key points, improve confidence, and connect with large groups of people.

Above all else, video and audio aids allow you to show and tell more effectively—and that will have a major impact on what your audience understands and recalls after the presentation. Research indicates that people retain 10 percent of what they read, 20 percent of what they hear, 30 percent of what they see, 50 percent of what they hear and see, and 70 percent of what is discussed with other people.[16]

There is an ever-growing range of new presentation products arriving each year, but the best tend to be the most tested and trusted. Here are some of the most popular presentation tools, their advantages and disadvantages, and how best to use them:

Flipchart

This is essentially an easel that holds a pad of large, white paper that can be easily flipped over the back.

Advantages: It is a portable, inexpensive, and does not require electricity. It is an easy-to-use aid for presenting simple drawings and keywords. It also serves as a good reminder for the speaker (you can list all the major points of your talk in sequence).

Disadvantages: It only suits small groups (generally no more than forty people). Flipping pages can be a distraction.

Tips: Prepare pages in advance, using thick marker pens and printing in large block letters (2″ high letters can be read by people forty feet away). Use different colors for contrast. Emphasize with headings, boxes, and circles, and itemize points with bullets. Leave plenty of white space.

Whiteboard

The whiteboard replaces the traditional classroom blackboard, enabling presenters to illustrate and list points on the fly.

Advantages: Like the flipchart, it is simple to use and does not require electricity. There is no preparation needed, and it is ideal for building on a message, point by point. It uses low-cost media (nonpermanent marker pens) and is commonly found in businesses and training facilities.

Disadvantages: Unlike the flipchart, you are limited in the amount of information you can present at one time (you cannot flip any number of pages, simply write, wipe, and start over). Writing on the fly is time-consuming and can be distracting to the audience—you need to develop the ability to speak and write simultaneously.

Tips: Use similar presentation principles as the flipchart, listing key points as you progress. Keep the board clean and uncluttered. Make text and illustrations large and legible. Do not talk while facing the board. Where possible, use a double-sided whiteboard so you can flip to a second side. This is ideal if you want to prepare extra information or intricate illustrations beforehand.

Overhead projector

This remains a popular tool today because it's portable, flexible, and effective in projecting images to small or medium-sized groups.

Advantages: Transparencies can be prepared beforehand, and you add information on the fly. You can create text and drawings by hand with OHP pens and acetates, you can design professional-looking pages on the computer, or photocopy printed material onto transparencies.

Disadvantages: Does not suit large audiences (more than one hundred). Some people may have difficulty viewing images or be distracted by continually switching transparencies. It is perceived by some as dated technology compared to other tools, such as computer presentations.

Tips: Be careful not to block individuals' view of the projection. Write large and legibly. Limit the number of pages, and present one major point per page, with no more than half a dozen lines of text. Number pages and ensure they are in sequence. "Reveal" information progressively by using a piece of paper to hide part of a page. Make copies of important transparencies for use as handouts.

When working with a flipchart, whiteboard, or overhead projector, think before using the ink—some colors are not well suited for presentations. The most visible colors are blue, black, and green. The most popular are blue followed by red (keep in mind that while red is popular, it isn't as legible as the others, so use it for highlighting text not blanketing a page). Avoid pink, purple, brown, and yellow—they tend to be distracting and harder to discern. When writing points or drawing graphics, it's best to work with three colors or less. That's enough to provide contrast; using more colors could be distracting.

Computer presentation

Presentation software, like Microsoft's PowerPoint and Apple's Keynote, enables speakers to create the most professional-looking presentations incorporating high-quality charts, tables, and graphics as well as multimedia video and audio.

Advantages: It is flexible—you can produce a range of speaking resources from the one package, including OHP and slides, speakers' notes, and audience handouts. It's suitable for any size audience and is relatively quick to produce using a variety of templates. You can make the most dynamic presentations, incorporating multilayered images, animation, and a consistent look and feel to all slides.

Disadvantages: The presentation software requires training. You will need a specialist to produce 35mm slides or access to an expensive data projector attached to a laptop for screening the presentation.

Tips: When using any equipment, check to see it is working properly prior to the presentation. As with other visual aids, limit the number of slides and the number of lines per slide (a maximum of six). Use bullet points instead of complete sentences. Present text in at least a 20-point font. Use graphs, charts, and graphics in place of or to complement text.

General hints on presenting visuals

Here are ten final tips when presenting visual aids to an audience:

- Rehearse using visual aids before you present
- Use color for variety, but don't abuse it
- Limit the number of visuals—less is more
- Make sure aids support your message and provide additional details
- Number the transparencies or pages
- Summarize the aid—don't read it
- Maintain eye contact while explaining the aid
- Step aside—don't block the audience's view of the screen or board
- Give the audience time to read and absorb it
- Have an alternate presentation in case the aids fail (for example, a hard copy and/or speaking notes)

Other speaker's aids

Handouts. Handouts are not a must for every speech, but they are advisable for sales conferences, media briefings, and workshops. Handouts can complement an address or they can be a curse. It all depends on the speaker, the listener, and the way the handouts are used. If they are provided before the presentation, the audience can—and usually does—leaf through them rather than give their full attention to the speech.

I prefer to give handouts to my audience after a presentation. I find this is the best way to retain interest in and understanding of the presentation. But I do tell people there will be handouts, just to alleviate any anxiety. I also encourage people to take their own notes, and I provide paper and pens, in case they don't.

Depending on what you are presenting and to whom, notes can be as extensive as you wish. Generally, they carry more detail than the visual aids but less than the speech. They can also include references to other resources, including URLs and a company's contact information. When presenting to the media, your handout would be one part of a larger press kit. You can elect to include a copy of the speech notes for accurate quotations.

Microphones. There are various types of microphones on the market, but the principles of correct use are virtually the same. If you haven't used one before, it's worthwhile testing the one you'll be using at your next event or visiting an audio store and getting a feel for the various styles available. If you will be using a handheld mic, but don't have access to one, rehearse your presentation holding an object of similar size and shape, such as a hairbrush.

Before you present your talk, familiarize yourself with the mic as you would any other equipment. Know where the on and off switch is. Do a sound-check, preferably a couple of hours before the event, so you'll know how close to hold it to your mouth and at what level to speak. As a general rule, speak at your normal level and hold the mic six inches from your mouth—any closer and your voice may be muffled.

Pointers. Just like microphones, there are various pointers on the market. The most popular is the laser pen. While pointers are useful in highlighting technical details on screen, it's really a personal choice whether they suit you and your presentation. Frankly, they're low on my list. I find the darting laser light distracting to both the audience and myself. It's even worse if you don't have a steady hand. Like all other tools, if you have a choice, try it before you commit to it.

Lectern. Lecterns can be restrictive or protective, depending on the speaker. They're excellent tools if you choose to read your speech, but some speakers feel a lectern stifles their performance. While it may be comforting to have a protective prop on stage, it restricts your movement and the audience's view. If appropriate, take greater command by speaking beside the lectern instead of behind it.

The best way to know what tools work best is to test them before going live. But don't use anything just because it's available. Remember, if it enhances your presentation, it's a tool; if it doesn't, it's a toy.

Handling Q&As

Once the formal part of your speech is over, another challenge begins—questions from the audience. The thought is enough to strike fear in many speakers' hearts. Why? Because they don't know what the audience will ask or what they should say. That's why it's just as important to prepare for Q&A as any other part of your speech.

Anticipate questions that may arise from your presentation, prepare ready-made answers, and practice your delivery. Ask others what questions they have after hearing your rehearsal—they will be more objective and may offer some interesting "left-of-field" queries. It's better to be surprised while preparing than presenting.

Tips to get the most out of Q&As

- Repeat the question for those who may not have heard it. Paraphrase if you need to clarify it. This technique also buys you a little extra time to think of a good answer.
- Don't respond to the questioner; deliver your answer to the audience as a whole.
- Respect the questioner, even if you don't agree with the query or the way it was asked.
- Answer a question even if you covered it in your presentation. The person may not have heard it, and this gives you a chance to re-emphasize points.
- If you don't know, say so. There's no point trying to bluff but you can offer to find out. Where appropriate, you can always throw the question to the audience—this is a good way to get people involved and solve the problem.
- Save some of your material, which you know will prompt questions, for the Q&A session. If the audience doesn't ask the "right" questions, you can lead into them with a prompter, such as "I'm often asked why . . . ," and then proceed to answer it.
- Close the Q&A with a prompter, such as "We're almost out of time" or "We have time for one final question."

Making a strong close (again)

As we've discussed, the closing of your speech is just as important as the opening. You want to leave your audience on a high, with a positive impression of you and your message. So how can you do that when your close is followed by a Q&A session? By preparing a second close, of course.

Too often speakers will finish on a high note, answer questions from the audience, and then appear lost as to how to finish the presentation. Once you've finished the Q&A, complete the presentation with a second closing statement that builds on the first and rounds out the entire event.

After the Speech

Just when you thought it was all over, it's not—or it shouldn't be. There are a few things you still need to do after the speech:

- Thank your audience for coming and for their time.
- Distribute handouts (if you haven't already).
- Make yourself available for any final questions, private comments, or feedback.

Evaluate your speech

The best way to improve your public speaking is to evaluate every performance. When possible, gain objective opinions from others and view a video of your talk. First, review the content:

- Did your speech have a proper opening, body, and closing?
- Were the major points organized in a logical sequence?
- Did the speech flow naturally?
- Did the illustrations support the key messages?
- Did the talk relate to the purpose?

Second, examine the presentation:

- Did you project a confident image (voice control, posture, eye contact)?
- Did your presentation hold the audience's attention?
- Did the audience react favorably to the overall talk?
- Did you adequately answer all questions during and afterwards?

And finally, consider:

- What was lacking from your presentation (content or performance)?
- How would you improve the presentation?
- What can you do to improve future presentations?

There are a great many benefits to mastering the art of public speaking.

It will benefit you professionally with the skills and confidence to address all kinds of interactions on stage and screen, in person, and on the phone. It will benefit you socially, by making you a better conversationalist. In fact, public speaking has the potential to assist you in all areas of your life, including your writing, by giving you the confidence to tackle areas and issues you wouldn't ordinarily undertake. So, even if you don't plan on taking the stage any time soon, it's in your best interest to learn and practice these principles, because your day in the spotlight will be here before you know it.

CHAPTER 18

Formalize Your Business for Long-Term Success

*What you receive by accomplishing your
goals is not nearly as important as what you
become by accomplishing your goals.*

Zig Ziglar (1926–)

One of the keys to managing a successful operation today and tomorrow is to automate as many processes as possible. Invest the time up front in developing a series of templates and they'll repay you many times over by saving you time and allowing you to concentrate on delivering quality work.

The other advantage of using forms or templates is that they allow you to document or formalize your business. This is a prerequisite for any reputable company, and it should be one for your business as well. Make it a rule to document anything of importance. If all important matters are put in writing, everyone—you, your clients, and any third parties—will know what's involved and what's required of them. This not only enables you to stay focused, it also protects you if things become unglued.

Get It In Writing
Document briefs

Before you commence any major task for a client, you should have a clear understanding of their objectives and expectations. That sounds obvious, but writers often miss the mark with a communication because they have misinterpreted what the client wants. Ordinarily, briefs are written. They can be a paragraph in length or a multipage document, depending on the complexity of the task. The fail-safe approach is to gain a formal, written brief from the client. If you are given an oral brief, I suggest you confirm in writing what the client requires of you.

Client Brief

If you do not receive a proper brief from a client, you can ask a series of questions to get a better understanding of their needs. I use a Client Briefing Form, especially when I'm dealing with new clients. This helps ensure I gather all relevant information needed to act on the project.

Feel free to adapt my Client Brief form:

---

market*Zing*
Business-to-Business Communications

Client Brief
Date _____
Client _____
Code _____
Contact Name _____
Position/title _____
Address _____
ZIP code _____
Phone _____
Fax _____
E-mail _____
Web URL _____

Company Background
Product/Services _____
Target Markets _____
Decision Makers _____
Major Competitors _____
Competitive Advantage/USP _____
Sales Force _____
How do you sell _____
Marketing activities _____ Advertising _____ PR _____ Direct Mail
Marketing support _____ Brochures _____ Profile _____ Newsletter
Internal/External Marketing _____

Campaign/project title
The client's project name _____

Objectives
The client's stated objectives _____

Target market
Details relating to the client's target prospect market _____

Client Brief, page 1

Reverse brief

Sometimes, you can walk away from a briefing meeting and still be unclear about what's required of you. In that situation, it's best to give the client a "reverse brief," which is a document that states your understanding of the client's vision. It's a good place to start, and it at least allows the client to correct your interpretation before you invest a lot of time.

Here's an example of a reverse brief I drafted for a client:

Sample
Reverse Brief

Dear John,

BRIEF: TWELVE-PAGE BROCHURE

Market*zing* has been contracted to arrange copywriting and design & layout of a twelve-page (inclusive) brochure for your company.

The brochure will comprise an outer cover featuring a simple design already established by your company as well as eight pages of text and pictures.

This will cover the three major products ranges and also focus on the professional service, support, and overall commitment of the team in Australia.

Specifically, the brochure will feature:

- One-page introduction to the company in Australia, focusing on the general features and benefits of the range

- Two facing pages on each of the generic features and benefits of the product ranges (six pages inclusive)

- One-page wrap-up on the company's customized solutions for all trucking needs, its technical excellence, and quality approach

John, this is my understanding of the vision you have for this brochure. Please advise any changes prior to commencement of this project.

Regards,

Michael Meanwell

Managing Director

As you can see, preparing a reverse brief is not a difficult proposition. It looks like a regular letter, but it's also an important tool you can use. It will not only save you valuable research time, it will also demonstrate to your client your professionalism.

Work-in-progress schedule

Once you and your client agree on the brief, you can begin developing a "work-in-progress" (WIP) schedule of tasks. You can develop a WIP as a simple spreadsheet or word processor document, which includes:

- Task (e.g., "press release")
- Status of the task (e.g., "awaiting more info")
- Action (e.g., "client to provide background info on product range")
- Responsibility (client initials and company code—see chapter four)
- Deadline

This is a simple but powerful tool you can use every working day. I don't just use one WIP; I use three. The first is my general WIP. It provides an overview of every project I am currently working on or will be working on in the near future. This helps me keep my work week in perspective and also shows me where I am headed in the near future. Long-term projects are listed and, as they get closer to fruition, can be added to my second WIP. The second WIP is a weekly schedule that contains all tasks that have to be achieved in that week. Each week, this version is updated accordingly and faxed to active clients and any relevant third parties so that everyone involved knows the role they will play. As you can see, the weekly WIP includes not only the tasks I must perform but also those that need to be handled by other people in the project team. And, finally, there's the daily WIP for all tasks I have to achieve today. Each night, I reevaluate my daily WIP, adding new tasks to be done and deleting those that have been completed.

The WIP is a vital tool, especially for freelancers who assume the responsibility of project manager or facilitator. It helps you stay focused, and it also allows you to keep others on the ball.

---

market*Zing*
Business-to-Business Communications

WORK IN PROGRESS

WEEK COMMENCING: July 1, 2004

TASK	STATUS	ACTION	BY	D'LINE

Quotation

Quoting on jobs should be as formal as client briefings. My standard quote template is two-pages. The front outlines the parameters and costs involved in the project; the back covers all of the terms and conditions of the quotation. My lawyer originally drew this up.

I'm supplying this document to give you an understanding of what you can use in your own business. You may need to adapt my template to suit your specific business requirements as well as the laws of your state.

market**Zing**
Business-to-Business Communications

QUOTATION

DATE: July 1, 2004

NO: 2394

CLIENT: Any Company, Inc., 1234 E Street, Any Town

ATTENTION: Mr. John Smith, Managing Director

ITEM	DESCRIPTION	COST
1.	Prepare press release on new product	
2.	Draft copy for direct mail campaign	
3.	Draft copy for print advertisement	
N.B.	This Quote is firm for thirty (30) days. The cost does not include out-of-pocket expenses such as stationery; fax and Internet transmissions; long-distance telephone calls and couriers, as outlined over the page.	

TOTAL $

Approved by: _____

Signature: _____

I have read the Terms & Conditions and accept this quotation and brief. On behalf of the company, I hereby commission Marketzing to undertake this project.

TERMS AND CONDITIONS OF TRADING BETWEEN Marketzing and CLIENT NAME (hereinafter referred to as "the Client").

WHEREAS the Client has appointed Marketzing to undertake the project, as outlined.

AND WHEREAS Marketzing has agreed to complete the project for the Client upon the terms and conditions as hereinafter appearing:

1. Appointment

The Client hereby appoints Marketzing to complete the project, as outlined.

2. Remuneration

The Client shall pay to Marketzing the following:

(a) For any and all services for which Marketzing has been commissioned by the Client, such work shall be charged to the Client at the amount quoted.

3. Terms of Payment

Marketzing shall submit invoices to the Client upon completion of the project, and the Client shall pay these invoices within fourteen (14) days of the date of the invoice.

4. Obligations of the Client

The Client agrees with Marketzing throughout the term of the project, as outlined:

(a) To support Marketzing in its duties and in particular:

(i) To notify Marketzing of any inquiries from the media;

(ii) To advise Marketzing of the opening of any new outlet of the Client and of the launch of any new product or service of the Client;

(iii) To permit Marketzing or its representatives to attend meetings with the advertising agents of the Client;

(iv) To make available a well briefed personable speaker for the Client on reasonable notice to represent the Client at media briefings or conferences arranged by Marketzing during the term;

(v) To make available to Marketzing, free of charge, its promotional material for use by Marketzing in the course of its duties;

(b) To indemnify and keep indemnified Marketzing from and against any and all loss, damage, or liability, whether criminal or civil suffered, and legal fees and costs incurred by Marketzing in the course of conducting the duties and resulting from:

(i) Any act, neglect or default of the Client's agents, employees or licensees, or customers;

(ii) The proven infringement of the intellectual property rights of any third party;

(iii) Any successful claim by any third party alleging libel or slander in respect of any matter arising from the conduct of the business, provided that such liability has not been incurred by Marketzing through any default in carrying out the terms of the Agreement;

(c) To pay Marketzing promptly being payment of Marketzing's quotation, as outlined, and any other sums payable to Marketzing pursuant to this Agreement.

5. Obligations of Marketzing

Marketzing shall throughout the term of this Agreement:

(a) At all times work diligently to protect and promote the interests of the Client in accordance with the project brief, as outlined;

(b) In all matters to act loyally and faithfully toward the Client;

(c) To advise the Client of all its meetings, discussions, and correspondence with representatives of the media concerning the Client, and the business of the Client in accordance with the project brief, as outlined;

(d) Not to exceed the project's budget without the prior written consent of the Client;

(e) To keep accurate and separate records and accounts in respect of the budget and sundry expenses in accordance with good accountancy custom;

(f) To meet agreed deadlines excepting force majeure, as outlined.

6. Signed Agreement

Signatures from representatives of Marketzing and the Client shall bind both parties to the Terms and Conditions of this Agreement. These Terms and Conditions shall be governed and construed in accordance with the law for the time being in force in the State of Victoria. The invalidity of any clause, or part of a clause, shall not affect any other clause, or any other part of the clause.

Approval form

It's essential that any work you produce for a client be formally approved by all parties involved, for your legal protection. That means getting a signature not just from your client but from their customer as well, if you have provided them with a quotation or obtained information from them. You can have something drawn up by your lawyer; however, I use my own approval form for press releases produced on behalf of clients:

The wording can be modified to suit any project you are working on.

Purchase orders

Just as it's important for you to quote on all projects, you should also provide purchase orders to all of your suppliers. With a purchase order, there can be no dispute over the costs of items or the parameters of the project. This is standard procedure for larger companies, and it makes common sense for freelancers' businesses as well.

Purchase orders are the ideal document to formalize all that is required and agreed upon with supplier (for example, a photographer shooting products for a catalog, a printer producing the catalog, and a mailing house distributing the catalog). Purchase orders should also be used when subcontracting to other freelance writers.

The easiest approach to purchase orders is to set up a database that allows you to log supplier details so that they can easily be added to each new purchase order. Your purchase order template should contain the following elements:

- Date of order
- Purchase order number (use a sequential number)
- Supplier's details (contact name, contractor name, physical address, phone, fax, and e-mail)
- Description (allow adequate room for detailing the various components of the order)
- Price (ensure your price allows for any tax, shipping, etc.)
- Deadline for order fulfillment
- Client code (include your client's three-letter code, as discussed in chapter four, so you know which client to bill)

- Approval (include your details on the purchase order and also allow room to authorize the order with your physical signature). When it comes to working with contractors, don't leave anything to chance. In your purchase order, always spell out what you require
- Request that the order number be included on the contractor's invoice
- Specify whether you require the contractor to arrange shipping or to contact your preferred courier

E-mail signature files

I use four different e-mail signatures depending on whom I am addressing. Three relate to the three businesses I run, and one allows for personal correspondence. The following is the signature I use for my freelance business. It includes all the information the recipient needs to contact me. It also allows for other people who may not know me, such as prospects, third parties, and individual members of the media.

```
=====================
Michael Meanwell
Managing Director
Marketzing Pty Ltd.
P.O. Box 9000, Any Town, NY 10010
Tel: (212) 345-7890
Fax: (212) 567-8910
Cell: (212) 123-4567
E-mail: contactme@michaelmeanwell.com

Put more zing in your marketing with:
• Media Announcements
• Direct Mail
• Customer & Staff Newsletters
• Product & Corporate Brochures

This e-mail and any files transmitted with it are confidential and
intended solely for the use of the individual or entity to whom they
are addressed.
=====================
```

Stationery

I used to spend a small fortune on stationery. Then I shifted to virtual stationery that is saved on my computer's hard drive. If you have a logo, simply scan and paste it onto a new page. Then add your contact details, as they would appear on regular stationery. Here is an example of my freelance company letterhead:

Business-to-Business Communications

April 1, 2004

Mr. Fred Nurk
Managing Director
Nurkem Inc.
123 Wilma Ave.
Flatstone, California

Dear Fred,
This is an easy template you can adapt for use in your business.

Why pay for printed letterhead when you can design and maintain your own template on computer?

Regards,

MICHAEL MEANWELL, MPRIA, AMAMI, AIMM
Managing Director

Marketzing Pty Ltd
P.O. Box 9000, Any Town, NY 10010

Tel: (212) 345-7890
Fax: (212) 567-8910
E-mail: contactme@whateverwebsite.com

CHAPTER 19

The Powerful No-Staffing Secret That Saved My Business

There are those who see an opportunity
and then there are those who SEIZE an
opportunity.

Joanie Warren

The term "outsourcing" shouldn't be foreign to any freelancer, since the bulk of our work comes from this handy little corporate strategy. But when was the last time you thought about using it in your own business? Yes, *your* business. As we've discussed, many small businesses suffer from the "feast or famine" phenomenon. You've either got too much work or not enough. Most of this book is dedicated to helping you resolve the "famines" in your business, but this chapter will show you how to deal with the "feasts" that come your way.

Feasts. They sound great, don't they? That is, until you're in the thick of one, with no time to think and yet another deadline looming. It doesn't take long before you're cursing the feast and your clients for making you so successful. The old saying "bite off more than you can chew, and chew like crazy" will only get you so far. You can't keep working at a frenetic pace forever and, apart from missing your life, it won't be long before you start making mistakes. So what do you do?

You Can Have Your Feast and Eat It, Too

What if I could show you a way of riding out the feast, keeping all of your clients happy, profiting by it, and still maintaining your sanity? Well, you know what I'm going to suggest—outsourcing. It's what saved my business when I returned to being a one-man band, back in 1996.

It wasn't long before I built the business up beyond my own abilities to service it. After putting in all that marketing effort, the last thing I wanted to do was drop clients, or worse, allow them to leave because of poor service. I also knew I didn't want to return to the days of maintaining a full-time staff. They were great when the work was there but a burden when it wasn't. I wanted the best of both worlds, so I advertised for freelance writers and received more than 250 responses. There are plenty of people out there who want to write, and there are also plenty of people out there who can help your writing business. After sifting through a mountain of résumés, I phoned forty or more people, short-listed less than half for interviews, and appointed about a handful to help me with current and future work.

It sounds easy, but it wasn't easy for me. The hardest part was actually deciding to take this route after having gone solo and heading a "real" company with "real" employees. But, I'm glad to say some years later, it's one of the best business decisions I've made. Outsourcing has allowed me to take control of my business again. I now can choose *when* and *how* I work. I can handle the difficult clients who I think are beyond my freelancers' call of duty, and I can take on larger tasks by using a team of professionals.

A good basic team, for me, comprises:

- A graphic designer to lay out newsletters, brochures, and ads
- A photographer for stills and videos
- A printer for handling print production
- A fulfillment house for managing databases and distribution
- An ad agency for creative assistance with and placement of advertising
- PR practitioners, marketers, and writers (some individuals fulfill all of these roles) for my own overload as well as for brainstorming and managing the business when I'm away

And, just in case any of these people are unavailable, I always have others in reserve.

The Dos and Don'ts of Outsourcing

We've talked about the positives, so now let's examine the negatives of outsourcing. The first is that you can potentially lose control of accounts. Keep in mind that your business is a people business, and you need to interact with your clients regularly and frequently. You need to be seen to be managing all client accounts and overseeing all client activities.

Second, by outsourcing, you are creating another layer of bureaucracy, so you need to make sure that your client's instructions are correctly understood by you, correctly communicated by you to your freelancer, and correctly executed by your freelancer.

Third, you need to find a balance between letting go and ensuring that your standards are not compromised.

Maintaining control of your clients

First, you need to tell your clients that you are adding some new people to the team. Tell them how this will benefit their business in terms of greater depth of experience, expertise (e.g., "we can now offer you a wider range of services"), and improved customer service. You can arrange a meeting and introduce key staff to key clients, or you can phone your clients and follow through with a letter which includes a few details about the new team's capabilities, as well as key members' strengths, experience, and client services.

Once the new team is in place, it's important to show your clients that you are still there managing their accounts personally. One of the major grievances suffered by corporate clients is how some agencies treat them once they win accounts. Often the larger agencies will go into a competitive pitch, with one or more directors guaranteeing a high level of professionalism. Within a short time, the suit is no longer available, and in his or her place is a regular consultant, or worse, a junior or trainee.

That's one of the secrets to my success—guaranteeing a hands-on role by a director of the firm: me. This is something both my partner and I did when the consultancy was bigger, and it's something I still guarantee now that I am the sole employee, with a team of contractors. So, once you have gained the trust of your clients, don't betray them by delegating responsibility to a second-stringer. Always maintain control of your accounts.

The best way to do this is to keep direct communication between your subcontractors and your clients to a minimum. If they need to interview your client, that's fine. But strategic meetings, consultations, proposals, and presentations must all come from you. What you need to remember is that the client hired your firm because of *you*. *Your* name and *your* reputation are at stake, so take responsibility by being responsible for

---

every major transaction between your contractors and your clients.

The second issue we outlined earlier is the extra layer of bureaucracy that occurs when you become a go-between with your clients and your contractors. It sounds messy, but there's no way around it unless you hand over more control to your contractor to work directly with your client. For me, I'll take the "messy" route because I think it's less risky for the business in the long run.

If It Moves, Document It

So, how do you manage the new bureaucracy? Document everything. When your client gives you an oral brief, put it in writing to your subcontractor. You may need to add further detail to the brief if the consultant is unfamiliar with the work, your approach, or the client's expectations. It's best to over-brief than under-brief. I'd prefer to insult someone's intelligence rather than leave something unsaid and risk the consequences.

When dealing with contractors, furnish them with all the information they need to complete tasks. That includes sending them previous press releases and other marketing collateral so they can familiarize themselves with the account. Prepare to invest time up front educating them to the client's needs and expectations, as well as your own requirements and the responsibilities of the contractor.

Check Your Workers' Work

One of the first thoughts you may have when outsourcing work is that it will make your day a little easier. That's true—otherwise you'd never hire anyone. But, you need to do something extra. You need to oversee the contractor's work to ensure that the job runs smoothly and meets objectives, deadlines, and the specifics of the brief. This may sound obvious, but it's easy to fall into the habit of trusting that the work has been done to your high standards. Never assume.

I'm not suggesting that the people you hire are not up to par. What I am suggesting is that this is *your* business. *You* are ultimately responsible. The worst that can happen to a contractor is that he loses an occasional freelance job. The worst that can happen to you is that you can lose a major account.

So stay sharp. Check everything twice. Don't hesitate to rework their work if you can improve on it. I must admit that it's a rare day when a contractor's work gets past me without a few corrections. It's an average day when a good slice of their work is streaked with my red pen. But it's a good idea to be a perfectionist in your own business.

Formalize your arrangement

Like anything important in your business, put your outsourcing arrangement in writing so all parties understand what is required of them, and you are legally protected should anything go wrong.

Before I hire anyone for any job, I have him sign two copies of the following document. This represents a contract between both parties. I've been fortunate in that I haven't had to test this document in court, as none of my freelancers or subcontractors has ever betrayed my confidences or divulged confidential client information. But if nothing else, it formalizes our agreement and certainly gives me peace of mind.

Terms and Conditions of Subcontracting

I understand and accept the Terms and Conditions of Subcontracting as outlined to me by Market*zing* Pty Ltd (hereinafter referred to as "the consultancy"). I accept the consultancy's terms and conditions of subcontracting, which are stated below:

1. That all client information, verbal or written, be treated in the strictest confidence and not used for any means other than for the benefit of the client or the consultancy;

2. That all consultancy information, verbal or written, be treated in the strictest confidence and not used for any means other than for the benefit of the consultancy;

3. That any clients of Market*zing* Pty Ltd will not be approached or solicited by myself or any colleague of mine for a period of two (2) years after the completion of my tenure with this consultancy.

I understand that if any of these conditions are not met by myself that Market*zing* Pty Ltd can exercise its rights to dismiss me immediately and will have recourse to other areas for recovery of damages.

_____   _____

(SUBCONTRACTOR)   DATE OF ACCEPTANCE

Preceding this contract, I also give subcontractors a briefing document that spells out what is required of them, plus the agreed pay rates. As you'll see, my standard document relates to writing PR releases and liaising with the media:

General Brief for Subcontractors

Market*zing* Pty Ltd provides various PR and marketing services for clients; however, the bulk of work requiring your assistance falls into two categories—generation of press releases and media liaison.

Press Releases:

All projects will be provided to you via verbal or written brief. They will include, wherever possible, further information from our client as well as contact details.

Unless otherwise instructed, Market*zing* will maintain all direct contact with our client. You will be required to source information, quotes and, where appropriate, photos from the allocated contacts. Draft releases will be sent to Market*zing* for vetting and client approval. We reserve the right to alter stories accordingly.

Wherever possible, we will try to gain the maximum amount of time for you to research and draft releases; however, stories are often required within twenty-four or forty-eight hours of brief.

Stories should typically be written between one and two pages in length (maximum of five hundred words) to suit client style. We will provide you with the client letterhead templates with the initial brief.

It is not necessary for us to meet on a regular basis. Projects will be sent to you via fax or e-mail, where possible, and we require draft releases to be returned via e-mail.

Media Relations:

Almost all press releases also require media phone follow-up after they are syndicated.

Projects you have worked on should be followed-up by you, since you have the most experience on that job.

Market*zing* will advise you of the project's syndication date. Projects will need to be followed-up typically within one or two days of syndication. Stories are generally issued to a range of media categories comprising 60 to 135 outlets. Ordinarily, media liaison can take 5 to 9 hours to complete over 1 or 2 days.

It's important to make contact with the media, however we understand that it's also important not to irritate journalists with several calls. We generally allow for 1 to 3 calls to be made before taking the hint.

When dealing with the media, please follow these commonsense rules:

1. State your full name, and that you are calling on behalf of the client, not Market*zing*.

2. Ask whether or not they recall seeing the story you are calling about, and whether it is of interest. (Journalists do not like being asked if the

story will be published and on which page, so try to use some tact when ascertaining their interest in the story). When you are put through to voicemail, it's wise to leave as extensive a message as possible (e.g., your name, what the story is about, and your number to call).

3. If the phone contact number is wrong, when you finally make contact, please also check the journalist's fax number, e-mail address, and physical address. Please advise Marketzing of the changes so we can update our database.

4. When phoning contacts, as a matter of course, please request their fax number and e-mail address if these are not listed on the contact sheets.

5. Marketzing generally e-mails stories as well as posts and/or faxes them to the media. Before or during the phone follow-up, we will advise you of any e-mails that were returned because of wrong/old address. Please update for our database.

6. Part of our service to our clients is to provide them with a report of media that have or intend to run a story. To assist us with this report, when the task is completed, please either fax back the sheets or advise via e-mail any changes for our database as well as those journalists who either have filed a story, or have interest/plan to write a story. Wherever possible, please indicate which issue the story may run (while observing # 2). Also, if you have gained any comments regarding the story (positive or negative), please also include for mentioning in our report.

Other Projects

As mentioned, these are the main fare of Marketzing at present. We do hope in the future to involve you in other client projects, such as direct mail campaigns, newsletters, brochures, and marketing campaigns, as they come to hand.

Michael Meanwell
Managing Director
Marketzing Pty Ltd

What to Pay Your Subcontractors

What do you pay for outsourcing work? You have two choices: You can pay your contractors on an hourly rate or you can pay them on a project rate. I do both.

For jobs where I have quoted the client on a project basis, I set a fair rate for the contractor. If it takes them longer, bad luck for them. If it's done in half the time expected, everyone's happy. For tasks like media liaison, where the hours are variable, I offer an hourly rate. Once a routine is in place, we standardize the rate.

So how much should you pay for outsourced work? For me, the short answer is between one-third and one-half of the fee I charge my client. The long answer is that, before I come up with a rate, I factor a number of variables into the equation, such as:

- My time spent winning the account (winning some accounts requires attending several meetings, preparing detailed proposals, and competitive pitches)
- My time spent servicing the account (for example, client meetings and rebriefings items for which I cannot charge my client)
- The quality of the contractor's work (some contractors work faster, some write better, some require less supervision—all of which have an effect on how much extra time I have to invest)
- The complexity of the project (the harder the job, the higher the rate)

If you've got your freelancer's hat on now, you may be thinking it's unfair to offer just 33 to 50 percent of the money for most of the work. Okay, now put your business hat back on, and you'll recognize a few home truths:

- This is your business, not your contractor's business. You set the rate. Contractors have the choice of working with you or not.
- These are your clients, not your contractor's. You have invested a great deal of time discovering them, winning their trust, and developing a solid business relationship. You deserve to be rewarded for your initiative and your ongoing efforts.
- Your cut will fund future business development, and potentially more work for them.
- Your cut also funds your efforts in ensuring that their work meets your client's needs. This is a win-win situation for all parties.
- Your cut also ensures that you remain viable and in business—another win-win situation.

At first, it may feel strange to "play client" and outsource work, but if you want to grow your business safely and painlessly, this is one of the best ways to do it.

CHAPTER 20

Bad Debts: Strategies to Avoid and Redeem Them

*Whoever said money can't buy happiness
didn't know where to shop.*

Anonymous

Maintaining a stable of clients, having regular work, and making money are the stuff of a successful business. But getting paid on time—that's the stuff of a *surviving* business.

Bad debts were the one thing I thought I would avoid in business. I would do my job right. I would always have satisfied clients. Why would anyone not pay their bills?

I started preparing for business about a year before taking the plunge. I read books, developed a rudimentary business plan, and constantly observed my boss, who was running a small business of three employees. He taught me a great deal, not just about my craft but about how to make money and how to get paid on time—or so I thought.

When it was time for me to spread my wings in business, I thought I had it made. I'd won three accounts, two of which promised a lot of regular work; I'd made the move from a bedroom at home to a real office in a professional suite within a couple of months. I had access to secretarial facilities, a boardroom, and even nightly cleaners and security staff. It wasn't long, however, before I discovered that my overheads had outstripped my revenue. That wasn't because of poor planning but poor cash flow. You see, two of the three clients for whom I was now working six days a week had stalled payment.

I didn't realize this until I presented invoices totaling $8,000 for two completed jobs. The computer retailer was happy with the finished brochures, and talked of other great things ahead. But for now, he had a cash flow problem, which meant I had to share his problem. I still remember the compassionate words he said to me when I pleaded for payment: "Welcome to the real world." That's okay, I told myself. I have plenty of other work and other clients to cover the shortfall. Or so I thought.

I continued working for another client, a business management consultancy and accountancy practice. The Managing Director was a charismatic person who had big ideas and promised tremendous things in the near future, including trips overseas to launch new ventures. In the meantime, I had set to work on four major projects for him, which promised to earn me around $10,000 a month. That amount at that time was more than enough to sustain me financially. The future looked bright. That is, until I discovered my second client was worse than my first.

He had no intention of paying me anything, *ever*. I didn't discover this right away, but after repeated efforts to have invoices paid, it became painfully apparent. As time went on, I learned that he was working under an alias and was wanted by the police in other states. It sounds like a movie, but it was my horror show, and it was getting worse. Within the first four to six months of starting my business, I had used up most of my cash reserves and was racking up bills on credit while feverishly trying to pay my creditors. I was more fortunate than some: My wife and I had a house. We sold the house and, after paying off the mortgage, the balance helped us weather the storm.

Fortunately for me, business improved. I picked up new accounts, the first client finally paid up, and my second client finally fled the scene (with my money in tow). It was an expensive lesson to learn early on, but it taught me a number of things, which this chapter will address.

How to Avoid Bad Debts

There are a number of simple steps you can take to reduce your exposure to bad debts.

Getting a credit rating

Before you begin work for a new client, check out the company's credit through one of the many credit agencies. If the company has a habit of not paying bills, that information will be on its credit report. A standard report will tell you:

- The trading address and registered office
- Incorporation information (including issued shares and paid-up capital)
- Details of the directors
- Outstanding court judgments as well as writs and summonses
- Default information (including written-off accounts and accounts referred to a collection agency)

Most companies trying to ascertain whether someone is a good credit risk settle for asking for a few credit references. This sounds good, but obviously no one is going to give you a bad credit reference. So, if you want to safeguard yourself, investigate a company's credit rating through an independent bureau. This is not an expensive exercise, and it can save you a lot of time and money in the long run.

Using quotations and purchase orders

In chapter eighteen, you saw my quote template. It sets out what the job involves, a client reference (e.g., a purchase order number), total sum, and payment terms. In addition, my quotations also include a brief but detailed contract documenting what is required of me and what's required of the client. The reason is simple—a contract is not complete until parties agree on terms, and it's not binding until signed.

Make sure that the client just doesn't receive the quote but also signs and returns it. I will not begin a job until I have a signed copy in my hand. This simple process has saved me several times over the years when a client has refused to pay or questioned an account. There have been instances where I have worked on a project, the person I've dealt with has left, and there's no record of our dealings or their promise to pay me. That's where a signed quotation with the accompanying contract is a lifesaver.

The best arrangement, however, is a signed quote and a purchase order from the company. Many companies use purchase orders as a matter of course. It makes life easier for them and it will help ensure that you get paid on time and according to your agreement. The purchase order should be numbered and should state all of the agreed points of the work you are undertaking, as well as the agreed cost of the job.

Making your invoices clear and simple

Your invoices should contain all of the information provided in your quotes. Include the job description, subtotals for the various tasks or stages of the project, and grand total, including tax, as well as the payment terms and any client purchase order number you have. Present this information as clearly and simply as possible so there can be no misunderstandings by the recipient.

Getting an advance payment

If you're working on a project that you can complete in a matter of days or a week, then there's probably little chance of getting an advance or part payment for the job. But if you are working on a project that may take several weeks or months to complete, I suggest you request that the fee be split into three equal parts: a third up front upon approval of the quote, a third during the job, and the final third upon completion.

This is fair and reasonable to request. It also achieves two things for you. You are receiving some money throughout the course of the project, so you don't starve. And if something goes wrong and the client refuses to pay, at least you have received some money for the work you have done.

Setting terms

When dealing with many newspapers and magazines, you won't have the opportunity to set the terms. They will tell you their standard terms, or what is acceptable to them. When dealing with corporate clients, however, you can set your own terms. I have two payment arrangements, depending on the nature of the work and the client. For new clients, my terms are fourteen days from the date of the invoice. For loyal clients, my terms are thirty days.

When I was running a much larger business, invoices were issued at the end of every month by my bookkeeper. This was fine because issue date corresponded with her monthly visits, but it did affect our cash flow. Some clients would get an extra fourteen days or more credit—free. If they were late payers (and many were), our cash flow was stretched even further. These days I issue invoices at the end of each project. It only takes a few minutes to transfer the information and costs from the approved quote or purchase order to the invoice.

Speeding up slow payers

You may have done everything right—gained client agreement to your payment terms, completed the job to the client's satisfaction, and delivered it to them on time—but now the invoice is overdue. This can happen even with old clients who have generally paid on time. Sometimes I've had to wait six to eight months for payment of a fourteen-day account. That's stretching the friendship and, in several instances, I've had to threaten legal action (something we'll discuss in the next section). There are two approaches you can take to motivate slow payers. You can provide an incentive to pay on time, or you can penalize them for slow payment.

In Victoria, Australia, the *Penalty Interest Rates Act* 1983 allows businesses to impose an interest fee for overdue accounts. So, to discourage late payers, all of my invoices and quotes include this notice at the bottom near the total cost of the project: "Please note: Interest will be charged on overdue accounts pursuant to the rate prescribed by the *Penalty Interest Rates Act* 1983 (Vic)."

When I do have a stubborn client, I first speak with their accounts department about the matter, and then with the person who commissioned the project. Then I issue a friendly but firm letter advising the company that their account is now overdue and that if they wish to avoid an interest fee, they should pay the account this week. (I've never enforced the interest fee, but it has motivated some people.)

Another approach you can take is to offer clients a 5- or 10-percent discount if the bill is paid within the set trading terms. This approach can be very effective if you have an acute cash flow problem or if your bills are worth several thousand dollars. However, my attitude is that if I deliver the work on time, within budget, and to the client's brief, then the least they can do is pay their account on time. I don't believe they should be given a reward for conducting business fairly.

Setting up a reserve bank account

Even if your clients have been doing the right thing by paying on time, there may come a time when they don't. It could be because the person handling your account is away sick or on vacation. It could be that the account is due over Christmas or that the company has gone into liquidation. Whatever the reason, these things do happen. So make sure that it doesn't hurt too much by setting up a separate bank account as a reserve for tough times. This is something we discussed earlier, and it's a good way to weather the storms of business—both those caused by slow payers and those caused by flat business.

How to Collect Bad Debts

According to David Sher, co-author of *How to Collect Debts and Still Keep Your Customers*,[17] around 18 percent of customers can be categorized as slow payers, and about 2 percent have no intention of ever paying. Here are some strategies you can apply.

Chasing up overdue accounts immediately

You have a better chance of getting paid if you chase up accounts as soon as they become overdue. By phoning your clients as soon as an account is overdue, you are doing two things: You are "training" them as to when to pay you, and you are training yourself as to when to expedite payment of overdue accounts. I tend to give my clients one to two week's grace before badgering them for payment. That allows for any unforeseen difficulties or mail delays.

Here's how to proceed:

Phone the accounts payable department and advise them that the invoice is now overdue. Give the person your full name and company name, the invoice number, the amount, and the due date for payment. Request payment by a certain date (a few days to a week). If your invoice included an interest fee for overdue accounts, make sure you remind the client of this fact. This will give them another incentive to resolve the issue quickly.

When discussing overdue accounts, it's important to speak to the right person. Make sure you are talking with the manager—someone who can make decisions. Ask if they would like you to fax a copy of the invoice (sometimes invoices can be lost between departments, sometimes people stall by saying they haven't seen the invoice). Also ask if there's any reason why the account cannot be paid within the new time frame. If there is a problem, such as cash flow, try to work out a compromise, such as partial payments over a short period of time.

This is generally all you need to do to ensure payment from slow payers. You may have to invest more time in speaking with the accounts payable staff as well as your client in order to ensure that you will be paid.

"The check is in the mail" may be an oldie, but it's not the only tall tale used to delay or avoid paying. Here are my magnificent seven, which one client used on me just recently over the course of about three weeks:

- I didn't get your invoice.
- Could you send your invoice again?
- The person you need to discuss this with is not here at the moment.
- The person you need to discuss this with is sick today.
- The person you need to discuss this with is on vacation.
- We will be doing a check run at the end of the month.
- The CEO is on a plane to Europe. He can't sign the check until he returns.

So much for those excuses, and so much for that client. I finally did get paid after harassing three different people and threatening legal action. That's always a last resort for me. When I reach that stage, I have completely lost confidence in the prospect of any future dealings with them, and usually choose to terminate the business relationship.

You may see that as drastic action, especially if you're starting out in business. You need all the work you can get, right? True. But you don't need deadbeat clients. I would rather work on my tan than work for free. I hope you feel the same way.

Making paying easier

In this electronic age, we no longer need to wait for the check to arrive. Companies can make direct payments into your bank account. This means less money paid out in bank fees for you and for them, and less time waiting for the money to materialize.

When you are establishing terms with a new account, request that they pay you electronically. You'll find that most major organizations already have a system in place, and a growing number of smaller firms are following suit.

Handling difficult cases

Depending on how much money is at stake, you may like to take the matter further. Beyond the phone calls and faxes, you can elect to send a registered letter, enclosing a copy of the original invoice plus a stern request for payment, with a deadline. If this approach does not work, then you can hire a lawyer to write a letter on your behalf. Seeing a letter from a lawyer is enough to get some people to pay. But for the harder nuts, you may need heavier hammers to crack them.

The final step you can take is to have your lawyer send the client a summons. This, I am told, almost always works, especially if the debt is only for a few thousand dollars. Of course, any action that involves a lawyer is going to cost you serious money. And, if you use a summons, you're looking at court costs, the cost of getting the summons served, as well as extra charges from the lawyer to prepare the case.

By now, the debt collection exercise is seriously eating into your profits. But if the debt is large, it may be worth investing funds to recoup it. Financially, such action may be less than profitable. But psychologically, it is important for your own self-respect—and for the message it sends to the business community.

How to Handle Clients After the Debt is Resolved

How you work with your clients after resolving a debt will depend on how you conduct yourself and how your client responds. If it was just a matter of one or two follow-up phone calls, then life can go on much as before. Make sure, however, that you monitor future payment activity. If the client's account becomes overdue again, don't waste any time calling them. Take prompt action so they get into the habit of paying on time, every time.

If the overdue account was a more protracted affair, you should request a partial payment up front as well as progress payments throughout the course of the project, if it is more than a week. For a quick project, you can request half up front and the balance on completion of the job.

If the outstanding debt reached the stage of legal action, my advice would be to terminate any future dealings with this client. Whether or not you finally get paid, chalk the incident up to experience and learn from it. There's no point in pursuing them endlessly, or in punishing yourself.

I have lost something in the region of $20,000 in bad debts over the years. Most of this occurred in the first few years of business, and none has occurred in the past decade. When I think back, some of the deadbeats could have been detected with a credit check, and others could have been swayed to pay with more stringent measures. Nowadays I am more careful about which clients I take on, and I'm also more persistent when a good account starts to go bad.

WORKING SMARTER, WRITING FASTER

If you're like most writers, when you first had an inkling you wanted to write, you would explore thoughts at will. You wrote when you felt like it and enjoyed every minute of the process.

Today, you still enjoy writing, but a few things may have changed. You can't just write when the muse takes you—you have to write when a client calls you. You can't always write about things that interest you when you are being paid to write for someone else.

In the next chapters, we'll explore issues like reinvigorating your creativity. We'll look at proven techniques for conducting bombproof interviews. We'll examine the dreaded writer's block and how to demolish it. We'll also consider ways of ensuring you enjoy the process of writing and develop it to your best advantage.

CHAPTER 21

The Art of Interviewing

*Wait for those unguarded moments. Relax
the mood and, like the child dropping off to
sleep, the subject often reveals his truest self.*

Barbara Walters (1931–)

There's an old journalists' saying—"You're only as good as your contacts"—but in reality, journalists are only as good as their interviews.
Good interviewing skills are not just a must-have for journalists; they're
vital tools for all freelance writers. Being a good interviewer enables you
to be a good researcher, unearth and gather the information you need to
understand your client's needs, and write well-rounded marketing copy.

Whether working with new or old clients, often I am given a one-
line brief regarding promoting a new product or producing a customer
testimonial. It's up to me to determine what information to gather and
where to find it. I couldn't do it if I didn't know which people to ask and,
just as importantly, what questions to ask.

Interview Methods

There are a number of ways to facilitate an interview, from using video
conferencing satellites and Internet chat rooms to e-mail, fax, telephone
and, of course, the traditional method, in person.

I prefer to conduct phone interviews. They offer most of the benefits
of in-person interviews in terms of instant and interactive communication,
without the time and cost disadvantages of travel. You can easily burn an

hour or two getting to and from a location, not to mention more time spent waiting for the subject to be available. That's why I rarely conduct face-to-face interviews—I don't see any distinct advantage for the type of work I do. In contrast to conventional journalism, there is not the same need to pick up on a person's body language or other cues. You can generally collect all of the information you need on the phone and send and receive documents and photos by fax or e-mail.

E-mail interviews, also known as e-interviews, are my second preference for interviewing, albeit a distant second. They are most useful when dealing with disparate time zones. While they require more work for the interviewee in typing answers to questions, the e-interview offers the subject an advantage in that she can invest more time considering and preparing responses compared with other methods.

Tools of the Trade

There are two basic forms of recording interviews: manually with a notepad or electronically with a conventional tape recorder, mini-disc recorder, or mp3 player (such as an iPod). There are pros and cons to both methods.

If you are simply taking notes, you will be able to review and write up the interview far quicker than if you recorded it. But, unless you are proficient in shorthand, the accuracy of your notes will be no match for that of a recording. Alternatively, taping the interview allows you to relax and focus more on the interview process. But transcribing can be a time-consuming exercise. So which is the best method?

Well, for me, both. I generally take notes while I tape the interview. This way, I have the key points and comments on paper and an accurate record on tape. By using both methods, my notes act as a guide, indicating which areas of the tape I need to listen to for more detailed information. The notes also act as a backup if the tape recording fails (I had to learn that one the hard way!).

If you take this dual approach, it's best to write copy based on your written notes, then fast-forward the tape to find specific quotes or information. This will save you time in transcribing the entire tape. I find that taking notes while taping not only ensures that I have solid facts on paper and insurance against tape failure, it also helps me focus on what is being said and often sparks questions I would not have thought of asking.

There's one other benefit to taping that most freelance writers don't consider, but commercial writers should. Depending on the quality and the nature of the interview, you could transform an audio recording or a video into a value-added communication. Sound bites or video footage, for example, could be posted on your client's Web site or included on a CD or DVD for use in a press kit. You will, of course, need to gain permission from the subject, which we will discuss later.

Whichever approach you take, here are a few commonsense tips that will ensure a successful interview. If taking notes:

- Bring backup supplies—an extra notepad and extra pens
- Learn shorthand, even if it's your own version, so you can keep accurate notes

If taping:

- Test your recorder to ensure it is in good working order
- Use new batteries and tapes, and have spares on hand
- Do a sound check before starting the interview
- If conducting an in-person interview, consider using an external, clip-on microphone rather than relying on the built-in mic (this is a judgment call—some people may feel uncomfortable about being recorded, so placing a mic on them could exacerbate their anxiety.)
- If conducting a phone interview, there is a range of recording devices that attach to the phone and produce reasonable quality recordings. Be aware there are legal ramifications involved with recording conversations, which will be covered later in the chapter.

Check that your subject agrees to being recorded *before* the interview. If there is a problem, you can put his mind at ease by assuring that you will stop taping any time the person wishes. This is usually all you have to do to gain his trust and compliance.

Retain Good Records

When freelancing for magazines and newspapers, you should retain your notes and tapes indefinitely as a form of insurance against any issues that may arise, such as allegations of misquoting. This is not as necessary when you are a freelance commercial writer.

When I am interviewing people on behalf of a client, I keep my interview notes and tapes until the project has been completed. My reasoning is that there's no need to keep notes after the copy has been formally approved by all parties interviewed (see chapter eighteen regarding approvals).

There is a distinct difference between interviews conducted by a freelance journalist and a freelance commercial writer. A journalist is required to produce direct quotes and information precisely. Generally speaking, an interviewee first sees their comments in print. This is not so when dealing with a writer for hire. The commercial writer can apply some license to their work, providing it is approved by the person interviewed (or the company they represent). In some cases, some of the interviewee's quotes may be "massaged" to read better and communicate messages more effectively. This is perfectly acceptable, provided the interviewee has seen and agreed to the copy. Needless to say, it's important to keep your signed approval forms and other documentation archived in a safe place.

Preparation and Research

The practice of interviewing can be as daunting as being interviewed. Some of my most challenging experiences as a young journalist involved interviews. I recall having to ask tough questions of a family whose famous father had just died, of having to quiz high-ranking politicians, leading business people, and pry into the lives of celebrities. Just the thought of interviewing can be daunting, but the task is much easier when you've prepared well in advance. That means thinking about what information you need and what questions you should ask, and that all begins with solid research.

Researching the subject

When I am contracted to interview a client's customer, I generally ask the client many of the same questions I will later ask the customer. Why? Ammunition. I ask the client (usually the salesperson who has intimate knowledge of the customer sale) why the product was purchased, what alternatives were considered, and what were the major features and benefits from the customer's viewpoint. Often the information they offer enables me to better shape the questions I will pose to the customer. Also, often a customer will overlook certain details, mainly because they have forgotten about them or didn't think they were important. By knowing in advance, I am able to ensure that important points are covered. This approach is most useful when you get a scant brief. It enables you to stimulate answers and produce more expansive communications.

Good research also allows you to speed through the interviewing process, which benefits everyone, particularly the subject. I try to keep interviews as short as possible, but that's not to say I don't conduct long interviews. I recently spent more than an hour and a half interviewing bestselling author Matthew Reilly. That's an extraordinarily long time to have a phone glued to your ear, but I covered possibly three hours worth of questions because I had invested considerable time researching before dialing.

The more knowledgeable you are about the topic or the customer's needs, the better equipped you are for the interview. Much will depend on the quality of the brief. In some instances, your client will provide you with background information and a list of topics and issues that have to be addressed in your interview. But, when your brief is a one-liner, you have a couple of choices. You can research the major issues on the Internet or with appropriate people within the company or the industry. But the simplest way to expand the brief is to ask your client what topics or issues they want addressed in the communication, then formulate your questions accordingly.

Remember, the better prepared you are, the more confident and relaxed you'll be when you conduct interviews. Not only will you be more knowledgeable on the subject, you will ask better questions and gain better responses because of the groundwork you have already done. Research also acts as mental preparation for many interviewers. Even seasoned journalists can get decidedly nervous before an interview, especially with someone they do not know. So make it easy on yourself with initial research.

When you're ready, try to make an appointment time within a few days of your initial contact. This should allow enough time for your subject to think about the interview but not too much time to forget about it. When you make initial contact, provide an overview of the areas you wish to cover in the interview. This will put her mind at ease and also allow time for the subject to consider her responses.

Preparing questions

When it comes to interview questions, some journalists prefer to fly by the seat of their pants and ask questions that seem appropriate at the time. Others prefer to use a fully scripted list of questions.

There are pros and cons to both approaches. Interviewing without a list of questions gives the interviewer complete freedom to adjust the questioning to suit the subject and the responses, but it leaves the interviewer open to running dry or asking dead-end questions. If, however, you rely solely on a list of prepared questions, you run the risk of limiting the interview, especially if you don't allow for follow-up questions (for example, if the subject reveals some interesting tidbits that you have not accounted for).

The best method for me, once again, is the dual approach. I use prepared questions as signposts, pointing me in the right direction, while still giving me the flexibility to stray off the main road with on-the-fly questions if something interests me. It's best to kick off the interview with your prepared questions but allow yourself the flexibility to respond to the interviewee's answers with follow-up queries. Once the issue has been addressed, get back on track with the rest of your list.

As mentioned earlier, some writers can get anxious about interviews and may even forget the questions they had in mind, but not so if they are printed in front of them. This way, whatever your reaction, you'll be assured of a good interview.

Whichever way you go, much like news stories, interviews generally should encompass the famous five Ws and one H: Who, What, When, Where, Why, and How. In fact, this is an excellent way to prepare for an interview. Keep in mind each of these elements as you consider the questions you'll ask.

If possible, arrange your questions so that there is a natural flow-on effect. Begin with an overview question about the topic, which leads to your next question, which progresses to the next, and so on. This will make the interview process easier for you and the interviewee.

Should you show before you tell?

Generally speaking, it's not a good idea to show your questions to the contact before the interview. Even though the commercial interviewer and interviewee are both on "the same side" (unlike some news journalists and their quarry), revealing your questions can remove spontaneity from the interview. If the subject has too much time to think about the questions, his answers may appear contrived and even uninspiring. There will be more than enough time for the subject to consider his responses after your media release or newsletter story is completed and you're gaining his formal approval.

If, however, the person is insistent, I suggest you do as I do: Provide a generalization of the areas you intend covering in the interview, rather than submitting the exact questions. This way, everybody wins—the person's mind is at ease and your interview method is still intact.

Getting Started

Start the interview with pleasantries. Thank the subject for her time and for agreeing to participate. Confirm the purpose of the interview, what topics you wish to cover, and how you expect the information to be used (for example, to form the basis of a brochure or speech). Also, reassure the person upfront that whatever you write will be forwarded to her for her approval, prior to use.

Check the spelling of her name even if it's a common name. You may think you're safe with a contact named "Jane Smith," but it could be spelled "Jayne Smyth." It's better to ask the embarrassing question at the beginning of the interview, rather than be embarrassed by misspelling it in print afterwards. (There is, however, an exception to this rule—when you're dealing with high-profile people, such as the President!)

In this preliminary phase, you should also gather other important information, such as the person's title and contact details (for example, fax number or e-mail address for sending the copy for approval). I also like to give the person an idea of what areas I wish to cover with my questions, if I haven't already done so. Also tell the subject the approximate time the interview will take.

Interview times depend on the complexity of the information you need. As a rule of thumb, I find commercial interviews can generally take anywhere from several minutes to half an hour. If you intend spending more time than this, it would be wise to alert the contact prior to the interview to ensure she makes allowances for it.

You may be tempted to skip this part of the interview process, but I recommend you do not. It's important to reassure the interviewee, because often you will be dealing with people who are not media savvy. In many instances, it will be the first time the person has been interviewed so, to get the best responses, you must put her mind at ease from the start. In fact, when dealing with someone new to the media process, sometimes I don't even refer to it as an interview but a "conversation" or "discussion." A simple change of phrase can alleviate an anxious or uninitiated interviewee.

Once the formalities are out of the way, you can ease your way into the interview process with some casual, icebreaker comment or question relating to a topic or the subject of the interview. Then begin with some simple, introductory questions, such as background relating to the topic before progressing to more complex or tough questions. (A similar approach is taken by news journalists. They usually save the "bombs" for later in the interview—just in case they cause a premature end to the interview.)

Eight Questioning Styles

A good interviewer understands and uses a mix of questioning styles to achieve the desired outcome. Here are the eight most-used questioning styles:

1. Concise Questions. Apply the KISS principle to your questions. Keep them brief, concise, and to the point. Generally speaking, limit your questions to a dozen or less words. As we've discussed, interviews can be stressful for both parties, so make it easy for you to ask questions and for your contact to understand and answer them.

2. "Bigger, Better, Faster" Questions. Whether you're writing a press release, sales letter, or product brochure, your marketing communication is about promoting the benefits of your client's product, service, or business. So don't forget to ask the "bigger, better, faster" questions, such as what makes this widget interesting, special, or worth reading about. They automatically answer the "so what?" question, which makes the copy you're writing more interesting to read.

3. "Dumb" Questions. When you're writing about a range of industries and interests, it's impossible to be an expert in every field. There will be times when you do not understand a specific term or an explanation given. When this happens, be honest and ask the interviewee to explain it in layperson's terms. There's no shame in not knowing, but there is when you don't rectify it. Remember the journalists' adage: *When in doubt, find out.*

4. "Closed" Questions. These are questions that elicit a "yes" or "no" response. Generally speaking, it's better to avoid using closed questions, unless you want a precise response that you have not received using other methods.

5. "Open" Questions. You can transform closed questions into open questions simply by adding one of the six fundamental queries outlined earlier. For example, the closed question, "Do you like using the XYZ widget?" can be instantly opened by adding, "*Why* do you like using the XYZ widget?"

Using open questions will ensure you get longer and more detailed answers. You can gain extra information by employing other fundamental questions, such as "*When* did begin using the XYZ widget?", "*What* product did you use before the XYZ widget?", and "*How* has the XYZ widget improved your business?"

You can get more expansive answers if you lead into the question with an encouraging statement, such as "Can you explain about . . .", "Take me through the whole story when . . .", or "Describe the . . .".

6. Rephrasing Questions. If at first you don't succeed, try rephrasing or repeating your question to gain more information. Politicians are used to this media tactic and will remind journalists by continuing to evade the same question repeated several different ways. But it's a useful strategy to employ with other contacts when they have avoided the question or you would like a more detailed response.

7. Loaded or Leading Questions. If an interview is going nowhere fast, loaded or leading questions are a good way to get answers, especially answers your client will be happy to hear. Here are a couple of approaches you can take: "Would you agree that . . ." or "Is it fair/accurate to say that . . .". This question style won't work, of course, if your contact does not agree with your leading question. But it's a good way to keep the interview moving and in the direction you would prefer.

8. The Silent Question. Silence can be a golden weapon in interviews. It is a useful method for stimulating a response from a stubborn subject as well as extending answers from compliant subjects. When there is silence in a conversation, a person generally feels obliged to fill the gap. Also, some subjects think slower than others and require more time to process.

Qualities of a Successful Interviewer

As you can see, there are many ways to conduct an interview, but the most successful interviewers embody certain qualities. Here are six qualities you can develop to ensure you get the best out of your interviews:

1. Attentiveness. It's important to listen not just hear the interviewee's voice. Some journalists are so intent on reciting questions or recording answers that they miss subtle cues and clues in what the interviewee is saying. Listen to what the person is saying, listen to how he is saying it, and listen for clues that can lead the interview in an unexpected direction.

2. Trustworthiness. Establishing trust with your interviewee is arguably the most important quality you can develop. Without it, there's no hope for your interview. An experienced interviewer builds rapport with the subject. She has empathy for the subject, displaying genuine interest in the conversation and encouraging frank and open comments.

3. Objectivity. Good interviewing requires balancing subjective qualities, such as those just mentioned, with the objectivity to sift interesting information from erroneous comments.

4. Flexibility. Whether you choose to work from prepared questions or on the fly, have the flexibility to change the tack of questions to suit a change in the course of the discussion.

5. Spontaneity. As we've discussed, it doesn't hurt to stray from your line of questions; in fact, it's a healthy approach. When appropriate, try an intelligent "left-of-field" question—you may be surprised at the results you get. (On more than one occasion, I have thrown a zinger at a subject, and the response has become the lead for a story.) Needless to say, this tactic requires some discretion, so choose your questions and your targets carefully.

---

6. Positive personality. Try to make an interview as painless as possible by staying positive from beginning to end. A positive, enthusiastic personality encourages a similar attitude in the subject and will generally ensure good responses.

Telephone Interviews

As mentioned at the start of this chapter, I prefer to interview by telephone. I find it offers most of the benefits of face-to-face meetings without the disadvantages of traveling time and cost. Also, like e-mail interviews (which we'll discuss soon), phone interviews enable you to communicate with people in other states or other countries.

Having said that, one of the disadvantages of telephone interviews is that they are not as personal as face-to-face conversations. You will not have the opportunity to pick up on a subject's body language or tour a facility. But there are some techniques you can use to ensure you will gain the best from your interviews.

Smile while you dial

As mentioned, you do not have the opportunity to see someone's body language, but you can often pick it up from his voice. This, of course, works both ways. If you get into the habit of smiling while talking on the phone, you'll find you come across in a more positive, confident manner. This is not a technique for everyone or every situation but, considering for the most part you will be conducting "soft" interviews, it's far more appropriate and even conducive than for news reporters asking the "hard" questions.

Be prepared

Time is of the essence, especially when you're handling a telephone interview. You can't keep the subject on the line while you frantically search for the next question to ask. Be prepared with your questions or key points before you pick up the phone.

Simplicity counts

Keep questions simple, especially when you're interviewing on the phone. Some people can have difficulty remembering long-winded questions, and some interviewers can become tongue-tied on novel-length queries. Keep them to a dozen words or less, if possible.

Recording and the Law

There are legal obligations regarding electronic recording of conversations, including face-to-face and phone interviews.

In some countries, the law requires only one person (which can be the interviewer who is recording) to consent to the taping of a conversation with another. This means that you do not need to advise the subject that you are taping the phone call.

U.S. federal law also requires only one-party consent; however, twelve states require consent from every person participating in the conversation.[18] It's important to note that if you're telephoning, for example, from New York (which only requires one-party consent) but you are recording a conversation with a subject in California (which requires all-party consent), then you are legally obligated to advise and gain permission to tape the interview before commencing. If you do not, you could be in violation of your subject's state law, even though the recording is lawful in your own state. The same principle applies when conducting international telephone interviews, where the laws in the subject's country require all-party notification.

Unlawful recordings can—and have—resulted in civil suits and even criminal prosecution. Whether conducting interstate or international interviews, it's best to operate on the safe side and presume that the more stringent law applies. Always be upfront with your subject and advise her that you wish to tape the interview before it begins, and get an "okay" on tape.

E-Mail Interviews

E-interviews are growing in popularity, particularly with cyber-based media as well as writers wishing to interview people in different countries or different time zones. It is a cost-effective way to communicate, but it is a time-intensive process for the interviewee who is responsible for writing answers to your questions.

I have been on both sides of e-interviews, so I can see the pros and cons for both parties. Freelancers can save a lot of time and money conducting interviews this way. Once you've established contact, it's just a matter of compiling a list of questions and working with the answers you receive.

You may need to clarify some responses with further questions and also tidy up the English of your subject but, for the most part, it's a simple and painless interview process. And, at the end of it, you will have an official record of what the subject stated, so there should be no fear of misquotation when you're armed with an e-mail interview.

There are, however, a few cons for a freelancer. First, it will take some time to get a response to your interview. Depending on the subject's work schedule and motivation, you can wait anywhere from a few days to a few weeks. For this reason, if appropriate, I'd suggest you include a deadline for the subject to respond.

Second, there's no guarantee that what you receive will be useable. You don't have the advantage of an in-person or telephone interview in pursuing a line of questions. Also, e-mail interviews, depending on the subject writing them, can suffer from a lack of spontaneity and enthusiasm. If that happens, I suggest you revise the subject's quotes and send them back for approval, much as you would do with a standard marketing communication.

There are positives and negatives for the e-mail interviewee as well. These interviews are labor intensive. A number of times, I have spent an entire day producing a 2,500-word response to a dozen or more e-mailed questions. But, on the plus side, e-interviews do give the subject time to think and consider their answers. In addition, some people feel pressured by journalists on a phone or in person, so the e-mail alternative makes it easier on the nerves.

The best way to request an e-interview is in a formal, one-page query. Introduce yourself, your background, and the purpose of the interview, including the areas you wish to cover and how the information will be used (for example, in a company newsletter). If appropriate, advise that the subject's comments will be sent to him for approval before being used. Remember to keep the query brief, to the point, and respectful.

Once you get the green light, thank the subject for his time and assistance and formulate questions in a logical, numbered sequence. This is something you should do with any interview, but it's even more crucial with an e-interview since the subject will be doing most of the work. Also, make sure your questions are properly phrased to avoid confusion.

If your interview involves more than a handful of questions, you should indicate this before the process begins. You can also stagger the interview by sending the subject a few questions, rather than bombarding him. Once these have been answered, you can continue with other questions. This will make the e-mail interview more interactive, less daunting to the subject, and generally provide you with more considered answers.

Other Electronic Interviews

There are other electronic methods for interviewing, such as the fax, as well as instant messaging, chat rooms, and public message boards on the Internet.

The online methods enable you to interact with your subject in real time, making them more effective communicators than e-mail and fax, which require lapses in time. And, because you're able to communicate with the interviewee simultaneously, like a true conversation, you are able to clarify points made and also take the interview in different directions based on her answers.

The other plus with chat rooms and message boards is that you are able to communicate with several people at once. But one disadvantage of message boards is that they are not private. Virtually anyone accessing the board can view your interview. This, of course, can be off-putting not only to you but to your subject.

The humble fax can be useful for interviewing in that most people have access to a machine. Like e-mail, it gives the subject time to think about how she wishes to answer.

Fax and on-line mediums are a valid method of gathering information but, like e-mail, they should not be your first choice for conducting interviews. Remember, there's a lot more to interviewing than just asking a list of questions. Interviewing is a matter of understanding and interpreting what is being said and adjusting your approach to get the most out of your subject. This is not an easy thing to do on a computer or a fax machine.

Checklist for Success

Here are some final thoughts on the art of interviewing:

Know your interviewee. The more you know about your subject and the topics you wish to cover, the more effective your interview. Where possible, research your subject and topic by reading background information online and seek further information from your client or other contacts.

Know your questions. It's not enough to list your questions—you need to know them. Run through them before you conduct your interview to ensure they make sense and flow naturally from one to the next.

Think like a reader. Consider the typical reader who will be receiving your marketing communication. What would he like to know and need to know from your interview? Consider this as you re-think your questions. Remember, as we discussed earlier, it's okay to ask "dumb" questions that your reader would like to know, but not stupid ones.

Be courteous. You're not a news reporter, and even if you were, you should always be courteous and treat your interviewee with respect. Never ask threatening, embarrassing, or offending questions.

Stay out of it. Despite what's been said before, this is not a conversation, it's an interview. There's no room for your opinion unless your subject asks for it. This interview is about the interviewee, so keep your own views and comments to yourself.

Stay on course. It's easy for an interview to veer off course. You ask a question and before you know it, it's been shanghaied by your subject. If this happens, gently steer the interview back to familiar territory with a subtle question, such as "That's interesting, but what do you think about . . .".

Go off with the tangent. Despite what I've just said in the earlier point, sometimes it works to go off on a tangent with your subject rather than to stay rigidly on course. Often, when I have allowed an interviewee to pursue a point I thought had been answered adequately, the extra information has given me a new angle or new insight on what I was writing. It's not always easy to know when the subject has had enough rope and it's time to reel him in—it's really up to you to make the judgment on an individual basis. If the subject continues for too long or too often, take charge.

Take note. A part of listening carefully to the interview means being aware of any interesting issues your subject mentions. If it is not appropriate to interrupt, take notes and address points raised with questions later or at the end.

Ask if there is anything else. One simple way to check if there is anything you missed in your interview is to ask your contact at the end. A simple question, like "Is there anything you'd like to add?", can often yield positive results.

Finish the interview. When you've finished, scan your notes quickly, looking for any holes in the information. If everything is okay, thank the subject for her time. It's also important to leave your subject with a sense of confidence in you and in what information she has shared. Confirm that the story will be sent for her approval, and provide a rough idea of how long that will take, based on previous approval experiences with your client. Give your phone number, in case she wishes to add or query anything. Always finish an interview on a positive note—you never know when your paths will cross again.

Perhaps the final word on the art of interviewing should go to "Doctor Ink" from the Poynter Institute, a highly regarded journalism school. Here's his formula for a successful interview:

1. Shut up.
2. Shut up some more.
3. Work from a list of questions, but veer off.
4. Shut up again.
5. Get there early, stay late.
6. Interview a person on his turf.
7. Ask for tours (of a photo album, book or music collection, memorabilia, set of golf clubs, wine cellar, favorite crack house, old neighborhood).
8. Write down things you see, not just answers to questions.
9. Use your notebook to show that you are conducting a formal interview.
10. Put your notebook away near the end, but keep talking.
11. If you've got time, hang around a person to watch and record his interactions with others.
12. Ask the most important questions more than once and in different forms.
13. Ask the "slam the door" questions last.
14. Shut up.
15. Fill out or copy your notes as quickly as possible.

CHAPTER 22

Strategies for Keeping the Creativity Flowing

You can't wait for inspiration.
You have to go after it with a club.

Jack London (1876–1916)

D on't you just love it when the words seem to flow effortlessly and eloquently? That's the time we all enjoy the job of being a writer, not those other times when you're racing against a deadline—when your brain is on hold, your body is numb, and the last thing you want to do is spend another minute staring at a computer screen. That's usually the time we consider some other occupation.

Trust Yourself

The problem might be writer's block (more on this in the next chapter), or it might be a different sort of dilemma: "What's the best way to explain this?" "Who really is the audience?" and "Is this argument going to convince anyone who doesn't already believe it?" Or you may just feel as if you've written yourself into a corner. "Trust yourself" is probably the last thing you want to hear at this time, but reminding yourself that you have all of the solutions to your creative problem puts you on the path to recovery.

You've been in this situation before, and you probably will face it again. When it comes, take time out. Take a mental deep breath and reassess your situation:

- What resources do you have available for the task (books, magazines, newspapers)?
- Which colleagues, family, or friends can best help you?
- Visit the library or surf the Net for ideas and inspiration.

And when you've done all that:

- Do something fun (this will shift your focus away from the problem).
- Interact with others (this will help ignite the creative process).
- Enjoy time alone (this will give you the chance to sift through ideas).

You can liken the first step to seeding your mind, as you would a newly plowed field. The second allows the seed to grow. This process is vital— if you plant roses, then roses will grow. If you plant cabbages, cabbages will grow. If you plant nothing, what will happen? Nothing? No. Weeds will grow, as will negativity, depression, and despair. The third step allows you time to sort the wheat from the chaff.

The key to creativity, for me, is to do something different. When I get stuck, the only way to break free is to change my approach, to change my thinking. And the best way to do that is to feed the mind with positive, new people, experiences, and ideas. This will assuredly jump-start your creativity again.

Make sure you are ready when the lightning strikes. Always have a notepad or laptop computer handy so you can capture the brilliance and return to work as soon as possible. My most recent example of this happened while writing this book.

I have written novels in the past but, when I decided I was going to write a different kind of book, my mind was feverish with activity. Within minutes I had ideas for not just one, but a dozen books. Within days, I had fleshed out each of them in my head. They were practically writing themselves. I outlined each of the subjects I wanted to cover and began writing. And that's when everything seized up.

My mental machinery, which had been greased with inspiration and anticipation only days before, was now stubbornly refusing to budge. Everything I wrote, I rejected. *There has to be a better way to start this book. There has to be a better way of expressing that idea. Maybe I should start another way. How about . . . What about . . .*

Before I knew it, no words were coming out, or none I would accept. So, how did I solve the problem? I stood back, surveyed the field, and decided to take a new approach to the project. By "stood back" I mean I stopped editing the words before they got onto the page. I simply let them come, trusting that what I wanted to say would ultimately find its way and I could revisit and revise later. I also took time out to relax. I took my focus off the problem and enjoyed life. I went for a walk (with pen and paper in hand). I picked up a book I had been meaning to read. I called some friends I hadn't spoken to in a while. I did anything I could to let the conscious mind cool off while the subconscious mind warmed up. By "surveyed the field" I mean I considered all of the resources I had available to me, and I reassessed the purpose of the book. I went back to the fundamental questions: Who is the audience? What am I trying to achieve with this book? What are the best ways of meeting my objectives?

Before long, the ideas came. The new approach allowed the right words to appear, and the book was on its way again. And that's what I've always done. I trust the creativity, and I know it will not fail me. This may sound a little esoteric for some, but if you don't have confidence in your ability to solve problems, then your subconscious can—and will—seed your mind with doubt.

Know Thyself

Two and a half millennia ago, Socrates discussed the importance and application of a simple moral maxim: "Know thyself." I believe this simple but profound wisdom also applies to our creative process. In order to stay vibrant and creative, in order to continue succeeding in any endeavor, we need confidence in ourselves and our abilities. But how can you have confidence in yourself if you don't know yourself?

I'm not talking about knowing your limitations, as so many people think they do. When it comes to our minds, I don't think anyone will ever know their true limitations, only the limitations they place upon themselves. What I'm talking about is knowing, remembering, and acknowledging all of the triumphs in your life. We are good at remembering the failures—especially when faced with a challenge in our lives—but what about all of the successes? If we think and act positively, we are tilling the soil of our mind, preparing it for more success.

Take any successful person you know, or one you've read about. The majority of successful people profess to having an inner confidence about their abilities and their future successes. They *know* what they can achieve and they *know* they will succeed again and again. That's not to say they don't experience fear from time to time—we all do—but they are able to conquer it, to *use* it to achieve their goals.

Dr. Maxwell Maltz made the point that the human mind cannot differentiate between real experience and one that is vividly imagined.[19] Great motivationalists, like Dr. Wayne Dyer, agree that if you can conceive it, you can achieve it.

We can all develop this ability by using what's been termed "possibility thinking." Daydream about what you'd like to achieve. See it in your mind's eye. Feel it, taste it, *know* that it is already part of your life and that it's within your power to tap into your talent and draw that success to you.

If you do this at the beginning of each day, you'll move closer to having the end result you want in your life. Again, this may be getting a little off base for some people. My point is simply that, in order to get the most out of your creative process, you need to cultivate it by thinking differently. If you want positive action in your life, you need to nourish your mind with positive thought:

- Set goals and work toward them
- Recite positive affirmations and mean them
- Visualize yourself achieving and "experience" the sensation of success

Try it. You might just surprise yourself.

CHAPTER 23

Tips, Tricks, and Tactics That Destroy Writer's Block

Close the door. Write with no one looking
over your shoulder. Don't try to figure out
what other people want to hear from you;
figure out what you have to say. It's the one
and only thing you have to offer.

Barbara Kingsolver (1955–)

Writer's block—that dreaded affliction that cripples most writers at some time in their lives. If you haven't experienced it yet, you'll know when it strikes, because you won't be able to write a thing. You won't feel like writing, you won't want to write, and you won't be able to write. And, if you're like most of us, that will leave you with a terrible, empty, sinking feeling inside.

Is writer's block real or is it some figment of the imagination? Whatever it is, it can become very real in our lives if we allow it. Writer's block can last a few minutes, hours, or days. For some writers, it can last for years. But it doesn't have to be that way or last that long.

Write, don't think

Writer's block comes in all shapes and sizes, but often the problem is not a lack of words but a lack of *good* words. The writer edits the words before they appear, and as a result, the words stop appearing altogether. Creativity grinds to a halt. Some have found a solution in writing anything. Even if you're writing, "I can't write anything. This is stupid. I can't write anything," at least the act of writing is in progress. If you continue with this procedure, sooner or later you will begin to write words worth reading.

Don't worry about what's coming out at this stage; just write for the sake of writing, and allow the creativity to begin to flow again.

If you need an audience, draft a letter to a friend, even if you begin by telling him or her that the reason you're writing the letter is because you can't complete your novel or can't finish an article. You can decide later to keep the letter or mail it. But, whatever you do, just write. Don't agonize and rationalize—just write.

Kick-start the words by brainstorming

Contrary to what I just stated, a lack of ideas or even enthusiasm about a project can quickly transform into writer's block. If this happens to you, apply the Mind Map principle outlined in chapter eleven. Think laterally about anything and everything related to your writing project. Don't judge (that's what got you into trouble in the first place), just let the ideas flow freely, listing them as you go. Before long, you'll be brimming with wonderful new thoughts and a newborn enthusiasm to get on with the task.

Find the cause and cure the effect

Writer's block is an emotional block that can be caused by any of a number of emotional issues. Finding the root cause of the block may give you the serum to reverse the block.

You may be blocked due to:

- Lack of confidence
- Fear of success
- Fear of failure
- Fear of the unknown (for example, a new writing project, style, subject, or genre)
- Disappointment with earlier work
- Physical or mental exhaustion

These are common problems, but maybe something else is the cause of your block. Do some soul-searching. Consider your work style before you started this project. What was different? Ask yourself what frightens you about this project. What's the worst thing that can happen to you if you begin writing? What's the worst thing that can happen to you when you finish writing? Once you have identified the core reason for the block, you can begin resolving it.

Tips, Tricks, and Tactics That Destroy Writer's Block

Change gears

Sometimes we get writer's block simply because we have been pushing the envelope too much, too often. As they say, a change is as good as a vacation. Maybe all you need is to shift gears and initiate a new writing project.

As we've discussed earlier, it makes good business sense to cultivate diverse writing talents so you can handle a variety of work. It also makes good sense from a productive and creative viewpoint. I've worked on a wide range of writing assignments for corporate clients to magazine and newspaper editors. The best tactic I've found is to work on something new when I'm blocked on something old.

Alternatively, if you're working on a difficult or technical project, you might take a break by attending to other duties in the office. Just spending an hour away from the project at hand can be enough to refresh that part of your mind that's been dedicated to the job. If the problem is bigger than that, then even more time away from the project seems to do the trick for me.

Another approach you can take is to alter your routine. Instead of always typing directly onto your computer, why not write in longhand first? You may find that this is enough to break the block. Or, instead of writing at your usual desk, why not take a pad out for a walk, find a comfortable park bench, and let your imagination take over?

Keep busy

Along the same line, it's important for you to keep busy. If you don't, you will dwell on your block and before long it will affect other areas of your life. Some writers say that when writer's block strikes they have an enormous amount of physical energy. If this happens to you, get out there and burn up that block. Physically exerting yourself is a natural way to relieve stress, and it's also a good way to take your mind off the issue that's stopping you from writing.

Talk it out

This is a technique I learned in my teens when I first became a newspaper journalist. If I came back to the office with a story but didn't know how to start it, I'd visit my Chief of Staff. All he had to do was ask me some basic questions, reporter-style, and I was back at that old Underwood typewriter, bashing out the story.

The same approach may work for you with any kind of writing project. Talking about it to someone can help you work through the problem. The person doesn't have to be a writer or even knowledgeable about the subject. Simply talking it out can be enough to get the creative juices flowing again.

Visualize your reader

You may initially be writing for you, but you will have a wider audience. Think about your reader, and imagine talking with them as you begin writing. Having this one-on-one relationship with your reader cannot only help resolve the block, it can also help improve your writing as a whole.

Remind yourself how good you are

Sometimes just a little encouragement from your biggest fan is enough to get you moving in the right direction. Read some of your best writing. Rediscover how good you are at your craft. Relive what you've achieved and remind yourself what you can achieve with this new piece you're working on.

Tell yourself how good you are

As we discussed in the previous chapter, positive affirmations are a good way to engender feelings of self-worth.

Instead of dwelling on the problem at hand, recite a series of positive affirmations at the start of each day and at the end of each night. Affirmations should always be positive (never include negative words, even when they're designed to be positive, e.g. "I don't worry about writer's block) and should be said in the present tense, as if you already have the ability or gift you are seeking. Here are some samples for you to try:

- I am a great writer.
- I am successful because I enjoy what I do.
- I love writing.
- I am a successful writer and people applaud my expertise.
- My writing is creative, productive, and profitable.

You can use these or make up your own. Say them loud, and say them with conviction. Mean what you say and allow them to come true in your life.

Imagine how good you are

We are visual creatures, by nature, so use your visual skills to enhance the image you have of yourself. Find a place where you will not be disturbed. Close your eyes. Visualize yourself as a successful writer. See yourself writing with ease. Picture yourself autographing copies of your new novel. Imagine yourself speaking at your book launch. Experience the joy of being praised by editors and paid well by clients. See yourself relaxing wherever you wish, writing at whim, and loving every moment of it. The images are up to you.

Repeat this pleasurable personal ritual before you go to sleep and when you wake up. Make it a regular part of your working day. Start with this visual exercise followed by positive affirmations and, before long, you'll find your fingers can't wait to get at the keyboard.

Call it a day

The writer's block will *not* persist. But if it lingers for a day or two, don't fight it. Call it a day and start fresh tomorrow. The old French proverb "sleep brings counsel" is true for us writers as well. Sleep on your writer's block. You may be surprised at what presents itself in the morning.

CHAPTER 24

Finding the Right Time to Write

There is no perfect time to write.
There's only now.

Barbara Kingsolver (1955–)

Chris is a good friend and fellow writer who used to share a house with me when we were both bachelors. He's the first person to tell you he keeps a pretty messy house, and I'm the first one to agree. Put politely, he's a casual guy who prefers to put his energies into more important areas.

But, when it comes time to start an important piece of writing, getting the first words down is usually the last thing on his mind. Let me put it this way—Chris's place becomes immaculate overnight. You can actually make out the original color of the carpet. The tabletops gleam. The house smells wonderful. And I'm almost ready to call *House & Garden*. But when he's full-steam-ahead writing a new book, you can't stop the guy. When he says, "I'll be there in five minutes," you'll end up waiting five hours. It's as though he's been lost in the Bermuda Triangle.

The funny thing is that there is a Chris in each writer. Have you done anything and everything you could before you settled down to write? I have. It happens to me most mornings. What about once you're really into a project—do you find that five hours fly by as fast as five minutes? I often do. In fact, it happened to me repeatedly while writing this book.

Finding that rhythm is another key to successful writing, and the key to finding that rhythm is in developing a ritual to your writing day. It doesn't matter whether you write every day or only when you can: Develop one or more rituals or routines to your writing life. You'll find you'll get into the rhythm much more quickly and more often.

A few writers like to begin their day with a quiet walk or contemplation, some prefer to complete house duties before they feel they're free to write, and other writers like to hit the ground running by writing as soon as they're out of bed and still in their pajamas. Whatever ritual or routine works best for you, here are some ideas you can apply to help enhance your productivity.

Avoid distractions

It's easy to get caught up in snail mail or e-mail. It's easy to find something more "urgent" to do than writing. Let's face it, the cat needs to have her teeth cleaned regularly, and that lawn is looking a little long. Before you know it, the best part of the day is gone and, along with it, most of your creative fire. So avoid the temptation, and start the day with a regular dose of writing.

Many people find that first thing in the morning offers the best results for fresh, creative writing. Once you've got a couple of hours under your belt, you can elect to continue if the mood takes you, or eat breakfast and attend to other duties. I go one step further: I tape any must-see television shows, transfer all e-mails to a separate folder, and put aside my daily mail and newspapers *until* I have finished the writing tasks which I've set for the day.

At the time I am writing this, it is 4:35 P.M. I haven't properly dressed yet. It didn't seem important when I started in the wee hours of the morning. I also haven't read my mail, watched television, or relaxed in general. I've got the rhythm, so why waste it? Apart from staying more focused, I also achieve a lot more in my writing day. A lot of the must-see television and must-read mail isn't that important, especially when you're getting around to it at the end of the day or the end of the week.

When I am deeply involved in an important piece with a strict deadline, I add the answering machine to my inventory of distraction-beaters. I can save a lot of time by screening calls or not answering the phone, if I am that busy. Unless it's extremely urgent, there's always tomorrow, but not so for my writing—there's just *today*.

Know your ritual and enjoy it

If your ritual is to read the newspaper so you know what's going on in the world, then so be it. Know it and enjoy it. And also know that once the ritual is complete, you are now ready for work.

Rituals are an important part in every worker's life. They're like warm-up exercises for an athlete. For some, the ritual is traveling to work, for others tasting their first coffee or just having a shower and getting dressed. Whatever it is, it's a necessary part of your preparation for work. If, however, you are finding that your morning ritual erodes your working day, then it's time to alter the process. Find a better way of preparing for the onslaught.

Seize the moment

I find that I'm thinking about the day as I am waking from sleep. Once I'm up, I meditate for half an hour, working on the goals I've set in my life. Soon after, I'm in bedroom number two (my office), hard at work.

I review my WIP for the day (which was completed the night before) and begin working on the most urgent or most difficult task for the day. I find that if I attack the "imperative" tasks while I am fresh, I generally complete them quicker and more easily than if I leave them until later in the day. Then I start on "important" tasks. If I leave any urgent, important, or even general writing tasks too long, I find that the creative fire has waned and it's almost impossible to rekindle the flame. But if I begin the day writing, I can usually continue through the day unhindered, with the furnace fully stoked with words.

How to Make the Time to Write

Time is the most valuable resource to a writer, yet it's arguably the single most under-used or abused element in many writers' lives. The obvious facts are that you need to devote time to your craft. You need to make it a priority. I shouldn't have to say this, since you already know it, but many writers still ignore it.

Here are some ways of getting you and your craft back on the same page.

Make writing a priority

Decide how much time you can devote to writing, and dedicate that time solely to the task. That means no interruptions from family, friends, housework, or hobbies. Your business is writing. This is your time to write, so use it wisely.

Set challenging but attainable goals

Part of the reason some writers lose their way is because they have no direction to start with. They have hopes and dreams and wishes, but they have not set any goals in their writing lives. Whether you are writing a press release, sales letter, or something more substantial, like a video script, you can complete it more quickly by adopting this commonsense approach.

Draft an outline covering all of the major points, then divide it into bite-sized chunks, thinking about and working on it point by point, rather than considering the whole communication. If you reduce a project to a series of steps, the project does not seem as large and overwhelming.

Another way of accomplishing writing goals is to set a daily target. Try something that's not easy but possible. It may be 100 words in a sitting or 1,000 words in a day. Once you get comfortable hitting this target, raise your sights a little higher. When you have a genuine expectation of achieving these goals, you'll be amazed at the progress you will make with your writing.

Write when it feels right to you

As we've already discussed, some people like to start the day writing. But you may find that your most productive time is after hours when the phone has stopped ringing and the children are asleep. Identify the best time for you and stick with it.

CHAPTER 25

The Final Word on Writing

There's one thing your writing must have to be any good at all.
It must have you. Your soul, your self, your heart, your guts,
your voice—you must be on every page. In the end,
you can't make the magic happen for your reader. You can only
allow the miracle of "being one with" to take place. So dare to be
yourself. Dare to reveal yourself. Be honest, be open, be true . . . If
you are, everything else will fall into place.

Elizabeth Ayres

I wrote this book to help you develop a profitable life as a writer. By profitable, I mean more than making money. I mean enjoying a real lifestyle. It's easy for any of us to get caught up in the daily affairs of our business. It's easy to let work spill from a 9 to 5 schedule to a 24/7 obsession. The hard part, for some, is knowing when and how to let go. I was one of those people. And, I admit, I still wrestle with it from time to time.

Balancing Your Business and Personal Lives

Here are some final thoughts on how you can find balance between your business life and your personal life.

Setting limits for work

The Peter Principle tells us that work expands to fill the time available. There was a time some years back when I was working not just seven days a week but several nights a week as well. It was a subtle defense mechanism. There was a lot going on in my life at the time, so it was easier to bury myself in paperwork than deal with my personal issues. And that's the "great thing" about working for yourself. There's always something to do. There's always bookkeeping and filing to do, strategies to develop, reports to write, and fires to put out. There's always an excuse to work late.

But you have a *choice*. Consider all of the things you really *have* to do today. Are they urgent? Can they wait until tomorrow or maybe next week? Will your business suffer? Will your reputation be tarnished forever? Probably not.

Remember what Mark Twain once said: "I am an old man. I have had many worries in my life. Most of which never happened." But I can guarantee that if you don't take time out for you and your family, then *all* of these worries will happen.

As Dr. Wayne Dyer says, you have a choice in life: enjoy vacations or endure hospital visits. So, setting limits means treating your playtime as seriously as you do your work time. When you invest in your leisure, you not only appreciate it more, you also will function better during your work periods.

Decide to go away for a weekend with loved ones. Plan a couple of nights out. Set aside time to read that book you've been wanting to finish or maybe take up a course in cooking, art, or something else that interests you.

At the very least, allow for one full day off a week. Sunday or Saturday seems to be a good day to take off for most people, just because family and friends are likely to have the day off, too.

If you're still having trouble with this concept of setting aside time for work and play, think of it this way. If you don't give yourself adequate time off, you are doing a disservice not just to yourself but to your business. You will get stale, and so will your business. If you still find it difficult, see time off as a form of maintenance or service on yourself to ensure you are in peak performance for the next work period.

Taking annual leave

Again, I know it's hard to take off a week or two when you represent the entire staff of your business. But it's important to your ongoing vitality, so take a vacation when your business requires your presence least.

Every industry has downtimes. For me, since I primarily work in the corporate market, that time is Christmas. In Australia, traditionally businesses shut down for two, three, or four weeks over the festive season, which is also our summer. That's usually the time I have available to close the office, and it gives me the chance to not only have a break from working but also to reassess where I am headed in the new year.

To make the transition as smooth as possible for all parties, give your clients as much notice as possible. Send them a card advising when your business will be closed. Give them at least a month's warning so you can complete tasks due over that time or defer projects until you return.

If you've got into the habit of never taking an annual break, you may think it's impossible for you to do so now. But it's not. It's just a matter of an attitude change. Let's face it, virtually every one of your clients is absent for vacations at some point during the year, and business continues, so why not the same for you?

Paying back the time

There are, of course, times when you just can't tear yourself away from the office. Maybe you're on deadline or a client has dropped a big project on you and it's due on Monday. If you have to work the whole weekend, then work it. But try to make up for it later. Take a day or two off the following week or enjoy a long weekend later in the month. Think of it as a reward for all of the hard work you've been putting in. This is something you should do, not just for yourself, but for your family.

Delegating to save time

When you are running a successful writing business, you don't have the time to undertake all of the menial tasks you used to, but you do have the money to delegate them to someone else.

When my business is running at a blistering pace, there are two household chores that are delegated. The first is gardening. I have never developed a green thumb and have never got much joy out of pushing a lawn mower around in circles. So, when business is good, that chore goes to a mowing service. I justify it this way: I can earn up to $125 an hour in my business. Lawn mowing costs a fraction of that. It doesn't take an Einstein to work out the logic in handing the mower to someone else. When business is quiet, then I resume my gardening chores. I tell myself it gives me a chance to get back in touch with nature, flex some muscles, and breathe good, clean air. That works most of the time.

I use the same philosophy in my working life. When I have serious troubles with my technology, I hire a technician to come out and fix it. I used to spend hours—which turned into days—trying to fix my computers. Now, it costs a bit, but the problem is fixed the same day. My justification is that technology is the lifeblood of my business. I cannot go a day without it working properly, so I delegate the job to a professional.

Exploring life beyond your four walls

There's a whole world out there beyond your office. I know, I saw it once on *Discovery*. Seriously, it's easy to rely on all of the technology that surrounds you—phone, fax, e-mail, and the Internet. But, just as we get stale from working too much, we also get stale from being cooped up inside. Get out. Make it a daily habit, even if it's just a half-hour walk or catching up for a coffee or lunch with friends, colleagues, or clients. Make the effort. You will feel and act more refreshed when you do.

Treating your staff well

Remember, you are your business's entire work force. You are management and staff, all rolled into one. If you had staff, as I have in previous years, you would treat them well. You would look out for their interests, make sure you weren't pushing them too hard, and ensure that any grievances were addressed promptly. So why not take the same approach with yourself? Be a good boss to yourself and you will be rewarded with higher staff productivity, a lower attrition rate, and greater job satisfaction.

Remembering you are one of the lucky ones

How many people do you know who love what they do for a living? I can only think of a few—and they're all writers. Yes, you and I are the lucky ones. We have chosen a profession, not for the money, not for the lifestyle, not for the prestige, but for the pure love of it. We enjoy what others call work. Always remember how fortunate you are to enjoy this labor of love. I continually remind myself, and it's made this current project that much easier and more enjoyable.

My Final Say

Well, dear reader, we have covered some territory. I hope you have enjoyed the journey as much as I have. Before I go, I would like to offer you one final piece of advice. Before you launch your writing business or take it to the next level, just sit here for a moment and think rather than act.

No doubt a lot has happened to you since you began reading this book. A lot of ideas have been created. Some attitudes have been shifted. And, I hope, a lot of enthusiasm has been ignited within you. It's because of this that you should reread the first two sections of this book, "Getting Started" and "Getting Organized." As you know, they lay the foundation for a solid enterprise.

No doubt you're tempted to just leap into your business, but I strongly recommend you hold off for a moment. Reread these sections first, but don't stop there. Reevaluate where your career is going and how you're going to take it there. Rewrite what you have drafted in your business plan and operations manual. Remember what I said to you at the beginning of this journey. The more time and careful thought you invest now, the more you will be rewarded throughout the course of your business life.

Thank you for coming along for the ride, and I wish you every success in your new journey ahead as a *Wealthy Writer*.

FAQs (FREQUENTLY ASKED QUESTIONS)

Here are some frequently asked questions put to me in media interviews and seminars:

Talking Personally

What inspires you as a writer?

Life. Ever since I can remember I have looked at the world in wonder. I have wondered why things are, I have wondered about my place in the world, and I have wondered how I can help myself and others make this a better place in which to live. Much of my writing reflects this. I get terrific ideas for characters and stories merely by observing life—seeing people interact at a train station, a shopping center, or virtually anywhere. Inspiration is all around us, if only we would stop and take note.

How did you get your first break as a freelance writer?

I had published material in newspapers and magazines soon after finishing high school, but I didn't get serious about freelancing until I endured a couple of dead-end sales jobs. Then, at the ripe age of eighteen, I decided to freelance full time. Fortunately, I was living with my parents at the time, so money wasn't the highest priority. Like everything, the hardest part was getting started.

In the beginning, publications wouldn't hire me because I didn't have any experience. So I would just continue to write and submit stories, and continue to gain rejection slips, week after week. Then I got a breakthrough with a local newspaper and I wrote a series of conservation-based articles. After a while, my articles started to get picked up in national magazines and my focus spread to other topics.

The following year I got a full-time job as a newspaper reporter and later sub-editor for a regional daily newspaper. From there, I became a columnist, feature writer, and journalist for various newspapers and national magazines. But, throughout that time, I continued to freelance.

What was the first article you sold and to whom?

I believe it was a personality piece on some celebrity of the day to *People* magazine. They paid me some enormous amount of money, which was more than I earned in a week in my "real job."

I recall hearing about the article while at work in my first sales job.

Someone bought the magazine and pinned the tear sheet to the company notice board. It was an amazing thing to see. For the first time, I felt I had been validated as a writer, and the fact that many of my co-workers knew added to the impact. Everyone who knew me then knew I didn't belong in that job—and that magazine article proved it to them *and* to me.

I didn't receive a check for a couple of weeks, but it was a great feeling. I remember seeing the publication logo on the front of the envelope and tearing it open in excitement to discover how much they paid me. In those days, I was too timid to ask about freelance rates, let alone negotiate with a magazine, so the amount they paid me (I have no idea how much, but it was a lot at the time) both surprised and shocked me. A moment later, my mind was working out how much I could earn if I freelanced full time.

How long did it take you to write The Wealthy Writer?

It took about six months to write but more than twenty years to research. That's the sum total of my life as a professional writer, and many of my experiences, lessons and, hopefully, a little wisdom gained from those years are in the book.

What idea sparked the writing of this book?

Everything I learn I pass on to others. I am very grateful to the mentors in my life, as they have made the learning curve easier for me. Helping others is the best way I know of repaying those who helped me.

I had the idea for this book some years ago after working with a number of professional writers. I have spent more than half my literary career running my own business, hiring both full-time and freelance writers. Some, like me, had a newspaper and magazine journalism background, others came from television and radio, and a few came from corporate marketing. In many cases, I hired people who had ten or twenty years or more in the industry and, with that, far more experience and skills. Some writers had worked on well-known and internationally respected publications, and some had enjoyed top salaries working for large corporations.

The point is that most of these professional writers had the credentials, track record, and ability to be major successes in their own writing businesses. And yet, without exception, none had risen to great heights working for themselves.

This got me thinking—"What am I doing that they are not doing?"—

and the germ for *The Enterprising Writer* (the original title for *The Wealthy Writer*) was born. It essentially formalizes what I have been doing for a number of years.

Did you make some tough decisions before making it in business?

Yes. I think that if you want to be a success at anything, you need to focus on what works and discard what doesn't. In my case, it wasn't a matter of just focusing on writing but focusing on the *right* kind of writing.

When I got my first full-time job as a reporter on a regional daily, I also became the paper's film critic. It was a lot of fun, and I didn't mind seeing and reviewing a few films a week in my spare time. But that experience led to other opportunities to review videos, music, and then books. Before long, I was spending a good portion of my spare time "researching" and writing weekly reviews. This didn't worry me at the time, because I was learning my craft, enjoying the fruits of my labor, and also interviewing celebrities and attending gala events.

When I took a job as a subeditor for a group of interstate newspapers, I also continued my moonlighting as an entertainment critic. By then, I was working a forty-hour job and spending at least another forty hours a week writing reviews, attending functions, and freelancing for other newspapers and magazines. It was exciting but time consuming, and it took me several years to figure out that my time could be better spent elsewhere. Once I finally cut the ties, I was able to move on to a better job and focus my freelance energies in more profitable areas.

It can be difficult to let go of things that have been a part of your life, even when you know your energies should be channeled elsewhere. That's why it's important to have clearly defined goals. To be a success at anything, you need to know what you truly want and what you are prepared to do to get it.

Talking Business

How can a writer win clients when he is starting a career in commercial writing?

When starting out, the goal is to develop a folio of work. This is chicken-and-egg stuff. You need a folio to gain work and you need work to develop a folio. So to get started, approach people you know in business—they can be family or friends. Offer your services at a low cost or, if you have to, at no cost. I am not suggesting you make a career out of working for free. I am only saying take this approach if you cannot find paid work. If you don't know of anyone in business, try various volunteer organizations, churches, and social groups. It's important to remind yourself that you are in a training phase, and that usually comes at a cost. In this case, the cost could be working for a reduced rate.

Once you have completed one or more jobs, seek testimonials from your clients. This will help support your growing folio and give potential clients confidence in your work. Once you have been in business for a while, you may find that you receive referrals and testimonials without even asking for them. That's what happens to me. This is generally far more powerful than asking for them, and it's a great vote of confidence in your abilities.

Now it's time to check out the job classifieds—not just for journalists, freelance, PR, or marketing writers—but for any sales and marketing roles. If a company is expanding its sales force, it will more than likely need marketing collateral, an ongoing PR program, or maybe just some overload services. Be proactive—write to the Marketing Manager, CEO, Managing Director, or Sales Manager (whoever is more appropriate), offering your services. But don't wait by the phone; call them within a few days of mailing the letter.

You have written for a wide range of disciplines. Do you think most freelance writers need to be multidisciplined to make a living?

Yes. I think it's good for your bank balance *and* your sanity. Also, it pays to try your hand at a number of areas—how do you know if you like a specific area or if you are any good at it if you have never experienced it?

Some freelance markets can dry up with little notice, so it pays to have other strings in your bow. In commercial writing, for example, I have written press releases, speeches, direct mail letters, and ads for radio and print. Each is considered a specific writing discipline. By being able to write for each of these disciplines, I instantly increase potential markets for my literary services. Also, once I begin working for a client in one area, it's not too difficult to expand and offer them a complete marketing communications service. This is something that larger agencies are offering now—integrated marketing. It's something I have been doing for several years, and I think it's one of the least-tapped strategies available to freelancers today.

In addition to writing various marketing communications, it also pays to expand your areas of industry expertise. I am experienced in a number of industries, so that means I have a smaller learning curve than another commercial writer approaching a new client in a specific industry.

That's where the sanity part comes in. Writing is an exciting occupation, and I think everyone reading this would agree. But if you are writing about power tools all day, every day, you will soon get stale and lose interest. That's why it's important to develop a number of industry interests, so you can swap accounts when it suits you.

It's not unusual for me to start the day working on a press release, then brainstorm for an ad, and maybe flesh out some ideas for a brochure or newsletter. That's not every day, of course. Some days I'll spend the whole time working on one project for one client, but I know there will be something different to do for someone else later in the week. That's what keeps things interesting and challenging.

How do you manage your disparate writing commitments?

That can sometimes be a tricky thing, but I have a method that has saved my sanity over the years.

Almost every client I have at some point needs a project completed "yesterday." It's just a matter of determining what really must be done now, prioritizing the other assignments, and negotiating sensible deadlines for completing each task. The key is sticking to my external *and* internal deadlines. The external deadline is the official one that I agree on with my client. The company may want a communication completed by Friday. I will then set an internal deadline of finishing the work by Wednesday or Thursday, at the latest. This internal deadline (which only I know about) gives me a little breathing space should something go wrong or I miscalculate the time needed. It's a simple but effective method for managing my time and my work, and ensuring my clients are satisfied. I live my commercial life by the maxim "meeting needs and exceeding expectations." And that's the main reason clients tell me they keep coming back. They don't want to know about excuses, only solutions. Internal deadlines offer me insurance against unforeseen delays.

Another way I handle disparate jobs is to use my downtime effectively. I enjoy a walk most evenings after work. I usually listen to an interesting interview or program or just some music, but I always take a tape recorder with me as well. Walking is one of the best brainstorming and mind-sorting exercises I know. It gives me a chance to get out of the office I also call home, and it gives me a chance to put everything into perspective.

Also, if I am working on a project and I feel myself getting bogged down, often I will take a break. I will take my notes to the park and sit and think. Before long, the problem is sorted out and I madly dash back to the office to put it down on screen.

What are the best marketing tools writers can use to promote themselves and attract business clients?

When I first launched my freelance writing business, I didn't have a lot of money to spend on marketing, but also I didn't need to spend a lot. I relied mainly on direct mail letters—sending letters to prospects—and it remains the main marketing tool I use today when needed.

In my view, direct mail and PR (by this, I mean, writing newsworthy articles that promote your business) are far more effective for freelance writers than conventional advertising. There's room to explain what you do and how you do it while building rapport with the prospect.

Direct mail is the best tool I know for generating business. First, it is extremely inexpensive to produce communications. Apart from your initial time in developing a letter, which can be duplicated or adapted to suit other prospects, your costs are simply postage stamps, stationery, and telephone calls to follow up the letters.

Second, direct mail is far more effective than cold calling, too. Consider that even before you pick up the phone, you have introduced yourself to a business and demonstrated your abilities as a professional writer as well as the benefits you can offer them. Once you begin working with some clients, you can seek referrals. This is also a simple but powerful tool for expanding your business. Whether your client is a marketing manager, an editor, or an agency director, they have friends and colleagues in the business and in different industries, and these are potential clients who will be more responsive to your inquiry following a personal recommendation.

Writers shouldn't be shy in asking for referrals. Satisfied clients are only too willing to help spread the word for you—but only if you ask them. Some will take the initiative, but it's best if you suggest it. I've generated a lot of business through referrals. In fact, I would say that referrals account for the majority of new business I have won. It's the cheapest form of marketing you can do—all it takes is providing exemplary customer service (which you should be doing anyway) and a few words in the right ear of the right client.

Why did you change from journalism to business writing?

I had gone as high as I could go as a journalist in terms of seniority. I had worked as a staff reporter, subeditor, and columnist for various newspapers along the east coast of Australia. From there, I worked as an editor for a stable of national business magazines, and that's where I got my first taste for commercial writing.

One day, I was reading a collection of news releases received from PR agencies and I thought, I can write these far better. That was part of my job anyway—to turn these thinly veiled advertisements into something worth printing. Often, I would sit on the phone, interviewing the PR agency's client, to discover the real "meat" of the story. Before long, the PR agencies' clients were praising my stories.

At twenty-five, and with the prospect of settling down in a few months, I was ready for a new challenge at work. That was when I decided to move from the mainstream media to public relations and marketing. I thought I would have immediate success by applying a fresh, journalistic approach to puffed-up PR releases, and I did; in fact, I also got more than I bargained for.

I got a job with a small agency. By small I mean it was myself, the boss (an ex-journalist like myself), and a receptionist. I don't begrudge my start in PR and marketing. I got a far better hands-on grounding in these disciplines than many colleagues I know who worked for the major agencies. Because the business was so small, I had to handle a wide range of activities and work across a variety of accounts. It was hard work, but it was a lot of fun. It's actually one of my most memorable experiences before starting my own consultancy a few years later.

I learned PR and marketing communications from an ex-journalist, so my news releases were written often as hard news and often printed verbatim. I still think and write PR as a journalist. I think it's the only way you're going to keep your clients in print. Before I got into PR, however,

I freelanced for an advertising agency, producing some direct mail, point-of-sale, and other material. That's where I got my first taste of the difference in writing PR copy vs. ad copy. Again, the small agency I worked for handled not just PR but also direct mail and advertising—virtually any kind of marketing—which broadened my skills.

Making It Happen

What advice do you have for fledging writers?

I have two pieces of advice:

First, never give up. That's not new advice, but it's the best I can offer. It's what has sustained me throughout the years and it's what will ultimately see me achieve my goals.

Talent is one thing, but drive is another. You can learn both, I believe, but the hungry writer will beat the talented writer every time in my book.

In fact, when I hire people in my business, either as full timers or as freelancers, I invariably choose hungry writers because I know they will give me their best, and then some.

The second piece of advice is about turning your dreams into reality. I don't care if you have been writing for five minutes or five years. If you have a dream, now is the time to turn it into a goal. Draw a line in the sand and commit yourself. Set a deadline for launching that full-time career, reaching a certain salary, or whatever you desire. Then set bite-sized goals—write a certain number of words a day, send out and follow up ten query letters a week, set a specific revenue target, and work toward it each week or month. Use these as stepping-stones to achieving the larger goal.

How can writers turn their hobbies into professions?

I think the most important thing writers should do is remind themselves that their hobby *is* their profession.

I have a lot of friends who are writers. Some are professionals, like me, some are amateurs who keep a journal and write the occasional article, and some are wannabes who dream for the day when they can see their name in print.

The problem I find, even with some of the professionals, is that they really don't see their writing as their profession. They don't use the right tools; they have not set themselves up in business; they do not prospect for work; they do not investigate and follow through properly on opportunities, and so on. Whether you sell cars or words for a living, there are certain things you need to do to be taken seriously in business—not just by your clients, but by you, too.

You need to find an office, even if it's a bedroom or an alcove in your home. You need to set up a business. You need to invest in the right tools so you can accomplish your tasks. Then you need to prospect for work, develop a folio, collect testimonials, and seek referrals. Then you need to build your business, expand your services, and your client list.

Putting a sign outside and waiting by the phone isn't enough in any business, especially this one. You need to be hungry for work. You need to be thick-skinned. You need to prove to yourself and others that you are a professional writer. And most of all, you need to stick with it. Don't quit. Keep writing. Keep reading. Keep believing in yourself and "seeing" yourself as a successful writer.

How can others fulfill their dreams?

I think you need three things to achieve any dreams:

1. Passion
2. Persistence
3. Confidence

You need to passionately want something. We all have dreams, but how many of us are willing to do anything to achieve them—forgo a secure job, move to a new state, give up security in our lives? I did all three to get what I wanted.

You also need to be persistent. Some people pursue their dreams all morning and sometimes continue throughout the week. Well, it has taken me over two decades to achieve my dream of having a book published. Sure, I self-published *The Enterprising Writer* a few years ago, but it's not the same as a print publisher that has invested thousands of dollars and a lot of effort to make this book appear on book shelves around the country.

And, as I said, it didn't come overnight. It took more than twenty years of continually honing my skills and perfecting my craft as a writer. It took twenty years of developing the experience in order to write this book.

That brings me to my third element—confidence. You have to have confidence in your ability to acquire your dream. I always knew I would be a writer; it's something I wanted to do when I was twelve, and it was something I started to do professionally at seventeen. My dream, back then, was to be a full-time author. I am not there yet, but I am well on my way, because I had confidence in my ability and in the validity of my dream.

What success principles can others apply to their lives?

I think the best way to achieve your dreams is to:

- Set and work toward goals
- Visualize a successful outcome
- Meditate and focus on your goals and your success

This is what I did, and continue to do today.

I have short and long-term goals. Things I want to achieve today, and dreams I want to realize in a year or ten years time. If you don't know where you want to be in a year, five years, or ten years, how can you expect to achieve your dreams? But it's not enough to have goals—they have to be clearly defined in your mind. I find the best way to set a goal is on paper.

We all know that human beings are visual creatures. When we read books, we conjure powerful images in our mind's eye, just as we do when we dream at night. And that's what you should do when you set goals. You should visualize the successful outcome.

If you want to be a writer, imagine yourself writing and imagine your creativity flowing from the keyboard each and every day. But don't stop there. See yourself receiving lucrative contracts and fat checks from clients. Picture your work winning awards. Visualize yourself enjoying all of the benefits that go with being a successful freelance writer—driving a new car, vacationing around the world, buying a big house, or whatever works for you.

And that brings me to the third point, meditation. I meditate each and every day, morning and night. I do it for a number of reasons. It improves my health and my well-being. It gives me a structure for the day and allows me to focus on what's important rather than getting sidetracked. It also is an integral part of the visualization process. When I am meditating for half an hour just before sunrise and just before going to bed, I imagine the goal I have set. I imagine the successful outcome of the goal. And I *revel* in it.

GLOSSARY

The following terms have been used in this book:

B2B: an abbreviation for "business to business" marketing.

B2C: an abbreviation for "business to consumer" marketing.

Download: to copy a file (text, graphic, sound, or video) from a Web site to your computer.

Dot-com: online business (e.g., www.yourcompany.com).

DM: an abbreviation for "direct mail."

E-book: a book that can be read online, on computer, or on handheld devices. They can also be printed.

E-publisher: an electronic publisher of e-books or other materials.

E-zines: electronic newsletters and magazines that can be downloaded from Web sites or e-mailed. Most are freely available to subscribers.

FAQ: an abbreviation for "frequently asked questions." Most major Web sites include a link to FAQs and relevant answers.

Forum: a haven where users can share information, files, and links. Forums can be accessed via the Web or e-mail.

HTML: HyperText Markup Language. This is the most common programming language for presenting online documents and creating Web sites.

Hyperlink: a dynamic link that connects one document to another or transfers to another Web site. By clicking on any highlighted words, your Web browser will take you to the appropriate linked file.

Inverted pyramid: a term that refers to the journalistic style of writing. Stories are structured so that the information is presented in order of importance. This approach has also become the most effective form of communication for online news articles and Web site copy.

Marcom: an abbreviation for "marketing communications."

Marketing collateral: an industry term for marketing material of a variety of types.

Newbie: Cyber-speak for "new user."

Opt-in e-mail or e-zine: communications you receive as a result of subscribing by volunteering your e-mail address.

PDF: Portable Document Format, a term coined by Adobe, which has become the industry de facto standard for producing electronic documents, such as e-books.

Press kit: a packet of promotional materials made available to the press, including a news release and one or more other items, such as photos, background releases, samples, brochures, CDs or DVDs, etc.

Spammer: an individual or company who sends someone "spam," or unsolicited e-mail. This practice is illegal in parts of the U.S., Europe, and Australia.

Syndicate: when referring to an individual writer or agency, this term means to send one's press release or story to a number of newspapers, periodicals, or other media.

Traffic: when referring to the Internet, traffic represents the number of visitors to a Web site.

URL: Uniform Resource Locator, Internet-speak for the address or directory path of a Web site or a specific file on a Web site (e.g., www.meanwellstore.com/about.htm).

Web site: a collection of Web pages, which may comprise text, images, graphics, and other files.

WIIFM: "What's in it for me?"

NOTES

1. *Wired News*, April 22, 2000: Interview with Melanie Rigney, former editor of *Writer's Digest*. Published online at www.wired.com/news/print/0,1294,35722,00.html (accessed February 2, 2004).

2. Among them Hal Mather, author of *How to Profitably Delight Your Customers* (Boca Raton, FL: CRC Press, 1999).

3. Peter Kent, *Making Money in Technical Writing* (New York: Macmillan USA, 1998).

4. Dr. Jakob Nielsen and John Morkes discuss this in their paper, "Concise, SCANNABLE, and Objective: How to Write for the Web" (1997), published online at www.useit.com/papers/webwriting/writing.html (accessed February 2, 2004).

5. Nielsen and Morkes, "Concise, SCANNABLE, and Objective: How to Write for the Web," cited above at note 3.

6. See Amy Gahran's Web siteat www.contentious.com.

7. Dr. Jakob Nielsen, "How Users Read on the Web" (October 1, 1997), published online at www.useit.com/alertbox/whyscanning.html (accessed February 2, 2004).

8. Nielsen/NetRatings (March 2003), published online at www.netratings.com, states that the average time a U.S. Web user spends exactly one minute reading one Web page from home and work. Most other western countries included in the survey reported lower average times, with Japan the lowest, at 0:34 per Web page.

9. Nielsen, "How Users Read on the Web," cited above at note 7.

10. A 2002 survey conducted by the Jenkins Group, an independent Michigan publisher.

11. Jim R. Macnamara, Councilor of the International Public Relations Association, "The Impact of PR on the Media" (2001), published online at www.masscom.com. (accessed February 2, 2004).

12. Dr. Kirk Hallahan, "A Short Chronology of Communication," published online in the course materials for students at http://lamar.colost ate.edu/~hallahan/jt100.htm (accessed February 2, 2004).

13. Tony Buzan developed the principles of the Mind Map in the late 1960s and has written several books on the subject. One of the best is one of his latest, *How to Mind Map: Make the Most of Your Mind and Learn to Create, Organize and Plan* (London: Thorsons, 2003).

14. Joe Vitale, "The 21 Most Powerful Copywriting Rules of All Time," published online at www.mrfire.com (accessed February 2, 2004).

15. Richard V. Benson, *Secrets of Successful Direct Mail* (Lincolnwood, IL: NTC 1991).

16. Ann Heide and Dale Henderson, *The Technological Classroom: A Blueprint for Success* (Toronto: Irwin Publishing, 1994).

17. David Sher and Martin Sher, *How to Collect Debts and Still Keep Your Customers* (New York: AMACOM Books, 1999).

18. At the time of writing, the following twelve U.S. states require all-party notification regarding electronic recording of conversations and interviews: California, Connecticut, Florida, Illinois, Massachusetts, Maryland, Michigan, Montana, New Hampshire, Nevada, Pennsylvania, and Washington. For further information, contact an attorney.

19. Dr. Maxwell Maltz, *Psycho-Cybernetics* (New York: Pocket Books, 1989).

FURTHER READING

Abrams, Rhonda; Kleiner, Eugene: *The Successful Business Plan: Secrets and Strategies* (Palo Alto, CA: The Planning Shop, 2003)—A comprehensive, step-by-step guide that covers all facets of establishing a business, including budgeting, forecasting, marketing, and ongoing operations.

Alred, Gerald; Brusaw, Charles; Oliu, Walter: *The Business Writer's Handbook* (New York: St. Martin's, 2003)—A no-nonsense reference that addresses the mechanics of writing various business communications.

Benson, Richard V.: *Secrets of Successful Direct Mail* (Lincolnwood, IL: NTC, 1991)—Authoritative reference which includes thirty-one "rules of thumb" that take much of the guesswork out of producing quality DM.

Bivins, Thomas: *Handbook for Public Relations Writing: The Essentials of Style and Format* (New York: McGraw Hill, 1999)—Covers the full gamut of PR writing, from media releases to newsletter and brochure copywriting and design.

Bly, Robert W.: *Secrets of a Freelance Writer: How to Make $85,000 a Year* (New York: Henry Holt, 1997)—Offers an excellent grounding in the major principles of running a successful freelance business as well as how to broach the top money-making markets.

——*The Copywriter's Handbook: A Step-by-Step Guide to Writing Copy that Sells* (New York: Henry Holt, 1990)—One of several definitive writing guides by one of the best copywriters in the business. It provides in-depth, how-to information on the full spectrum of above and below-the-line copywriting.

——*The Online Copywriter's Handbook: Everything You Need to Know to Write Electronic Copy That Sells* (New York: McGraw Hill, 2003)—The latest, proven principles for writing interactive online copy Web sites, e-mail direct mail, banner ads, and e-zines.

Brogan, Kathryn; Brewer, Robert: *2004 Writer's Market* (Cincinnati: Writer's Digest Books, 2003)—A wide range of listings on everything from newspapers and magazines to publishers and agents. It also offers advice on various literary and commercial topics as well as a detailed guideline to consulting fees. An online guide is also available at www.writersmarket.com.

Brown, Michael: *Making Effective Media Happen* (Sydney, Australia: Allen & Unwin, 2002)—A practical, hands-on approach to managing various media activities, showing you how to prepare and deliver successful communications, deal with difficult interviewers, and get your message across firmly and confidently.

Burton, Philip Ward: *Advertising Copywriting* (New York; McGraw Hill, 1999)—Covers the full spectrum of copywriting techniques, from drafting headlines and text to writing ads for different industries.

Buzan, Tony: *How to Mind Map: Make the Most of Your Mind and Learn to Create, Organize and Plan* (London: Thorsons, 2003)—One of the latest and most complete books on the principle of Mind Mapping, a vital technique to develop for any writer.

Cutts, Martin: *The Plain English Guide: How to Write Clearly and Communicate Better* (New York: Oxford University Press, 1996)—A handy reference that covers all the basics of good communication, including punctuation, active and passive writing, and sentence structure and length.

Dunn, Irina: *The Writer's Guide* (Sydney, Australia: Allen & Unwin, 2002)—A wide range of ideas and practical advice for all genres and writing types from fiction and nonfiction, freelancing, screenwriting, and cyber writing. Ideal for those who want to write outside the box.

Evoy, Ken: *Make Your Site SELL!* (Montreal: SiteSell Inc., 2003)—Everything you need to know to set up a Web site for promoting yourself and selling your information products and services. It addresses product and site selling, traffic building, and fulfillment as well as how to price, position, and test products for the Net. Available as an e-book from http://myss.sitesell.com.

Evoy, Ken; Robson, Joe: *Make Your Words Sell!* (Montreal: SiteSell Inc., 2003)—A detailed, nuts-and-bolts guide for empowering Web and e-mail communications. Available as an e-book from http://myws.sitesell.com.

Goldberg, Natalie: *Wild Mind: Living the Writer's Life* (New York: Bantam, 1990)—A user-friendly introduction to the writing life, with plenty of hints, tips, and a few Zen techniques for making the most of it.

Harper, Timothy: *The ASJA Guide to Freelance Writing : A Professional Guide to the Business, for Nonfiction Writers of All Experience Levels* (New York: Griffin, 2003)—Solid advice and guidance on a wide range of topics by working writers. Subjects include establishing a freelance business, self-promotion, research tools, writing for the Web, contracts, taxes, and deductions, and working with editors and agents.

Kaplan, Bruce: *Editing Made Easy* (Melbourne: Penguin, 2003)—Solid rules and practical information on the rudiments of good grammar and style. Ideal for editing your own work and others.

Katz, Michael J.: *E-Newsletters That Work, The Small Business Owner's Guide To Creating, Writing and Managing An Effective Electronic Newsletter* (Philadelphia: Xlibris, 2003)—Concise advice on how to develop compelling copy for e-newsletters, presented in a simple FAQ format. Topics include content, format, and design as well as writing approaches, outsourcing, and database management.

Kent, Peter: *Making Money in Technical Writing* (New York: Macmillan USA, 1998)—Shows you how to develop and fine-tune technical communications as well as how to develop your writing business and increase your income. Suits new and seasoned technical writers.

Moore, Chris: *Freelance Writing* (London: Robert Hale, 2001)—Takes a realistic look at the realities of freelancing, and offers solid advice on various topics, including developing a work strategy.

Ogilvy, David: *Ogilvy on Advertising* (New York: Vintage, 1985)—Ogilvy was the grand master of advertising, and this book is a good example of why. It contains many timeless techniques and gems about the business that are still relevant today. (If you're interested in advertising, devour any Ogilvy book you can find.)

Rekulak, Jason: *The Writer's Block: 786 Ideas to Jump-Start Your Imagination* (Philadelphia: Running Press, 2001)—Hundreds of wonderful and left-of-field ideas for making writing more pleasurable and productive.

Roberts, Stevan; Feit, Michelle; Bly, Robert W.: *Internet Direct Mail: The Complete Guide to Successful E-Mail Marketing Campaigns* (Lincolnwood, IL: NTC, 2000)—An up-to-date guide to Internet marketing. Bly and friends apply proven marketing principles to the Internet, providing a step-by-step guide to developing successful e-mail campaigns that get measurable results.

Sedorkin, Gail; McGregor, Judy: *Interviewing: A Guide for Journalists and Writers* (Sydney, Australia: Allen & Unwin, Australia, 2002)—One of the most comprehensive guides on interviewing. It balances a plethora of tips, techniques, and checklists with a variety of colorful and insightful anecdotes.

Silver, Ken: *Ebook Secrets* (Wellington, New Zealand: Ken Silver Publishing, 2003)—An excellent, practical guide to publishing and selling your own e-books, covering everything from e-book production and Web site design to online marketing and promotion. Available as an e-book from www.kensilver.com.

Zinsser, William: *On Writing Well: The Classic Guide to Writing Nonfiction—25th Anniversary Edition* (New York: HarperResource, 2001)—A must-have volume for any scribe. It covers not only the mechanics of good communication but also addresses various topics of interest to the commercial writer.

MORE INFORMATION

For more information on Michael and his books, visit his Web site: www.m ichaelmeanwell.com.

It includes background information on the author, other books he has produced, and a free subscription to a writers' e-zine. You can also discuss ideas with like-minded writers on the Meanwell Forum.

THANKS

My sincere thanks to the following organizations for kindly giving me permission to reproduce marketing collateral with which I have been involved: Australia Post, BJR Distilleries, BureauScan, Burgundy Lunch Box, Come2gether.com, Kodak Australasia, PACCAR Australia, Pin Point Tele Marketing, Océ Australia, Simplot Australia, Telstra Corporation.

PERMISSIONS

"8 Easy Steps to Improving Your Profits." *Talking Chips.* © Simplot Australia Pty Ltd.

Post Review newsletter issues and booklet "How to Produce Your Own Newsletter." © Australia Post.

SnapShots. © 1997-1998 Kodak (Australasia) Pty Ltd.

Marketing e-mails, e-zine, press pack, speechex, features, radio ads. © Telstra Corporation Ltd.

Direct mail letter to prospects. © 1992 Pin Point Tele Marketing Pty Ltd.

In Print newsletters. © Océ-Australia Limited.

"Bottom line isn't always the bottom line for Findlay," "Kenworth backs program to improve forestry operations," and "Lamattina delivers fresh to market with Kenworth" press releases. © PACCAR Australia Pty Ltd.

BJR product labels. © BJR Distilleries Pty Ltd.

Burgundy Lunch Box promotional material. © Burgundy Lunch Box.

Direct mail letter regarding Creative Steps merger and Come2gether. com brochure. © Dan Fogel.

BureauScan company brochure. © BureauScan Pty Ltd.

Index